Collins easy learning

French
Grammar

Je vais
souvent à Paris.

Ce livre est à toi.

Published by Collins
An imprint of HarperCollins Publishers
Westerhill Road
Bishopbriggs
Glasgow G64 2QT

Third edition 2016

ISBN 978-0-00-814199-8

10 9 8 7 6 5 4 3

© HarperCollins Publishers 2004, 2016

www.collinsdictionary.com
www.collins.co.uk/languagesupport

Typeset by Davidson Publishing Solutions,
Glasgow

Printed and bound by CPI Group (UK)
Ltd, Croydon, CR0 4YY

A catalogue record for this book is available
from the British Library.

If you would like to comment on any aspect
of this book, please contact us at the given
address or online.
E-mail: dictionaries@harpercollins.co.uk
www.facebook.com/collinsdictionary
@collinsdict

Acknowledgements
We would like to thank those authors and
publishers who kindly gave permission for
copyright material to be used in the Collins
Corpus. We would also like to thank Times
Newspapers Ltd for providing valuable data.

MANAGING EDITOR
Maree Airlie

CONTRIBUTORS
Laurence Larroche
Maggie Seaton

FOR THE PUBLISHER
Gerry Breslin
Craig Balfour
Chloe Osborne

CONTENTS

FOREWORD FOR LANGUAGE TEACHERS

The *Easy Learning French Grammar* is designed to be used with both young and adult learners, as a group reference book to complement your course book during classes, or as a recommended text for self-study and homework/coursework.

The text specifically targets learners from beginner to intermediate or GCSE level, and therefore its structural content and vocabulary have been matched to the relevant specifications up to and including Higher GCSE.

The approach aims to develop knowledge and understanding of grammar and to improve the ability of learners to apply it by:

- defining parts of speech at the start of each major section, with examples in English to clarify concepts
- minimizing the use of grammar terminology and providing clear explanations of terms both within the text and in the **Glossary**
- illustrating all points with examples (and their translations) based on topics and contexts which are relevant to beginner and intermediate course content

The text helps you develop positive attitudes to grammar learning in your classes by:

- giving clear, easy-to-follow explanations
- prioritizing content according to relevant specifications for the levels
- sequencing points to reflect course content, e.g. verb tenses
- highlighting useful **Tips** to deal with common difficulties
- summarizing **Key points** at the end of sections to consolidate learning

In addition to fostering success and building a thorough foundation in French grammar, the optional **Grammar Extra** sections will encourage and challenge your learners to further their studies to higher and advanced levels.

INTRODUCTION FOR STUDENTS

Whether you are starting to learn French for the very first time, brushing up on topics you have studied in class, or revising for your GCSE exams, the *Easy Learning French Grammar* is here to help. This easy-to-use guide takes you through all the basics you will need to speak and understand modern, everyday French.

Newcomers can sometimes struggle with the technical terms they come across when they start to explore the grammar of a new language. The *Easy Learning French Grammar* explains how to get to grips with all the parts of speech you will need to know, using simple language and cutting out jargon.

The text is divided into sections, each dealing with a particular area of grammar. Each section can be studied individually, as numerous cross-references in the text point you to relevant points in other sections of the book for further information.

Every major section begins with an explanation of the area of grammar covered on the following pages. For quick reference, these definitions are also collected together on pages viii–xii in a glossary of essential grammar terms.

What is a verb?
A **verb** is a 'doing' word which describes what someone or something does, what someone or something is, or what happens to them, for example, *be*, *sing*, *live*.

Each grammar point in the text is followed by simple examples of real French, complete with English translations, to help you understand the rules. Underlining has been used in examples throughout the text to highlight the grammatical point being explained.

➤ If you are talking about a part of your body, you usually use a word like *my* or *his* in English, but in French you usually use the definite article.

Tourne <u>la</u> tête à gauche.	Turn your head to the left.
Il s'est cassé <u>le</u> bras.	He's broken his arm.
J'ai mal à <u>la</u> gorge.	My throat hurts.

In French, as with any foreign language, there are certain pitfalls which have to be avoided. **Tips** and **Information** notes throughout the text are useful reminders of the things that often trip learners up.

Key points sum up all the important facts about a particular area of grammar, to save you time when you are revising and help you focus on the main grammatical points.

If you think you would like to continue with your French studies to a higher level, check out the **Grammar Extra** sections. These are intended for advanced students who are interested in knowing a little more about the structures they will come across beyond GCSE.

Finally, the supplement at the end of the book contains **Verb Tables**, where 93 important French verbs (both regular and irregular) are declined in full. Examples show you how to use these verbs in your own work. If you are unsure of how a verb conjugates in French, you can look up the **Verb Index** on pages 95–105 to find either the conjugation of the verb itself, or a cross-reference to a model verb, which will show you the pattern that verb follows.

We hope that you will enjoy using the *Easy Learning French Grammar* and find it useful in the course of your studies.

Glossary of Grammar Terms

ABSTRACT NOUN a word used to refer to a quality, idea, feeling or experience, rather than a physical object, for example, *size, reason, happiness*. Compare with **concrete noun**.

ADJECTIVE a 'describing' word that tells you more about a person or thing, such as their appearance, colour, size or other qualities, for example, *pretty, blue, big*.

ADVERB a word usually used with verbs, adjectives or other adverbs that gives more information about when, where, how or in what circumstances something happens, for example, *quickly, happily, now*.

AGREE (to) to change word endings according to whether you are referring to masculine, feminine, singular or plural people or things.

AGREEMENT changing word endings according to whether you are referring to masculine, feminine, singular or plural people or things.

APOSTROPHE s an ending ('s) added to a noun to show who or what someone or something belongs to, for example, *Danielle's dog, the doctor's wife, the book's cover*.

ARTICLE a word like *the, a* and *an*, which is used in front of a noun. See also **definite article, indefinite article** and **partitive article**.

AUXILIARY VERB a verb such as *be, have* and *do* when it is used with a main verb to form tenses, negatives and questions.

BASE FORM the form of the verb without any endings added to it, for example, *walk, have, be, go*. Compare with **infinitive**.

CARDINAL NUMBER a number used in counting, for example, *one, seven, ninety*. Compare with **ordinal number**.

CLAUSE a group of words containing a verb.

COMPARATIVE an adjective or adverb with *-er* on the end of it or *more* or *less* in front of it that is used to compare people, things or actions, for example, *slower, less important, more carefully*.

COMPOUND NOUN a word for a living being, thing or idea, which is made up of two or more words, for example, *tin-opener, railway station*.

CONCRETE NOUN a word that refers to an object you can touch with your hand, rather than to a quality or idea, for example, *ball, map, apples*. Compare with **abstract noun**.

CONDITIONAL a verb form used to talk about things that would happen or would be true under certain conditions, for example, *I would help you if I could*. It is also used to say what you would like or need, for example, *Could you give me the bill?*

CONJUGATE (to) to give a verb different endings according to whether you are referring to *I, you, they* and so on, and according to whether you are referring to past, present or future, for example, *I have, she had, they will have*.

CONJUGATION a group of verbs which have the same endings as each other or change according to the same pattern.

CONJUNCTION a word such as *and*, *because* or *but* that links two words or phrases of a similar type or two parts of a sentence, for example, *Diane* *and* *I have been friends for years.*; *I left* *because* *I was bored.*

CONSONANT a letter of the alphabet which is not a vowel, for example, *b*, *f*, *m*, *s*, *v* etc. Compare with **vowel**.

CONSTRUCTION an arrangement of words together in a phrase or sentence.

DEFINITE ARTICLE the word *the*. Compare with **indefinite article**.

DEMONSTRATIVE ADJECTIVE one of the words *this*, *that*, *these* and *those* used with a noun to point out a particular person or thing, for example, *this* *woman*, *that* *dog*.

DEMONSTRATIVE PRONOUN one of the words *this*, *that*, *these* and *those* used instead of a noun to point out people or things, for example, *That* *looks fun*.

DIRECT OBJECT a noun referring to the person or thing affected by the action described by a verb, for example, *She wrote* *her name.*; *I shut* *the window*. Compare with **indirect object**.

DIRECT OBJECT PRONOUN a word such as *me*, *him*, *us* and *them* which is used instead of a noun to stand in for the person or thing most directly affected by the action described by the verb. Compare with **indirect object pronoun**.

EMPHATIC PRONOUN a word used instead of a noun when you want to emphasize something, for example,

Is this for *me?*; *'Who broke the window?'* *– 'He did.'* Also called **stressed pronoun**.

ENDING a form added to a verb, for example, *go* → *goes*, and to adjectives and nouns depending on whether they refer to masculine, feminine, singular or plural things.

EXCLAMATION a word, phrase or sentence that you use to show you are surprised, shocked, angry and so on, for example, *Wow!*; *How dare you!*; *What a surprise!*

FEMININE a form of noun, pronoun or adjective that is used to refer to a living being, thing or idea that is not classed as masculine.

FUTURE a verb tense used to talk about something that will happen or will be true.

GENDER whether a noun, pronoun or adjective is feminine or masculine.

IMPERATIVE the form of a verb used when giving orders and instructions, for example, *Shut the door!*; *Sit down!*; *Don't go!*

IMPERFECT one of the verb tenses used to talk about the past, especially in descriptions, and to say what was happening or used to happen, for example, *I used to walk to school*; *It was sunny at the weekend*. Compare with **perfect**.

IMPERSONAL VERB one which does not refer to a real person or thing and where the subject is represented by *it*, for example, *It's going to rain*; *It's 10 o'clock*.

INDEFINITE ADJECTIVE one of a small group of adjectives used to talk about people or things in a general way, without saying who or what they are, for example, *several*, *all*, *every*.

INDEFINITE ARTICLE the words *a* and *an*. Compare with **definite article**.

INDEFINITE PRONOUN a small group of pronouns such as *everything*, *nobody* and *something*, which are used to refer to people or things in a general way, without saying exactly who or what they are.

INDIRECT OBJECT a noun used with verbs that take two objects. For example, in *I gave the carrot to the rabbit*, *the rabbit* is the indirect object and *carrot* is the direct object. Compare with **direct object**.

INDIRECT OBJECT PRONOUN a pronoun used instead of a noun to show the person or the thing the action is intended to benefit or harm, for example, *me* in *He gave me a book* and *Can you get me a towel?* Compare with **direct object pronoun**.

INDIRECT QUESTION used to tell someone else about a question and introduced by a verb such as *ask*, *tell* or *wonder*, for example, *He asked me what the time was; I wonder who he is*.

INFINITIVE the form of the verb with *to* in front of it and without any endings added, for example, *to walk*, *to have*, *to be*, *to go*. Compare with **base form**.

INTERROGATIVE ADJECTIVE a question word used with a noun to ask *who?*, *what?* or *which?* for example, <u>*What*</u> *instruments do you play?*; <u>*Which*</u> *shoes do you like?*

INTERROGATIVE PRONOUN one of the words *who*, *whose*, *whom*, *what* and *which* when they are used

instead of a noun to ask questions, for example, <u>*What's*</u> *happening?*; <u>*Who's*</u> *coming?*

INVARIABLE used to describe a form which does not change.

IRREGULAR VERB a verb whose forms do not follow a general pattern or the normal rules. Compare with **regular verb**.

MASCULINE a form of noun, pronoun or adjective that is used to refer to a living being, thing or idea that is not classed as feminine.

NEGATIVE a question or statement which contains a word such as *not*, *never* or *nothing*, and is used to say that something is not happening, is not true or is absent, for example, *I never eat meat; Don't you love me?*

NOUN a 'naming' word for a living being, thing or idea, for example, *woman, desk, happiness, Andrew*.

NUMBER used to say how many things you are referring to or where something comes in a sequence. See also **ordinal number** and **cardinal number**.

OBJECT a noun or pronoun which refers to a person or thing that is affected by the action described by the verb. Compare with **direct object**, **indirect object** and **subject**.

OBJECT PRONOUN one of the set of pronouns including *me*, *him* and *them*, which are used instead of the noun as the object of a verb or preposition. Compare with **subject pronoun**.

ORDINAL NUMBER a number used to indicate where something comes in an order or sequence, for example, *first, fifth, sixteenth*. Compare with **cardinal number**.

PART OF SPEECH a word class, for example, *noun*, *verb*, *adjective*, *preposition*, *pronoun*.

PARTITIVE ARTICLE the words *some* or *any*, used to refer to part of a thing but not all of it, for example, *Have you got <u>any</u> money?*; *I'm going to buy <u>some</u> bread*.

PASSIVE a form of the verb that is used when the subject of the verb is the person or thing that is affected by the action, for example, *we were told*.

PAST PARTICIPLE a verb form which is used to form perfect and pluperfect tenses and passives, for example, *watched*, *swum*. Some past participles are also used as adjectives, for example, *a <u>broken</u> watch*.

PERFECT one of the verb tenses used to talk about the past, especially about actions that took place and were completed in the past. Compare with **imperfect**.

PERSON one of the three classes: the first person (*I*, *we*), the second person (*you* singular and *you* plural), and the third person (*he*, *she*, *it* and *they*).

PERSONAL PRONOUN one of the group of words including *I*, *you* and *they* which are used to refer to yourself, the people you are talking to, or the people or things you are talking about.

PLUPERFECT one of the verb tenses used to describe something that <u>had</u> happened or had been true at a point in the past, for example, *I'<u>d</u> <u>forgotten</u> to finish my homework*.

PLURAL the form of a word which is used to refer to more than one person or thing. Compare with **singular**.

POSSESSIVE ADJECTIVE one of the words *my*, *your*, *his*, *her*, *its*, *our* or *their*, used with a noun to show that one person or thing belongs to another.

POSSESSIVE PRONOUN one of the words *mine*, *yours*, *hers*, *his*, *ours* or *theirs*, used instead of a noun to show that one person or thing belongs to another.

PREPOSITION is a word such as *at*, *for*, *with*, *into* or *from*, which is usually followed by a noun, pronoun or, in English, a word ending in *-ing*. Prepositions show how people and things relate to the rest of the sentence, for example, *She's <u>at</u> home*; *a tool <u>for</u> cutting grass*; *It's <u>from</u> David*.

PRESENT a verb form used to talk about what is true at the moment, what happens regularly, and what is happening now, for example, *I'<u>m</u> a student*; *I <u>travel</u> to college by train*; *I'm <u>studying</u> languages*.

PRESENT PARTICIPLE a verb form ending in *-ing* which is used in English to form verb tenses, and which may be used as an adjective or a noun, for example, *What are you <u>doing</u>?*; *the <u>setting</u> sun*; *<u>Swimming</u> is easy!*

PRONOUN a word which you use instead of a noun, when you do not need or want to name someone or something directly, for example, *it*, *you*, *none*.

PROPER NOUN the name of a person, place, organization or thing. Proper nouns are always written with a capital letter, for example, *Kevin*, *Glasgow*, *Europe*, *London Eye*.

QUESTION WORD a word such as *why, where, who, which* or *how* which is used to ask a question.

REFLEXIVE PRONOUN a word ending in *-self* or *-selves*, such as *myself* or *themselves*, which refers back to the subject, for example, *He hurt himself.; Take care of yourself.*

REFLEXIVE VERB a verb where the subject and object are the same, and where the action 'reflects back' on the subject. A reflexive verb is used with a reflexive pronoun such as *myself, yourself, herself*, for example, *I washed myself.; He cut himself.*

REGULAR VERB a verb whose forms follow a general pattern or the normal rules. Compare with **irregular verb**.

RELATIVE PRONOUN a word such as *that, who* or *which*, when it is used to link two parts of a sentence together.

SENTENCE a group of words which usually has a verb and a subject. In writing, a sentence has a capital letter at the beginning and a full stop, question mark or exclamation mark at the end.

SINGULAR the form of a word which is used to refer to one person or thing. Compare with **plural**.

STEM the main part of a verb to which endings are added.

STRESSED PRONOUN used instead of a noun when you want to emphasize something, for example, *Is this for me?; 'Who broke the window?' – 'He did.'* Also called **emphatic pronoun**.

SUBJECT the noun in a sentence or phrase that refers to the person or thing that does the action described by the verb or is in the state described by the verb, for example, *My cat doesn't drink milk.* Compare with **object**.

SUBJECT PRONOUN a pronoun such as *I, he, she* and *they* which is used instead of a noun as the subject of a sentence. Pronouns stand in for nouns when it is clear who is being talked about, for example, *My brother isn't here at the moment. He'll be back in an hour.* Compare with **object pronoun**.

SUBJUNCTIVE a verb form used in certain circumstances to express some sort of feeling, or to show doubt about whether something will happen or whether something is true. It is only used occasionally in modern English, for example, *If I were you, I wouldn't bother.; So be it.*

SUPERLATIVE an adjective or adverb with *-est* on the end of it or *most* or *least* in front of it that is used to compare people, things or actions, for example, *thinnest, most quickly, least interesting*.

SYLLABLE consonant+vowel units that make up the sounds of a word, for example, *ca-the-dral* (3 syllables), *im-po-ssi-ble* (4 syllables).

TENSE the form of a verb which shows whether you are referring to the past, present or future.

VERB a 'doing' word which describes what someone or something does, what someone or something is, or what happens to them, for example, *be, sing, live*.

VOWEL one of the letters *a, e, i, o* or *u*. Compare with **consonant**.

Nouns

What is a noun?
A **noun** is a 'naming' word for a living being, thing or idea, for example, *woman*, *happiness*, *Andrew*.

Using nouns

➤ In French, all nouns are either <u>masculine</u> or <u>feminine</u>. This is called their <u>gender</u>. Even words for things have a gender.

➤ Whenever you are using a noun, you need to know whether it is masculine or feminine as this affects the form of other words used with it, such as:

- adjectives that describe it
- articles (such as **le** or **une**) that go before it
- pronouns (such as **il** or **elle**) that replace it

➡ *For more information on **Adjectives**, **Articles** or **Pronouns**, see pages 25, 12 and 42.*

➤ You can find information about gender by looking the word up in a dictionary. When you come across a new noun, always learn the word for *the* or *a* that goes with it to help you remember its gender.

- **le** or **un** before a noun tells you it is masculine
- **la** or **une** before a noun tells you it is feminine

➤ We refer to something as <u>singular</u> when we are talking about just one of them, and as <u>plural</u> when we are talking about more than one. The singular is the form of the noun you will usually find when you look a noun up in the dictionary. As in English, nouns in French change their form in the plural.

➤ Adjectives, articles and pronouns are also affected by whether a noun is singular or plural.

Tip
Remember that you have to use the right word for *the*, *a* and so on according to the gender of the French noun.

2 Nouns

Gender

1 Nouns referring to people

➤ Most nouns referring to men and boys are <u>masculine</u>.

un homme	a man
un roi	a king

➤ Most nouns referring to women and girls are <u>feminine</u>.

une fille	a girl
une reine	a queen

➤ When the same word is used to refer to either men/boys or women/girls, its gender usually changes depending on the sex of the person it refers to.

un camarade	a (male) friend
une camarade	a (female) friend
un Belge	a Belgian (man)
une Belge	a Belgian (woman)

Grammar Extra!

Some words for people have only <u>one</u> possible gender, whether they refer to a male or a female.

un bébé	a (male or female) baby
un guide	a (male or female) guide
une personne	a (male or female) person
une vedette	a (male or female) star

➤ In English, we can sometimes make a word masculine or feminine by changing the ending, for example, English<u>man</u> and English<u>woman</u>, or *prince* and *princess*. In French, very often the ending of a noun changes depending on whether it refers to a man or a woman.

un Anglais	an Englishman
une Anglaise	an Englishwoman
un prince	a prince
une princesse	a princess
un employé	a (male) employee
une employée	a (female) employee

➡ *For more information on **Masculine and feminine forms of words**, see page 7.*

For further explanation of grammatical terms, please see pages viii–xii.

2 Nouns referring to animals

➤ In English we can choose between words like *bull* or *cow*, depending on the sex of the animal we are referring to. In French too there are sometimes separate words for male and female animals.

un taureau   a bull
une vache   a cow

➤ Sometimes, the same word with different endings is used for male and female animals.

un chien   a (male) dog
une chien**ne**   a (female) dog, a bitch

> *Tip*
>
> When you do not know or care what sex the animal is, you can usually use the masculine form as a general word.

➤ Words for other animals do not change according to the sex of the animal. Just learn the French word with its gender, which is always the same.

un poisson   a fish
une souris   a mouse

3 Nouns referring to things

➤ In English, we call all things – for example, *table, car, book, apple* – '*it*'. In French, however, things are either masculine or feminine. As things do not divide into sexes the way humans and animals do, there are no physical clues to help you with their gender in French. Try to learn the gender as you learn the word.

➤ There are lots of rules to help you:

- words ending in **-e** are generally feminine (**une boulangerie** a baker's; **une banque** a bank)

- words ending in a consonant (any letter except *a, e, i, o* or *u*) are generally masculine (**un aéroport** an airport; **un film** a film)

➤ There are some exceptions to these rules, so it is best to check in a dictionary if you are unsure.

4 Nouns

➤ These endings are often found on <u>masculine nouns</u>.

Masculine ending	Examples
-age	**un vill<u>age</u>** a village **un voy<u>age</u>** a journey **un ét<u>age</u>** a floor **le from<u>age</u>** cheese BUT: **<u>une</u> image** a picture **<u>une</u> page** a page **<u>la</u> plage** the beach
-ment	**un apparte<u>ment</u>** a flat **un bâti<u>ment</u>** a building **le ci<u>ment</u>** cement **un vête<u>ment</u>** a garment
-oir	**un mir<u>oir</u>** a mirror **un coul<u>oir</u>** a corridor **le s<u>oir</u>** the evening **un mouch<u>oir</u>** a handkerchief
-sme	**le touri<u>sme</u>** tourism **le raci<u>sme</u>** racism
-eau	**un cad<u>eau</u>** a present **un chap<u>eau</u>** a hat **un gât<u>eau</u>** a cake **le rid<u>eau</u>** the curtain BUT: **<u>la</u> peau** skin **l'<u>eau</u>** water
-eu	**un j<u>eu</u>** a game
-ou	**un ch<u>ou</u>** a cabbage **le gen<u>ou</u>** the knee
-ier	**le cah<u>ier</u>** the exercise book **un quart<u>ier</u>** an area **un escal<u>ier</u>** a staircase
-in	**un magas<u>in</u>** a shop **un jard<u>in</u>** a garden **un dess<u>in</u>** a drawing **le v<u>in</u>** the wine BUT: **<u>la</u> fin** the end **<u>une</u> main** a hand

For further explanation of grammatical terms, please see pages viii–xii.

-on	**un champignon** a mushroom **un ballon** a ball **le citron** the lemon BUT: **une maison** a house **la saison** the season

➤ The following types of word are also masculine:

- names of the days of the week, and the months and seasons of the year

le lundi	Monday
septembre prochain	next September
le printemps	Spring

- the names of languages

le français	French
le portugais	Portuguese
Tu apprends le français depuis combien de temps?	How long have you been learning French?

- most metric weights and measures

un gramme	a gramme
un mètre	a metre
un kilomètre	a kilometre

- English nouns used in French

le football	football
un tee-shirt	a tee-shirt
un sandwich	a sandwich

➤ These endings are often found on <u>feminine nouns</u>.

Feminine ending	Examples
-ance -anse -ence -ense	**la chance** luck, chance **une danse** a dance **la patience** patience **la défense** defence BUT: **le silence** silence
-ion	**une région** a region **une addition** a bill **une réunion** a meeting **la circulation** traffic BUT: **un avion** a plane
-té -tié	**une spécialité** a speciality **la moitié** half BUT: **un été** a summer **le pâté** pâté

Grammar Extra!

A few words have different meanings depending on whether they are masculine or feminine. These are the most common:

Masculine	Meaning	Example	Feminine	Meaning	Example
<u>un</u> livre	a book	**un livre de poche** a paperback	<u>une</u> livre	a pound	**une livre sterling** a pound sterling
un mode	a method	**le mode d'emploi** the directions for use	**la** mode	fashion	**à la mode** in fashion
<u>un</u> poste	a set (*TV/radio*); a post (*job*); an extension (*phone*)	**un poste de professeur** a teaching job	**la** poste	post the post office	**mettre quelque chose à la poste** to post something
<u>un</u> tour	a turn; a walk	**faire un tour** to go for a walk	<u>une</u> tour	tower	**la tour Eiffel** the Eiffel Tower

---

Key points

 Most nouns referring to men, boys and male animals are <u>masculine</u>; most nouns referring to women, girls and female animals are <u>feminine</u>. The ending of a French noun often changes depending on whether it refers to a male or a female.

✔ Generally, words ending in **-e** are feminine and words ending in a consonant are masculine, though there are many exceptions to this rule.

✔ These endings are often found on masculine nouns:
-age, -ment, -oir, -sme, -eau, -eu, -ou, -ier, -in and **-on**.

✔ These endings are often found on feminine nouns:
-ance, -anse, -ence, -ense, -ion, -té, -tié.

✔ Days of the week, months and seasons of the year are masculine. So are languages, most metric weights and measures, and English nouns used in French.

For further explanation of grammatical terms, please see pages viii–xii.

4 Masculine and feminine forms of words

➤ In French there are sometimes very different words for men and women, and for male and female animals, just as in English.

un homme	a man
une femme	a woman
un taureau	a bull
une vache	a cow
un neveu	a nephew
une nièce	a niece

➤ Many masculine French nouns can be made feminine simply by changing the ending. This is usually done by adding an **-e** to the masculine noun to form the feminine.

un ami	a (male) friend
une amie	a (female) friend
un employé	a (male) employee
une employée	a (female) employee
un Français	a Frenchman
une Française	a Frenchwoman

➤ If the masculine singular form already ends in **-e**, no further e is added.

un élève	a (male) pupil
une élève	a (female) pupil
un camarade	a (male) friend
une camarade	a (female) friend
un collègue	a (male) colleague
une collègue	a (female) colleague

Tip

If a masculine noun ends in a vowel, its pronunciation does not change when an **-e** is added to form the feminine. For example, **ami** and **amie** (meaning *friend*) are both pronounced the same.

If a masculine noun ends with a consonant that is not pronounced, for example, **-d**, **-s**, **-r** or **-t**, you DO pronounce that consonant when an **-e** is added in the feminine. For example, in **étudiant** (meaning *student*), you cannot hear the **t**; in **étudiante**, you can hear the **t**.

Tip

Some masculine nouns, such as **voisin** (meaning *neighbour*), end in what is called a <u>nasal vowel</u> and an **-n**. With these words, you pronounce the vowel 'through your nose' but DO NOT say the **n**. When an **-e** is added in the feminine – for example, **voisine** – the vowel becomes a normal one instead of a nasal vowel and you DO pronounce the **n**.

5 Some other patterns

➤ Some changes to endings from masculine to feminine are a little more complicated but still fall into a regular pattern.

Masculine ending	Feminine ending	Example	Meaning
-f	-ve	<u>un</u> veu<u>f</u>/<u>une</u> veu<u>ve</u>	a widower/a widow
-x	-se	<u>un</u> épou<u>x</u>/<u>une</u> épou<u>se</u>	a husband/a wife
-eur	-euse	<u>un</u> dans<u>eur</u>/ <u>une</u> dans<u>euse</u>	a (male) dancer/ a (female) dancer
-teur	-teuse -trice	<u>un</u> chan<u>teur</u>/ <u>une</u> chan<u>teuse</u> <u>un</u> ac<u>teur</u>/<u>une</u> ac<u>trice</u>	a (male) singer/ a (female) singer an actor/an actress
-an	-anne	<u>un</u> pays<u>an</u>/ <u>une</u> pays<u>anne</u>	a (male) farmer/ a (female) farmer
-ien	-ienne	<u>un</u> Paris<u>ien</u>/ <u>une</u> Paris<u>ienne</u>	a (male) Parisian/ a (female) Parisian
-on	-onne	<u>un</u> li<u>on</u>/<u>une</u> li<u>onne</u>	a lion/a lioness
-er	-ère	<u>un</u> étrang<u>er</u>/ <u>une</u> étrang<u>ère</u>	a (male) foreigner/ a (female) foreigner
-et	-ette	<u>le</u> cad<u>et</u>/<u>la</u> cad<u>ette</u>	the youngest (male) child the youngest (female) child
-el	-elle	<u>un</u> professionn<u>el</u>/ <u>une</u> professionn<u>elle</u>	a (male) professional/ a (female) professional

Key points

✔ Many masculine French nouns can be made to refer to females by adding an **-e**. If the masculine singular form already ends in **-e**, no further **e** is added.

✔ The pronunciation of feminine nouns is sometimes different from that of the corresponding masculine nouns.

✔ Other patterns include:

-f → -ve	-teur → -teuse or -trice	-er → -ère
-x → -se	-an, -en and -on → -anne,	-et → -ette
-eur → -euse	-enne and -onne	-el → -elle

For further explanation of grammatical terms, please see pages viii–xii.

Forming plurals

1 Plurals ending in -s

➤ In English we usually make nouns plural by adding an -s to the end (*garden* → *gardens*; *house* → *houses*), although we do have some nouns which are <u>irregular</u> and do not follow this pattern (*mouse* → *mice*; *child* → *children*).

> ### Tip
>
> Remember that you have to use **les** with plural nouns in French. Any adjective that goes with the noun has to agree with it, as does any pronoun that replaces it.
>
> ⇨ *For more information on **Adjectives**, **Articles** and **Pronouns**, see pages 25, 12 and 42.*

➤ Most French nouns also form their plural by adding an **-s** to their singular form.

un jardin	a garden
des jardins	gardens
une voiture	a car
des voitures	cars
un hôtel	a hotel
des hôtels	hotels

➤ If the singular noun ends in **-s**, **-x** or **-z**, no further **-s** is added in the plural.

un fils	a son
des fils	sons
une voix	a voice
des voix	voices
un nez	a nose
des nez	noses

2 Plurals ending in -x

➤ The following nouns add an **-x** instead of an **-s** in the plural:

- nouns ending in **-eau**

un chapeau	a hat
des chapeaux	hats

- most nouns ending in **-eu**

un jeu	a game
des jeux	games

- a FEW nouns ending in **-ou** (MOST nouns ending in **-ou** add **-s** as usual)

un bijou	a jewel
des bijoux	jewels
un caillou	a pebble
des cailloux	pebbles
un chou	a cabbage
des choux	cabbages
un genou	a knee
des genoux	knees
un hibou	an owl
des hiboux	owls
un joujou	a toy
des joujoux	toys
un pou	a louse
des poux	lice

Tip

Adding an **-s** or **-x** to the end of a noun does not usually change the way the word is pronounced. For example, **professeur** and **professeurs** and **chapeau** and **chapeaux** sound just the same when you say them out loud.

➤ If the singular noun ends in **-al** or **-ail**, the plural usually ends in **-aux**.

un journal	a newspaper
des journaux	newspapers
un animal	an animal
des animaux	animals
un travail	a job
des travaux	jobs

For further explanation of grammatical terms, please see pages viii–xii.

> **Tip**
> The plural of **un œil** (*an eye*) is **des yeux** (*eyes*).

3 Plural versus singular

➤ A few words relating to clothing are plural in English but <u>NOT</u> in French.

un slip	pants
un short	shorts
un pantalon	trousers

➤ A few common words are plural in French but <u>NOT</u> in English.

les affaires	business
les cheveux	hair
des renseignements	information

Grammar Extra!

When nouns are made up of two separate words, they are called <u>compound nouns</u>, for example, **les grands-parents** (meaning *grandparents*), **des ouvre-boîtes** (meaning *tin-openers*). The rules for forming the plural of compound nouns are complicated and it is best to check in a dictionary to see what the plural is.

Key points

✔ Most French nouns form their plural by adding an **-s** to their singular form. If the singular noun ends in **-s**, **-x** or **-z**, no further **-s** is added in the plural.

✔ Most nouns ending in **-eau** or **-eu** add an **-x** in the plural.

✔ Most nouns ending in **-ou** take an **-s** in the plural, with a few exceptions.

✔ If the singular noun ends in **-al** or **-ail**, the plural usually ends in **-aux**.

✔ Adding an **-s** or **-x** to the end of a noun does not generally affect the way the word is pronounced.

✔ A few common words are plural in English but not in French, and vice versa.

Articles

> **What is an article?**
> In English, an **article** is one of the words *the*, *a*, and *an* which is given in front of a noun.

Different types of article

➤ There are three types of article:

- the <u>definite</u> article: *the* in English. This is used to identify a particular thing or person.

  I'm going to <u>the</u> supermarket.
  That's <u>the</u> woman I was talking to.

- the <u>indefinite</u> article: *a* or *an* in English, *some* or *any* (or no word at all) in the plural. This is used to refer to something unspecific, or that you do not really know about.

  Is there <u>a</u> supermarket near here?
  I need <u>a</u> day off.

- the <u>partitive</u> article: *some* or *any* (or no word at all) in English. This is used to talk about quantities or amounts.

  Can you lend me <u>some</u> sugar?
  Did you buy <u>any</u> wine?
  Do you like chocolate?

The definite article: le, la, l' and les

1 The basic rules

➤ In English we only have <u>one</u> definite article: the. In French, there is more than one definite article to choose from. All French nouns are either masculine or feminine and, just as in English, they can be either singular or plural. The word you choose for *the* depends on whether the noun it is used with is masculine or feminine, singular or plural. This may sound complicated, but it is not too difficult.

⇨ *For more information on **Nouns**, see page 1.*

	with masculine noun	with feminine noun
Singular	le (l')	la (l')
Plural	les	les

> ## Tip
> **le** and **la** change to **l'** when they are used in front of a word starting with a vowel and most words starting with **h**.

➤ **le** is used in front of <u>masculine singular nouns</u>.

le roi	the king
le chien	the dog
le jardin	the garden

➤ **la** is used in front of <u>feminine singular nouns</u>.

la reine	the queen
la souris	the mouse
la porte	the door

➤ **l'** is used in front of <u>singular nouns that start with a vowel</u> (*a, e, i, o,* or *u*), whether they are masculine or feminine.

l'ami (*masculine*)	the friend
l'eau (*feminine*)	the water
l'étage (*masculine*)	the floor

ℹ️ Note that **l'** is also used in front of most words starting with **h** but some others take **le** or **la** instead.

l'hôpital	the hospital
le hamster	the hamster
la hi-fi	the stereo

> ## Tip
>
> It is a good idea to learn the <u>article</u> or the <u>gender</u> with the noun when you come across a word for the first time, so that you know whether it is masculine or feminine. A good dictionary will also give you this information.

➤ **les** is used in front of <u>plural nouns</u>, whether they are masculine or feminine and whatever letter they start with.

<u>les</u> chiens	the dogs
<u>les</u> portes	the doors
<u>les</u> amis	the friends
<u>les</u> hôtels	the hotels

i Note that you have to make the noun plural too, just as you would in English. In French, as in English, you usually add an **-s**.

➩ *For more information on **Forming plurals**, see page 9.*

> ## Tip
>
> When **les** is used in front of a word that starts with a consonant, you DO NOT say the **s** on the end of **les**: **les chiens** *the dogs*.
>
> When **les** is used in front of a word that starts with a vowel, most words starting with **h**, and the French word **y**, you DO pronounce the **s** on the end of **les**. It sounds like the *z* in the English word *zip*: **les amis** *the friends*, **les hôtels** *the hotels*.

2 Using à with le, la, l' and les

➤ The French word **à** is translated into English in several different ways, including *at* or *to*. There are special rules when you use it together with **le** and **les**.

➩ *For more information on the preposition **à**, see page 163.*

➤ When **à** is followed by **le**, the two words become **au**.

<u>au</u> cinéma	to/at the cinema
<u>au</u> professeur	to the teacher

➤ When **à** is followed by **les**, the two words become **aux**.

    <u>aux</u> maisons   to the houses
    <u>aux</u> étudiants   to the students

➤ When **à** is followed by **la** or **l'**, the words do not change.

    <u>à la</u> bibliothèque   to/at the library
    <u>à l'</u>hôtel   to/at the hotel

Tip

le and la change to l' when they are used in front of a word starting with a vowel and most words starting with **h**.

3 Using de with le, la, l' and les

➤ The French word **de** is translated into English in several different ways, including *of* and *from*. There are special rules when you use it together with **le** and **les**.

➡ *For more information on the preposition **de**, see page 166.*

➤ When **de** is followed by **le**, the two words become **du**.

    <u>du</u> cinéma   from/of the cinema
    <u>du</u> professeur   from/of the teacher

➤ When **de** is followed by **les**, the two words become **des**.

    <u>des</u> maisons   from/of the houses
    <u>des</u> étudiants   from/of the students

➤ When **de** is followed by **la** or **l'**, the words do not change.

    <u>de la</u> bibliothèque   from/of the library
    <u>de l'</u>hôtel   from/of the hotel

Tip

le and la change to l' when they are used in front of a word starting with a vowel and most words starting with **h**.

Key points

✔ With masculine singular nouns → use **le**.

✔ With feminine singular nouns → use **la**.

✔ With nouns starting with a vowel, most nouns beginning with **h** and the French word **y** → use **l'**.

✔ With plural nouns → use **les**.

✔ à + le = au

   à + les = aux

   de + le = du

   de + les = des

☐4 **Using the definite article**

➤ The definite article in French (**le**, **la**, **l'** and **les**) is used in more or less the same way as we use *the* in English, but it is also used in French in a few places where you might not expect it.

➤ The definite article is used with words like *prices*, *flu* and *time* that describe qualities, ideas or experiences (called <u>abstract nouns</u>) rather than something that you can touch with your hand. Usually, *the* is missed out in English with this type of word.

Les prix montent.	Prices are rising.
J'ai <u>la</u> grippe.	I've got flu.
Je n'ai pas <u>le</u> temps.	I don't have time.

📝 Note that there are some set phrases using **avoir**, **avec** or **sans** followed by a noun, where the definite article is <u>NOT</u> used.

avoir faim	to be hungry (*literally: to have hunger*)
avec plaisir	with pleasure
sans doute	probably (*literally: without doubt*)

➤ You also use the definite article when you are talking about things like *coffee* or *computers* that you can touch with your hand (called <u>concrete nouns</u>) if you are talking generally about that thing. Usually, *the* is missed out in English with this type of word.

Je n'aime pas <u>le</u> café.	I don't like coffee.
Les ordinateurs coûtent très cher.	Computers are very expensive.
Les professeurs ne gagnent pas beaucoup.	Teachers don't earn very much.

For further explanation of grammatical terms, please see pages viii–xii.

➤ If you are talking about a part of your body, you usually use a word like *my* or *his* in English, but in French you usually use the definite article.

Tourne <u>la</u> tête à gauche.	Turn your head to the left.
Il s'est cassé <u>le</u> bras.	He's broken his arm.
J'ai mal à <u>la</u> gorge.	I've got a sore throat.

➤ In French you have to use the definite article in front of the names of countries, continents and regions.

<u>la</u> Bretagne	Brittany
<u>l'</u>Europe	Europe
<u>La</u> France est très belle.	France is very beautiful.
J'ai acheté ce poster <u>au</u> Japon.	I bought this poster in Japan.
Je viens <u>des</u> États-Unis.	I come from the United States.

[i] Note that if the name of the country comes after the French word **en**, meaning *to* or *in*, you do not use the definite article. **en** is used with the names of countries, continents and regions that are feminine in French.

Je vais <u>en Écosse</u> le mois prochain.	I'm going to Scotland next month.
Il travaille <u>en Allemagne</u>.	He works in Germany.

➪ *For more information on the preposition* **en**, *see page 168.*

➤ You often use the definite article with the name of school subjects, languages and sports.

Tu aimes <u>les</u> maths?	Do you like maths?
J'apprends <u>le</u> français depuis trois ans.	I've been learning French for three years.
Mon sport préféré, c'est <u>le</u> foot.	My favourite sport is football.

[i] Note that the definite article is not used after **en**.

Comment est-ce qu'on dit 'fils' <u>en anglais</u>?	How do you say 'fils' in English?
Sophie est nulle <u>en chimie</u>.	Sophie's no good at chemistry.

➤ When you use the verb **parler** (meaning *to speak*) in front of the name of the language, you do not always need to use the definite article in French.

Tu parles espagnol?	Do you speak Spanish?
Il parle bien <u>l'</u>anglais.	He speaks English well.

➤ You use **le** with dates, and also with the names of the days of the week and the seasons when you are talking about something that you do regularly or that is a habit.

Elle part le 7 mai.	She's leaving on the seventh of May.
Je vais chez ma grand-mère le dimanche.	I go to my grandmother's on Sundays.

i Note that you do not use the definite article after **en**.

En hiver nous faisons du ski.	In winter we go skiing.

➤ You often find the definite article in phrases that tell you about prices and rates.

6 euros le kilo	6 euros a kilo
3 euros la pièce	3 euros each
On roulait à 100 kilomètres à l'heure.	We were doing 100 kilometres an hour.

Key points

✔ The definite article is used in French with:
- abstract nouns
- concrete nouns (*when you are saying something that is true about a thing in general*)
- parts of the body
- countries, continents and regions
- school subjects, languages and sports
- dates
- days of the week and the seasons (*when you are talking about something that you do regularly or that is a habit*)
- prices and rates

The indefinite article: un, une and des

1 The basic rules

➤ In English we have the indefinite article *a*, which changes to *an* in front of a word that starts with a vowel. In the plural we say either *some*, *any* or nothing at all.

➤ In French, you choose from **un**, **une** and **des**, depending on whether the noun is masculine or feminine, and singular or plural.

	with masculine noun	with feminine noun
Singular	un	une
Plural	des	des

➤ **un** is used in front of <u>masculine singular nouns</u>.

un roi	a king
un chien	a dog
un jardin	a garden

➤ **une** is used in front of <u>feminine singular nouns</u>.

une reine	a queen
une souris	a mouse
une porte	a door

➤ **des** is used in front of <u>plural nouns</u>, whether they are masculine or feminine, and whatever letter they start with.

des chiens	(some/any) dogs
des souris	(some/any) mice
des amis	(some/any) friends

i Note that **des** is also a combination of **de** + **les** and has other meanings, such as saying who something belongs to or where something is from.

➡ *For more information on **des**, see page 166.*

> ### Tip
>
> When **des** is used in front of a word that starts with a consonant (any letter except *a, e, i, o* or *u*), you DO NOT say the **s** on the end of **des**: **des chiens** *(some/any) dogs*.
>
> When **des** is used in front of a word that starts with a vowel, and most words starting with **h**, you DO pronounce the **s** on the end.
>
> It sounds like the z in the English word *zip*: **des amis** *(some/any) friends*, **des hôtels** *(some/any) hotels*.

20 Articles

2 The indefinite article in negative sentences

➤ In English we use words like *not* and *never* to indicate that something is not happening or is not true. The sentences that these words are used in are called <u>negative</u> sentences.

> I <u>don't</u> know him.
> I <u>never</u> do my homework on time.

➤ In French, you use word pairs like **ne ... pas** (meaning *not*) and **ne ... jamais** (meaning *never*) to say that something is not happening or not true. When **un**, **une** or **des** is used after this type of expression, it has to be changed to **de**.

> **Je n'ai pas de vélo.**   I don't have a bike.
> **Nous n'avons pas de cousins.**   We don't have any cousins.

⇨ *For more information on **Negatives**, see page 138.*

> ### Tip
> **de** changes to **d'** in front of a word starting with a vowel and most words starting with **h**.
>
> **Je n'ai pas d'ordinateur.**   I don't have a computer.
> **Il n'y a pas d'horloge dans la salle.**   There isn't a clock in the room.

Grammar Extra!

There are some very common adjectives, like **beau**, **bon** and **petit**, that can come <u>BEFORE</u> the noun instead of after it. When an adjective comes before a plural noun, **des** changes to **de**.

> **J'ai reçu de beaux cadeaux.**   I got some lovely presents.
> **Cette région a de très jolis villages.**   This area has some very pretty villages.

⇨ *For more information on **Word order with adjectives**, see page 32.*

---

3 The meaning of des

➤ **des** can mean different things in English, depending on the sentence. *Some* is often the best word to use.

> **J'ai un chien, deux chats et des souris.**   I've got a dog, two cats and <u>some</u> mice.
> **Tu veux des chips?**   Would you like <u>some</u> crisps?

➤ In questions and negative sentences **des** means *any*, or is not translated at all.

Tu as <u>des</u> frères?	Have you got <u>any</u> brothers?
Il n'y a pas <u>d'</u>œufs.	There aren't <u>any</u> eggs.
Avez-vous <u>des</u> timbres?	Do you have stamps?

> *Tip*
>
> As an English speaker, you will know what sounds right in your own language. The important thing to remember is that **des** can <u>NEVER</u> be missed out in French, even if there is no word in English.

4 Using the indefinite article

➤ The indefinite article is used in French in much the same way as we use *a*, *some* and *any* in English, but there are two places where the indefinite article is <u>NOT</u> used:

- with the adjective **quel** (meaning *what a*), in sentences like

Quel dommage!	What <u>a</u> shame!
Quelle surprise!	What <u>a</u> surprise!
Quelle bonne idée!	What <u>a</u> good idea!

⇨ *For more information on **quel**, see page 148.*

- when you say what jobs people do

Il est professeur.	He's <u>a</u> teacher.
Ma mère est infirmière.	My mother's <u>a</u> nurse.

> *Tip*
>
> When you use **c'est** (to mean *he/she is*), you <u>DO</u> use **un** or **une**. When you use **ce sont** (to mean *they are*), you <u>DO</u> use **des**.
>
> | | |
> |---|---|
> | **C'est <u>un</u> médecin.** | He's/She's a doctor. |
> | **Ce sont <u>des</u> acteurs.** | They're actors. |
>
> ⇨ *For more information on **c'est** and **ce sont**, see page 65.*

> **Key points**
> ✔ With masculine singular nouns → use **un**.
> ✔ With feminine singular nouns → use **une**.
> ✔ With plural nouns → use **des**.
> ✔ **un**, **une** and **des** → change to **de** or **d'** in negative sentences.
> ✔ The indefinite article is not usually used when you say what jobs people do, or in exclamations with **quel**.

The partitive article: du, de la, de l' and des

1 The basic rules

➤ **du**, **de la**, **de l'** and **des** can all be used to give information about the amount or quantity of a particular thing. They are often translated into English as *some* or *any*.

➤ In French, you choose between **du**, **de la**, **de l'** and **des**, depending on whether the noun is masculine or feminine, singular or plural.

	with masculine noun	with feminine noun
Singular	du (de l')	de la (de l')
Plural	des	des

> *Tip*
>
> **de + le** and **de la** change to **de l'** when they are used in front of a word starting with a vowel, most words starting with **h**, and the French word **y**.

➤ **du** is used in front of <u>masculine singular nouns</u>.

| **du** beurre | (some/any) butter |
| **du** jus d'orange | (some/any) orange juice |

i Note that **du** is also a combination of **de + le** and has other meanings, such as saying who something belongs to or where something is from.

➪ *For more information on **du**, see page 166.*

➤ **de la** is used in front of <u>feminine singular nouns</u>.

| **de la** viande | (some/any) meat |
| **de la** margarine | (some/any) margarine |

➤ **de l'** is used in front of <u>singular nouns that start with a vowel</u> and most nouns starting with **h**, whether they are masculine or feminine.

de l'argent (*masculine*)	(some/any) money
de l'eau (*feminine*)	(some/any) water
de l'herbe (*feminine*)	(some/any) grass

➤ **des** is used in front of <u>plural nouns</u>, whether they are masculine or feminine and whatever letter they start with.

des gâteaux	(some/any) cakes
des lettres	(some/any) letters
des hôtels	(some/any) hotels

ⓘ Note that **des** is also a combination of **de** + **les** and has other meanings, such as saying who something belongs to or where something is from.

⇨ *For more information on **des**, see page 166.*

2 The partitive article in negative sentences

➤ In French, you use word pairs like **ne ... pas** (meaning *not*) and **ne ... jamais** (meaning *never*) to say that something is not happening or not true. In this type of expression, **du**, **de la**, **de l'** and **des** all change to **de**.

Nous n'avons pas de beurre.	We don't have any butter.
Je ne mange jamais de viande.	I never eat meat.
Il n'y a pas de timbres.	There aren't any stamps.

⇨ *For more information on **Negatives**, see page 138.*

Tip

de changes to **d'** in front of a word starting with a vowel and most nouns starting with **h**.

Il n'a pas d'argent.	He doesn't have any money.
Il n'y a pas d'horloge dans la salle.	There isn't a clock in the room.

Grammar Extra!

There are some very common adjectives, like **beau**, **bon** and **petit**, that can come <u>BEFORE</u> the noun instead of after it. When an adjective comes before a plural noun, **des** changes to **de**.

J'ai reçu de beaux cadeaux.	I got some lovely presents.
Cette région a de très jolis villages.	This area has some very pretty villages.

⇨ *For more information on **Word order with adjectives**, see page 32.*

3 The meaning of du, de la, de l' and des

➤ **du**, **de la**, **de l'** and **des** are often translated into English as *some* or *any*, but there are times when no word is used in English to translate the French.

Il me doit <u>de l'</u>argent.	He owes me (some) money.
Je vais acheter <u>de la</u> farine et <u>du</u> beurre pour faire un gâteau.	I'm going to buy (some) flour and butter to make a cake.
Est-ce qu'il y a <u>des</u> lettres pour moi?	Are there any letters for me?
Elle ne veut pas <u>de</u> beurre.	She doesn't want any butter.
Je ne prends pas <u>de</u> lait.	I don't take milk.

Tip

Remember that **du**, **de la**, **de l'** and **des** can <u>NEVER</u> be missed out in French, even if there is no word in English.

Key points

✔ With masculine singular nouns → use **du**.

✔ With feminine singular nouns → use **de la**.

✔ With singular nouns starting with a vowel and some nouns beginning with **h** → use **de l'**.

✔ With plural nouns → use **des**.

✔ **du**, **de la**, **de l'** and **des** → change to **de** or **d'** in negative sentences.

For further explanation of grammatical terms, please see pages viii–xii.

Adjectives

> **What is an adjective?**
> An **adjective** is a 'describing' word that tells you more about a person or thing, such as their appearance, colour, size or other qualities, for example, *pretty*, *blue*, *big*.

Using adjectives

➤ Adjectives are words like *clever*, *expensive* and *silly* that tell you more about a noun (a living being, thing or idea). They can also tell you more about a pronoun, such as *he* or *they*. Adjectives are sometimes called 'describing words'. They can be used right next to a noun they are describing, or can be separated from the noun by a verb like *be*, *look*, *feel* and so on.

> a <u>clever</u> girl
> an <u>expensive</u> coat
> a <u>silly</u> idea
> He's just being <u>silly</u>.

➪ *For more information on* **Nouns** *and* **Pronouns**, *see pages 1 and 42.*

➤ In English, the only time an adjective changes its form is when you are making a comparison.

> She's <u>cleverer</u> than her brother.
> That's the <u>silliest</u> idea I ever heard!

➤ In French, however, most adjectives <u>agree</u> with what they are describing. This means that their endings change depending on whether the person or thing you are referring to is masculine or feminine, and singular or plural.

un mot français	a French word
une chanson français<u>e</u>	a French song
des traditions français<u>es</u>	French traditions

➤ In English we put adjectives <u>BEFORE</u> the noun they describe, but in French you usually put them <u>AFTER</u> it.

      un chat <u>noir</u>   a <u>black</u> cat

⇨ *For further information, see **Word order with adjectives** on page 32.*

Key points

✔ Most French adjectives change their form, according to whether the person or thing they are describing is masculine or feminine, singular or plural.

✔ In French adjectives usually go after the noun they describe.

Making adjectives agree

1 The basic rules

➤ In dictionaries, regular French adjectives are usually shown in the masculine singular form. You need to know how to change them to make them agree with the noun or pronoun that they are describing.

➤ To make an adjective agree with the noun or pronoun it describes, you simply add the following endings in most cases:

	with masculine noun	with feminine noun
Singular	-	-e
Plural	-s	-es

un chat noir	a black cat
une chemise noire	a black shirt
des chats noirs	black cats
des chemises noires	black shirts

2 Making adjectives feminine

➤ With most adjectives you add an **-e** to the masculine singular form to make it feminine.

> **un chat noir** a black cat → **une chemise noire** a black shirt
>
> **un sac lourd** a heavy bag → **une valise lourde** a heavy suitcase

➤ If the adjective already ends in an **-e** in the masculine, you do not add another **-e**.

> **un sac jaune** a yellow bag → **une chemise jaune** a yellow shirt
>
> **un garçon sage** a good boy → **une fille sage** a good girl

➤ Some changes to endings are a little more complicated but still follow a regular pattern. Sometimes you have to double the consonant as well as adding an **-e**. On the next page there is a table showing these changes.

Masculine ending	Feminine ending	Example	Meaning
-f	-ve	neuf/neuve	new
-x	-se	heureux/heureuse	happy
-er	-ère	cher/chère	dear, expensive
-an -en -on	-anne -enne -onne	paysan/paysanne européen/européenne bon/bonne	farming, country European good, right
-el	-elle	cruel/cruelle	cruel
-eil	-eille	pareil/pareille	similar
-et	-ette -ète	net/nette complet/complète	clear complete, full

un **bon** repas a good meal → de **bonne** humeur in a good mood

un homme **cruel** a cruel man → une remarque **cruelle** a cruel remark

Tip

If a masculine adjective ends in a vowel (*a, e, i, o* or *u*), its pronunciation does not change when an **-e** is added to form the feminine. For example, **joli** and **jolie** are both pronounced the same.

If a masculine adjective ends with a consonant that is not pronounced, such as **-d, -s** or **-t**, you <u>DO</u> pronounce that consonant when an **-e** is added in the feminine. For example, in **chaud** (meaning *hot, warm*), you cannot hear the **d** when it is said out loud; in the feminine form **chaude**, you can hear the **d** sound.

This is also true when you have to double the consonant before the **-e** is added, for example, **gros** (meaning *big, fat*), where you cannot hear the **s**, and the feminine form **grosse**, where you can hear the **s** sound.

Some masculine adjectives, such as **bon** (meaning *good*) or **italien** (meaning *Italian*), end in what is called a <u>nasal vowel</u> and an **-n**. With these words, you pronounce the vowel 'through your nose' but do not say the **n**. When the consonant is doubled and an **-e** is added in the feminine – **bonne, italienne** – the vowel becomes a normal one instead of a nasal vowel and you do pronounce the **n**.

➤ Some very common adjectives have irregular feminine forms.

Masculine form	Feminine form	Meaning
blanc	blanche	white, blank
doux	douce	soft, sweet, mild, gentle
faux	fausse	untrue
favori	favorite	favourite
frais	fraîche	fresh, chilly, cool
gentil	gentille	nice, kind
grec	grecque	Greek
gros	grosse	big, fat
long	longue	long
nul	nulle	useless
roux	rousse	red, red-haired
sec	sèche	dry, dried
turc	turque	Turkish

mon sport favori my favourite sport → **ma chanson favorite** my favourite song

un ami grec a Greek (male) friend → **une amie grecque** a Greek (female) friend

➤ A very small group of French adjectives have an extra masculine singular form that is used in front of words that begin with a vowel (a, e, i, o or u) and most words beginning with **h**. These adjectives also have an irregular feminine form.

Masculine form in front of a word beginning with a consonant	Masculine form in front of a word beginning with a vowel or most words beginning with h	Feminine form	Meaning
beau	bel	belle	lovely, beautiful, good-looking, handsome
fou	fol	folle	mad
nouveau	nouvel	nouvelle	new
vieux	vieil	vieille	old

un **bel** appartement	a beautiful flat
le **Nouvel** An	New Year
un **vieil** arbre	an old tree

3 Making adjectives plural

➤ With most adjectives you add an **-s** to the masculine singular or feminine singular form to make it plural.

> **un chat noir** a black cat → **des chats noirs** black cats
> **une valise lourde** a heavy suitcase → **des valises lourdes** heavy suitcases

> *Tip*
>
> When an adjective describes a masculine <u>and</u> a feminine noun or pronoun, use the masculine plural form of the adjective.
>
> | | |
> |---|---|
> | **La maison et le jardin sont** <u>**beaux**</u>. | The house and garden are beautiful. |
> | **Sophie et son petit ami sont très** <u>**gentils**</u>. | Sophie and her boyfriend are very nice. |

➤ If the masculine singular form already ends in an **-s** or an **-x**, you do not add an **-s**.

> **un fromage français** a French cheese → **des fromages français** French cheeses
> **un homme dangereux** a dangerous man → **des hommes dangereux** dangerous men

➤ If the masculine singular form ends in **-eau** or **-al**, the masculine plural is usually **-eaux** or **-aux**.

> **le nouveau professeur** the new teacher → **les nouv<u>eaux</u> professeurs** the new teachers
> **le rôle principal** the main role → **les rôles princip<u>aux</u>** the main roles

> *Tip*
>
> Adding an **-s** or an **-x** does not change the pronunciation of a word. For example, **noir** and **noirs** sound just the same, as do **nouveau** and **nouveaux**.
>
> When the **-s** or **-x** ending comes before a word starting with a vowel or most words starting with **h**, you have to pronounce the **s** or **x** on the end of the adjective. It sounds like the z in the English word *zip*.
>
> | | |
> |---|---|
> | **les ancien<u>s é</u>lèves** | the former pupils |
> | **de grand<u>s h</u>ôtels** | big hotels |

4 Invariable adjectives

➤ A small number of adjectives (mostly relating to colours) do not change in the feminine or plural. They are called <u>invariable</u> because their form <u>NEVER</u> changes, no matter what they are describing. These adjectives are often made up of more than one word – for example, **bleu marine** (meaning *navy blue*), or else come from the names of fruit or nuts – for example, **orange** (meaning *orange*), **marron** (meaning *brown*).

des chaussures <u>marron</u>	brown shoes
une veste <u>bleu marine</u>	a navy blue jacket

Key points

✔ To make an adjective agree with a feminine singular noun or pronoun, you usually add **-e** to the masculine singular. If the adjective already ends in an **-e**, no further **-e** is added.

✔ Several adjectives ending in a consonant double their consonant as well as adding **-e** in the feminine.

✔ **beau**, **fou**, **nouveau** and **vieux** have an irregular feminine form and an extra masculine singular form that is used in front of words that begin with a vowel and most words beginning with **h**: **bel**, **fol**, **nouvel**, **vieil**.

✔ To make an adjective agree with a masculine plural noun or pronoun, you usually add **-s** to the masculine singular. If the adjective already ends in an **-s** or an **-x**, no further **-s** is added.

✔ If the adjective ends in **-eau** or **-al**, the masculine plural is usually **-eaux** or **-aux**.

✔ To make an adjective agree with a feminine plural noun or pronoun, you usually add **-es** to the masculine singular.

✔ Some adjectives relating to colours never change their form.

Word order with adjectives

1 The basic rules

➤ When adjectives are used right beside the noun they are describing, they go <u>BEFORE</u> it in English. French adjectives usually go <u>AFTER</u> the noun.

l'heure <u>exacte</u>	the <u>right</u> time
la page <u>suivante</u>	the <u>following</u> page

➤ Adjectives describing colours, shapes or nationalities always go <u>AFTER</u> the noun.

des cravates <u>rouges</u>	red ties
une table <u>ronde</u>	a round table
un mot <u>français</u>	a French word

➤ Some very common adjectives usually come <u>BEFORE</u> the noun.

beau	lovely, beautiful, good-looking, handsome
bon	good, right
court	short
grand	tall, big, long, great
gros	big, fat
haut	high
jeune	young
joli	pretty
long	long
mauvais	bad, poor
meilleur	better
nouveau	new
petit	small, little
premier	first
vieux	old
une belle journée	a lovely day
Bonne chance!	Good luck!

➤ There is a small group of common adjectives whose meaning changes depending on whether they come before the noun or go after it.

Adjective	Example before noun	Meaning	Example after noun	Meaning
ancien	un ancien collègue	a <u>former</u> colleague	un fauteuil ancien	an <u>antique</u> chair
cher	Chère Julie	<u>Dear</u> Julie	une robe chère	an <u>expensive</u> dress
propre	ma propre chambre	my <u>own</u> bedroom	un mouchoir propre	a <u>clean</u> handkerchief

For further explanation of grammatical terms, please see pages viii–xii.

Tip

dernier (meaning *last*) and **prochain** (meaning *next*) go <u>AFTER</u> nouns relating to time, for example, **semaine** (meaning *week*) and **mois** (meaning *month*). Otherwise they go <u>BEFORE</u> the noun.

la semaine <u>dernière</u>	last week
la <u>dernière</u> fois que je t'ai vu	the last time I saw you
la semaine <u>prochaine</u>	next week
la <u>prochaine</u> fois que j'y vais	the next time I go there

Grammar Extra!

When certain adjectives are used with certain nouns, they take on a meaning you cannot always guess. You may need to check these in your dictionary and learn them. Here are a few:

mon petit ami	my boyfriend
les petits pois	peas
les grandes vacances	the summer holidays
une grande personne	an adult, a grown-up

2 Using more than one adjective

➤ In French you can use more than one adjective at a time to describe someone or something. If one of the adjectives usually comes <u>BEFORE</u> the noun and the other usually goes <u>AFTER</u> the noun, the word order follows the usual pattern.

une <u>jeune</u> femme <u>blonde</u>	a young blonde woman
un <u>nouveau</u> film <u>intéressant</u>	an interesting new film

➤ If both adjectives usually come <u>AFTER</u> the noun, they are joined together with **et** (meaning *and*).

un homme mince <u>et</u> laid	a thin, ugly man
une personne intelligente <u>et</u> drôle	an intelligent, funny person

Key points

✔ Most French adjectives go after the noun they describe.
✔ Some very common adjectives usually come before the noun: **bon/mauvais, court/long, grand/petit, jeune/nouveau/vieux, gros, haut, beau, joli, premier, meilleur**.
✔ The meaning of some adjectives such as **ancien**, **cher** and **propre** varies according to the position in the sentence.

Comparatives and superlatives of adjectives

1 Making comparisons using comparative adjectives

What is a comparative adjective?
A **comparative adjective** in English is one with -er on the end of it or *more* or *less* in front of it, that is used to compare people or things, for example, *slower*, *less important*, *more beautiful*.

➤ In French, to say that something is *easier*, *more expensive* and so on, you use **plus** (meaning *more*) before the adjective.

Cette question est <u>plus</u> facile.	This question is easier.
Cette veste est <u>plus</u> chère.	This jacket is more expensive.

➤ To say something is *less expensive*, *less complicated* and so on, you use **moins** (meaning *less*) before the adjective.

Cette veste est <u>moins</u> chère.	This jacket is less expensive.
un projet <u>moins</u> compliqué	a less complicated plan

➤ To introduce the person or thing you are making the comparison with, use **que** (meaning *than*).

Elle est plus petite <u>que</u> moi.	She's smaller than me.
Cette question est plus facile <u>que</u> la première.	This question is easier than the first one.

➤ To say that something or someone is *as ... as* something or someone else, use **aussi ... que**.

Il est <u>aussi</u> inquiet <u>que</u> moi.	He's as worried as me.
Cette ville n'est pas <u>aussi</u> grande <u>que</u> Bordeaux.	This town isn't as big as Bordeaux.

2 Making comparisons using superlative adjectives

What is a superlative adjective?
A **superlative adjective** in English is one with -est on the end of it or *most* or *least* in front of it, that is used to compare people or things, for example, *thinnest*, *most beautiful*, *least interesting*.

➤ In French, to say that something or someone is *easiest*, *prettiest*, *most expensive* and so on, you use:

- **le plus** with <u>masculine singular</u> adjectives

- **la plus** with <u>feminine singular</u> adjectives
- **les plus** with <u>plural</u> adjectives (for both masculine and feminine)

le guide <u>le plus</u> utile	the <u>most</u> useful guidebook
la question <u>la plus</u> facile	the easi<u>est</u> question
<u>les plus</u> grands hôtels	the big<u>gest</u> hotels
<u>les plus</u> petites voitures	the small<u>est</u> cars

➤ To say that something or someone is *the least easy*, *the least pretty*, *the least expensive* and so on, you use:

- **le moins** with <u>masculine singular</u> adjectives
- **la moins** with <u>feminine singular</u> adjectives
- **les moins** with <u>plural</u> adjectives (for both masculine and feminine).

le guide <u>le moins</u> utile	the <u>least</u> useful guidebook
Cette question est <u>la moins</u> facile.	This question is the <u>least</u> easy (*or* the hard<u>est</u>).
les mois <u>les moins</u> agréables	the <u>least</u> pleasant months
<u>les moins</u> belles photos	the <u>least</u> attractive photos

---

Tip

When the adjective comes <u>AFTER</u> the noun, you repeat the definite article (**le**, **la** or **les**).

    les mois <u>les</u> moins agréables   the least pleasant months

When the adjective comes <u>BEFORE</u> the noun, you do not repeat the definite article.

    les moins belles photos   the least attractive photos

⇨ *For more information on **Word order with adjectives**, see page 32.*

➤ In phrases like *the biggest hotel in London* and *the oldest person in the village*, you use **de** to translate *in*.

le plus grand hôtel <u>de</u> Londres	the biggest hotel in London
la personne la plus âgée <u>du</u> village	the oldest person in the village

⇨ *For more information on **de** and **du**, see page 166.*

3 Irregular comparative and superlative adjectives

➤ Just as English has some irregular comparative and superlative forms – *better* instead of '*more good*', and *worst* instead of '*most bad*' – French also has a few irregular forms.

36 Adjectives

Adjective	Meaning	Comparative	Meaning	Superlative	Meaning
bon	good	meilleur	better	le meilleur	the best
mauvais	bad	pire plus mauvais	worse	le pire le plus mauvais	the worst
petit	small	moindre plus petit	smaller, lesser	le moindre le plus petit	the smallest, the least, the slightest

J'ai une <u>meilleure</u> idée.   I've got a <u>better</u> idea.
Il ne fait pas <u>le moindre</u> effort.   He doesn't make the <u>slightest</u> effort.

Tip

Choose the right form of the adjective to match the noun or pronoun, depending on whether it is masculine or feminine, singular or plural. Don't forget to change **le** to **la** or **les** too in superlatives.

Grammar Extra!

bien and its comparative and superlative forms **mieux** and **le mieux** can be both adjectives and adverbs.

Il est <u>bien</u>, ce restaurant. (=*adjective*) This restaurant is good.
Elle va <u>mieux</u> aujourd'hui. (=*adverb*) She's better today.

⇨ *For more information on **Adverbs**, see page 152.*

Key points

✔ To compare people or things in French you use **plus** + adjective, **moins** + adjective or **aussi … que**.
✔ *than* in comparatives corresponds to **que**.
✔ French superlatives are formed with **le/la/les plus** + adjective and **le/la/les moins** + adjective.
✔ *in* after superlatives corresponds to **de**.
✔ **bon**, **mauvais** and **petit** have irregular comparatives and superlatives: **bon/meilleur/le meilleur**, **mauvais/pire/le pire**, **petit/moindre/le moindre**.

Demonstrative adjectives: ce, cette, cet and ces

> **What is a demonstrative adjective?**
> A **demonstrative adjective** is one of the words *this*, *that*, *these* and *those* used with a noun in English to point out a particular thing or person, for example, *this* woman, *that* dog.

➤ In French you use **ce** to point out a particular thing or person. Like all adjectives in French, **ce** changes its form depending on whether you are referring to a noun that is masculine or feminine, singular or plural.

	Masculine	Feminine	Meaning
Singular	ce (cet)	cette	this that
Plural	ces	ces	these those

> *Tip*
>
> **cet** is used in front of masculine singular nouns which begin with a vowel and most words beginning with **h**.
>
> | cet oiseau | this/that bird |
> | cet hôpital | this/that hospital |

➤ **ce** comes <u>BEFORE</u> the noun it refers to.

Combien coûte <u>ce</u> manteau?	How much is this/that coat?
Comment s'appelle <u>cette</u> entreprise?	What's this/that company called?
<u>Ces</u> livres sont très intéressants.	These/Those books are very interesting.
<u>Ces</u> couleurs sont jolies.	These/Those colours are pretty.

➤ If you want to emphasize the difference between something that is close to you and something that is further away, you can add:

- **-ci** on the end of the noun for things that are closer
  | Prends cette valise-<u>ci</u>. | Take this case. |

- **-là** on the end of the noun for things that are further away

Est-ce que tu reconnais cette personne-là?   Do you recognize that person?

Key points

✔ The adjective **ce** corresponds to *this* and *that* in the singular, and *these* and *those* in the plural.

✔ The forms are **ce** and **cette** in the singular, and **ces** in the plural. **cet** is used with masculine singular nouns beginning with a vowel and most words beginning with **h**.

✔ You can add **-ci** on the end of the noun for things that are closer, or **-là** for things that are further away, to emphasize the difference between them.

Possessive adjectives

> **What is a possessive adjective?**
> In English a **possessive adjective** is one of the words *my, your, his, her, its, our* or *their* used with a noun to show that one person or thing belongs to another.

➤ Here are the French possessive adjectives. Like all French adjectives, these agree with the noun they refer to.

with masculine singular noun	with feminine singular noun	with plural noun (masculine or feminine)	Meaning
mon	ma (mon)	mes	my
ton	ta (ton)	tes	your
son	sa (son)	ses	his her its one's
notre	notre	nos	our
votre	votre	vos	your
leur	leur	leurs	their

> *Tip*
> You use **mon**, **ton** and **son** with feminine singular nouns in front of words that begin with a vowel and most words beginning with **h**. This makes them easier to say.
>
> | | |
> |---|---|
> | <u>mon</u> assiette | my plate |
> | <u>ton</u> histoire | your story |
> | <u>son</u> erreur | his/her mistake |
> | <u>mon</u> autre sœur | my other sister |

➤ Possessive adjectives come <u>BEFORE</u> the noun they describe.

Voilà <u>mon</u> mari.	There's my husband.
<u>Mon</u> frère et <u>ma</u> sœur habitent à Glasgow.	My brother and sister live in Glasgow.
Est-ce que <u>tes</u> voisins vendent <u>leur</u> maison?	Are your neighbours selling their house?
Rangez <u>vos</u> affaires.	Put your things away.

> *Tip*
>
> Possessive adjectives agree with what they describe, <u>NOT</u> with the person who owns that thing. For example, **sa** can mean *his, her, its* and *one's*, but can only ever be used with a feminine singular noun.
>
> | | |
> |---|---|
> | **Paul cherche <u>sa</u> montre.** | Paul's looking for <u>his</u> watch. |
> | **Paul cherche <u>ses</u> lunettes.** | Paul's looking for <u>his</u> glasses. |
> | **Catherine a appelé <u>son</u> frère.** | Catherine called <u>her</u> brother. |
> | **Catherine a appelé <u>sa</u> sœur.** | Catherine called <u>her</u> sister. |

➤ The equivalent of *your* in French is **ton/ta/tes** for someone you call **tu**, or **votre/vos** for someone you call **vous**.

⇨ *For more information on the difference between* **tu** *and* **vous***, see page 43.*

[i] Note that possessive adjectives are <u>not</u> normally used with parts of the body. Use **le**, **la**, **l'** or **les** instead.

    J'ai mal <u>à la main</u>.   My hand hurts.

⇨ *For more information on* **Articles***, see page 12.*

Key points

✔ The French possessive adjectives are:
  - **mon/ton/son/notre/votre/leur** in the masculine singular
  - **ma/ta/sa/notre/votre/leur** in the feminine singular
  - **mes/tes/ses/nos/vos/leurs** in the plural

✔ Possessive adjectives come before the noun they refer to. They agree with what they describe, rather than with the person who owns that thing.

✔ You use **mon**, **ton** and **son** with feminine singular nouns when the following word begins with a vowel. You also use them with most words beginning with **h**.

✔ Possessive adjectives are not normally used with parts of the body. Use **le**, **la**, **l'** or **les** instead.

Indefinite adjectives

> **What is an indefinite adjective?**
> An **indefinite adjective** is one of a small group of adjectives that are used to talk about people or things in a general way without saying exactly who or what they are, for example, *several*, *all*, *every*.

➤ In French, this type of adjective comes <u>BEFORE</u> the noun it refers to. Here are the most common French indefinite adjectives:

Masculine singular	Feminine singular	Masculine plural	Feminine plural	Meaning
autre	autre	autres	autres	other
chaque	chaque	-	-	every, each
même	même	mêmes	mêmes	same
-	-	quelques	quelques	some, a few
tout	toute	tous	toutes	all, every

J'ai d'<u>autres</u> projets.	I've got other plans.
J'y vais <u>chaque</u> année.	I go every year.
J'ai le <u>même</u> manteau.	I have the same coat.
Il a <u>quelques</u> amis à Paris.	He has some friends in Paris.
Il reste <u>quelques</u> bouteilles.	There are a few bottles left.
Il travaille <u>tout</u> le temps.	He works all the time.

Tip

You can also use **tout** to talk about how often something happens.

tous les jours	every day
tous les deux jours	every other day

ⓘ Note that these words can also be used as <u>pronouns</u>, standing in place of a noun instead of being used with one. **chaque** and **quelques** have a slightly different form when they are used in this way.

⇨ *For more information on **Pronouns**, see page 42.*

> **Key points**
> ✔ The most common French indefinite adjectives are **autre**, **chaque**, **même**, **quelques** and **tout**.
> ✔ They come before the noun when they are used in this way.

Pronouns

> **What is a pronoun?**
> A **pronoun** is a word you use instead of a noun, when you do not need
> or want to name someone or something directly, for example, *it*, *you*, *none*.

➤ There are several different types of pronoun:

- Personal pronouns such as *I*, *you*, *he*, *her* and *they*, which are used to refer
  to yourself, the person you are talking to, or other people and things. They
  can be either subject pronouns (*I*, *you*, *he* and so on) or object pronouns
  (*him*, *her*, *them* and so on).

- Possessive pronouns like *mine* and *yours*, which show who someone or
  something belongs to.

- Indefinite pronouns like *someone* or *nothing*, which refer to people or things
  in a general way without saying exactly who or what they are.

- Relative pronouns like *who*, *which* or *that*, which link two parts of a
  sentence together.

- Demonstrative pronouns like *this* or *those*, which point things or people
  out.

- Reflexive pronouns, a type of object pronoun that forms part of French
  reflexive verbs like **se laver** (meaning *to wash*) or **s'appeler** (meaning
  to be called).

⇨   *For more information on **Reflexive verbs**, see page 88.*

- The two French pronouns, **en** and **y**, which are used in certain
  constructions.

- The pronouns **qui?** (meaning *who?, whom?*), **que?** (meaning *what?*), **quoi?**
  (meaning *what?*) and **lequel?** (meaning *which one?*), which are used in
  asking questions.

⇨   *For more information on **Questions**, see page 142.*

➤ Pronouns often stand in for a noun to save repeating it.
>   I finished my homework and gave <u>it</u> to my teacher.
>   Do you remember Jack? I saw <u>him</u> at the weekend.

➤ Word order with personal pronouns is usually different in French and English.

Personal pronouns: subject

> **What is a subject pronoun?**
> A **subject pronoun** is a word such as *I, he, she* and *they*, which performs the action expressed by the verb. Pronouns stand in for nouns when it is clear who is being talked about, for example, *My brother isn't here at the moment. He'll be back in an hour.*

1 Using subject pronouns

➤ Here are the French subject pronouns:

Singular	Meaning	Plural	Meaning
je (j')	I	**nous**	we
tu *or* **vous**	you	**vous**	you
il	he it	**ils**	they (*masculine*)
elle	she it	**elles**	they (*feminine*)
on	one (we/you/they)		

    Je pars en vacances demain.   I'm going on holiday tomorrow.
    Nous habitons à Nice.   We live in Nice.

> *Tip*
> **je** changes to **j'** in front of words beginning with a vowel, most words beginning with **h**, and the French word **y**.
>   **J'arrive!**   I'm just coming!
>   **Bon, j'y vais.**   Right, I'm off.

2 tu or vous?

➤ In English we have only <u>one</u> way of saying you. In French, there are <u>two</u> words: **tu** and **vous**. The word you use depends on:

- whether you are talking to one person or more than one person
- whether you are talking to a friend or family member, or someone else

➤ If you are talking to one person <u>you know well</u>, such as a friend, a young person or a relative, use **tu**.
    Tu me prêtes ce CD?   Will you lend me this CD?

➤ If you are talking to one person <u>you do not know so well</u>, such as your teacher, your boss or a stranger, use **vous**.

> **<u>Vous</u> pouvez entrer.**   You may come in.

Tip

If you are in doubt as to which form of *you* to use, it is safest to use **vous** and you will not offend anybody.

➤ If you are talking to <u>more than one person</u>, you have to use **vous**, no matter how well you know them.

> **<u>Vous</u> comprenez, les enfants?**   Do you understand, children?

[i] Note that the adjectives you use with **tu** and **vous** have to agree in the feminine and plural forms.

> **Vous êtes <u>certain</u>, Monsieur Leclerc?** (*masculine singular*)   Are you sure, Mr Leclerc?
>
> **Vous êtes <u>certains</u>, les enfants?** (*masculine plural*)   Are you sure, children?

Grammar Extra!

Any past participles (the form of the verb ending in **-é, -i** or **-u** in French) used with **être** in tenses such as the perfect also have to agree in the feminine and plural forms.

> **Vous êtes <u>partie</u> quand, Estelle?** (*feminine singular*)   When did you leave, Estelle?
>
> **Estelle et Sophie – vous êtes <u>parties</u> quand?** (*feminine plural*)   Estelle and Sophie – when did you leave?

➪ *For more information on the **Past participle**, see page 111.*

---

3 il/elle and ils/elles

➤ In English we generally refer to things (such as *table, book, car*) only as *it*. In French, **il** (meaning *he, it*) and **elle** (meaning *she, it*) are used to talk about a thing, as well as about a person or an animal. You use **il** for <u>masculine nouns</u> and **elle** for <u>feminine nouns.</u>

> **<u>Il</u> est déjà parti.**   He's already left.
>
> **<u>Elle</u> est actrice.**   She's an actress.
>
> **<u>Il</u> mord, ton chien?**   Does your dog bite?
>
> **Prends cette chaise. <u>Elle</u> est plus confortable.**   Take this chair. It's more comfortable.

➤ **il** is also used to talk about the weather, the time and in certain other set phrases, often in the same way as some phrases with *it* in English.

Il pleut.	It's raining.
Il est deux heures.	It's two o'clock.
Il faut partir.	We/You have to go.

➤ **ils** (meaning *they*) and **elles** (meaning *they*) are used in the plural to talk about things, as well as about people or animals. Use **ils** for <u>masculine nouns</u> and **elles** for <u>feminine nouns</u>.

Ils vont appeler ce soir.	They're going to call tonight.
'Où sont Anne et Rachel?' –	'Where are Anne and Rachel?' –
'Elles sont à la piscine.'	'They're at the swimming pool.'
'Est-ce qu'il reste des billets?'	'Are there are any tickets left?' –
– 'Non, ils sont tous vendus.'	'No, they're all sold.'
'Tu aimes ces chaussures?' –	'Do you like those shoes?' – 'No,
'Non, elles sont affreuses!'	they're horrible!'

➤ If you are talking about a masculine and a feminine noun, use **ils**.

Que font <u>ton père et ta mère</u> quand <u>ils</u> partent en vacances?	What do your father and mother do when they go on holiday?
'Où sont <u>le poivre et la moutarde</u>?' – '<u>Ils</u> sont déjà sur la table.'	'Where are the pepper and the mustard?' – 'They're already on the table.'

4 on

➤ **on** is frequently used in informal, everyday French to mean *we*.

On va à la plage demain.	We're going to the beach tomorrow.
On y va?	Shall we go?

➤ **on** can also have the sense of *someone* or *they*.

On m'a volé mon porte-monnaie.	Someone has stolen my purse.
On vous demande au téléphone.	There's a phone call for you.

Tip

on is often used to avoid a passive construction in French.

On m'a dit que tu étais malade.   I was told you were ill.

⇨ *For more information on the **Passive**, see page 122.*

➤ You can also use **on** as we use *you* in English when we mean people in general.

On peut visiter le château en été.	You can visit the castle in the summer.
D'ici on peut voir les côtes françaises.	From here you can see the French coast.

> *Tip*
>
> The form of the verb you use with **on** is the same as the **il/elle** form.
>
> ⇨ *For more information on **Verbs**, see pages 69–137.*

Key points

✔ The French subject pronouns are: **je (j')**, **tu**, **il**, **elle**, **on** in the singular, and **nous**, **vous**, **ils**, **elles** in the plural.

✔ To say *you* in French, use **tu** if you are talking to one person you know well or to a young person. Use **vous** if you are talking to one person you do not know so well or to more than one person.

✔ **il/ils** (masculine singular/plural) and **elle/elles** (feminine singular/plural) are used to refer to things, as well as to people or animals. **il** is also used in certain set phrases.

✔ If there is a mixture of masculine and feminine nouns, use **ils**.

✔ **on** can mean *we*, *someone*, *you*, *they*, or people in general. It is often used instead of a passive construction.

Personal pronouns: direct object

> **What is a direct object pronoun?**
> A **direct object pronoun** is a word such as *me*, *him*, *us* and *them*, which is used instead of the noun to stand in for the person or thing most directly affected by the action expressed by the verb.

1 Using direct object pronouns

➤ Direct object pronouns stand in for nouns when it is clear who or what is being talked about, and save having to repeat the noun.

> I've lost my glasses. Have you seen <u>them</u>?
> 'Have you met Jo?' – 'Yes, I really like <u>her</u>!'

➤ Here are the French direct object pronouns:

Singular	Meaning	Plural	Meaning
me (m')	me	**nous**	us
te (t')	you	**vous**	you
le (l')	him it	**les**	them (*masculine and feminine*)
la (l')	her it		

Ils vont <u>nous</u> aider.	They're going to help us.
Je <u>la</u> vois.	I can see her/it.
'Tu aimes les carottes?' – **'Non, je <u>les</u> déteste!'**	'Do you like carrots?' – 'No, I hate them!'

ⓘ Note that you cannot use direct object pronouns after a preposition like **à** or **de**, or when you want to emphasize something.

➪ *For more information on **Emphatic pronouns**, see page 51.*

> *Tip*
>
> **me** changes to **m'**, **te** to **t'**, and **le/la** to **l'** in front of words beginning with a vowel, most words beginning with **h**, and the French word **y**.
>
> | **Je <u>t'</u>aime.** | I love you. |
> |---|---|
> | **Tu <u>m'</u>entends?** | Can you hear me? |

➤ In orders and instructions telling someone to do something, **moi** is used instead of **me**, and **toi** is used instead of **te**.

Aidez-<u>moi</u>!	Help me!
Assieds-<u>toi</u>.	Sit down.

➤ **le** is sometimes used to refer back to an idea or information that has already been given. The word *it* is often missed out in English.

'Ta chemise est très sale.' –	'Your shirt's very dirty.' –
'Je <u>le</u> sais.'	'I know.'

2 Word order with direct object pronouns

➤ The direct object pronoun usually comes <u>BEFORE</u> the verb.

Je <u>t'</u>aime.	I love you.
<u>Les</u> voyez-vous?	Can you see them?
Elle ne <u>nous</u> connaît pas.	She doesn't know us.

[i] Note that in orders and instructions telling someone to do something, the direct object pronoun comes <u>AFTER</u> the verb.

Asseyez-<u>vous</u>.	Sit down.

➤ In tenses like the perfect that are formed with **avoir** or **être** and the past participle (the part of the verb that ends in **-é**, **-i** or **-u** in French), the direct object pronoun comes <u>BEFORE</u> the part of the verb that comes from **avoir** or **être**.

Il <u>m'</u>a vu.	He saw me.

➤ When a verb like **vouloir** (meaning *to want*) or **pouvoir** (meaning *to be able to, can*) is followed by another verb in the infinitive (the '*to*' form of the verb), the direct object pronoun comes <u>BEFORE</u> the infinitive.

Il voudrait <u>la</u> revoir.	He'd like to see her again.
Puis-je <u>vous</u> aider?	Can I help you?

> **Key points**
> ✔ The French direct object pronouns are: **me (m')**, **te (t')**, **le/la (l')** in the singular, and **nous**, **vous**, **les** in the plural.
> ✔ Except in orders and instructions telling someone to do something, the direct object pronoun comes before the verb.

Personal pronouns: indirect object

> **What is an indirect object pronoun?**
> When a verb has two objects (a <u>direct</u> one and an <u>indirect</u> one), the **indirect object pronoun** is used instead of a noun to show the person or thing the action is intended to benefit or harm, for example, *me* in *He gave <u>me</u> a book; Can you get <u>me</u> a towel?*

1 Using indirect object pronouns

➤ It is important to understand the difference between direct and indirect object pronouns in English, as they can have different forms in French:

- an <u>indirect object</u> answers the question *who to/for?* or *to/for what?*

  He gave me a book. → *Who did he give the book to?* → me (=*indirect object pronoun*)

  Can you get me a towel? → *Who can you get a towel for?* → me (=*indirect object pronoun*)

- if something answers the question *what* or *who*, then it is the <u>direct object</u> and <u>NOT</u> the indirect object

  He gave me a book. → *What did he give me?* → a book (=*direct object*)

  Can you get me a towel? → *What can you get me?* → a towel (=*direct object*)

➤ Here are the French indirect object pronouns:

Singular	Meaning	Plural	Meaning
me (m')	me, to me, for me	**nous**	us, to us, for us
te (t')	you, to you, for you	**vous**	you, to you, for you
lui	him, to him, for him her, to her, for her it, to it, for it	**leur**	them, to them, for them (*masculine and feminine*)

Il **nous** écrit tous les jours. — He writes to us every day.
Ils **te** cachent quelque chose. — They're hiding something from you.

> **Tip**
>
> **me** changes to **m'** and **te** to **t'** in front of words beginning with a vowel, most words beginning with **h**, and the French word **y**.
>
> | | |
> |---|---|
> | Il <u>m'</u>a donné un livre. | He gave me a book. |
> | Tu <u>m'</u>apportes une serviette? | Can you get me a towel? |

➤ The pronouns shown in the table are used instead of the preposition **à** with a noun.

J'écris <u>à Suzanne</u>. I'm writing to Suzanne. → **Je <u>lui</u> écris.** I'm writing to her.
Donne du lait <u>au chat</u>. Give the cat some milk. → **Donne-<u>lui</u> du lait.** Give it some milk.

➤ Some French verbs like **demander à** (meaning *to ask*) and **téléphoner à** (meaning *to phone*) take an <u>indirect object</u> even though English uses a <u>direct object</u>.

    Il <u>leur</u> téléphone tous les soirs.   He phones <u>them</u> every evening.

➤ On the other hand, some French verbs like **attendre** (meaning *to wait for*), **chercher** (meaning *to look for*) and **regarder** (meaning *to look at*) take a <u>direct object</u> even though English uses an <u>indirect object</u>.

    Je <u>les</u> attends devant la gare.   I'll wait for <u>them</u> outside the station.

2 Word order with indirect object pronouns

➤ The indirect object pronoun usually comes <u>BEFORE</u> the verb.

Dominique <u>vous</u> écrit une lettre.	Dominique's writing you a letter.
Il ne <u>nous</u> parle pas.	He doesn't speak to us.
Il ne veut pas <u>me</u> répondre.	He won't answer me.

> *i* Note that in orders and instructions telling someone to do something, the indirect object pronoun comes <u>AFTER</u> the verb.
>
>   **Donne-<u>moi</u> ça!**   Give me that!

> **Key points**
> ✔ The French indirect object pronouns are: **me (m')**, **te (t')**, **lui** in the singular, and **nous**, **vous**, **leur** in the plural.
> ✔ Except in orders and instructions telling someone to do something, the direct object pronoun comes <u>before</u> the verb.

Emphatic pronouns

> **What is an emphatic pronoun?**
> An **emphatic pronoun** is used instead of a noun when you want to
> emphasize something, for example *Is this for me?*

1 Using emphatic pronouns

➤ In French, there is another set of pronouns which you use after prepositions,
when you want to emphasize something and in certain other cases. These are
called emphatic pronouns or stressed pronouns.

Singular	Meaning	Plural	Meaning
moi	I me	nous	we us
toi	you	vous	you
lui	he him	eux	they (*masculine*) them
elle	she her	elles	they (*feminine*) them
soi	oneself (yourself, ourselves)		

Je pense souvent à toi.	I often think about you.
C'est pour moi?	Is this for me?
Venez avec moi.	Come with me.
Il a besoin de nous.	He needs us.

➤ **soi** (meaning *oneself*) is used with the subject pronoun **on** and with words like
tout le monde (meaning *everyone*) or **chacun** (meaning *each one*).

Il faut avoir confiance en soi.	You have to have confidence in yourself.
Tout le monde est rentré chez soi.	Everyone went home.

2 When to use emphatic pronouns

➤ Emphatic pronouns are used in the following circumstances:
- after a preposition

C'est pour moi?	Is this for me?

- for emphasis, especially where a contrast is involved

Toi, tu ressembles à ton père, mais <u>elle</u> non.	You look like your father, she doesn't.
Il m'énerve, <u>lui</u>!	He's getting on my nerves!

- on their own without a verb

'Qui a cassé la fenêtre?' – '<u>Lui</u>.'	'Who broke the window?' – 'He did.'
'Je suis fatiguée.' – '<u>Moi</u> aussi.'	'I'm tired.' – 'Me too.'

- after **c'est** and **ce sont** (meaning *it is*)

C'est <u>toi</u>, Simon?	Is that you, Simon?
Ce sont <u>eux</u>.	It's them.

⇨ *For more information on **c'est** and **ce sont**, see page 65.*

- in comparisons

Tu es plus jeune que <u>moi</u>.	You're younger than me.
Il est moins grand que <u>toi</u>.	He's smaller than you (are).

- when the subject of the sentence is made up of two pronouns, or of a pronoun and a noun

Mon père et elle ne s'entendent pas.	My father and she don't get on.

Grammar Extra!

You can add **-même** or **-mêmes** to the emphatic pronouns when you particularly want to emphasize something. These forms correspond to English *myself, ourselves* and so on.

Form with -même	Meaning
moi-même	myself
toi-même	yourself
lui-même	himself, itself
elle-même	herself, itself
soi-même	oneself (yourself, ourselves)
nous-mêmes	ourselves
vous-même **vous-mêmes**	yourself yourselves
eux-mêmes	themselves (*masculine*)
elles-mêmes	themselves (*feminine*)

Je l'ai fait <u>moi-même</u>.	I did it myself.
Elle l'a choisi <u>elle-même</u>.	She chose it herself.

For further explanation of grammatical terms, please see pages viii–xii.

Key points

✔ The French emphatic pronouns are: **moi**, **toi**, **lui**, **elle**, **soi** in the singular, and **nous**, **vous**, **eux**, **elles** in the plural.

✔ They are used:
- after a preposition
- for emphasis
- on their own without a verb
- after **c'est** and **ce sont**
- in comparisons
- when the subject of the sentence is made up of two pronouns, or of a pronoun and a noun

✔ You can add **-même** or **-mêmes** to the emphatic pronouns when you particularly want to emphasize something.

Possessive pronouns

> **What is a possessive pronoun?**
> A **possessive pronoun** is one of the words *mine, yours, hers, his, ours* or *theirs*, which are used instead of a noun to show that one person or thing belongs to another, for example, *Ask Carole if this pen is <u>hers</u>*.

➤ Here are the French possessive pronouns:

Masculine singular	Feminine singular	Masculine plural	Feminine plural	Meaning
le mien	la mienne	les miens	les miennes	mine
le tien	la tienne	les tiens	les tiennes	yours
le sien	la sienne	les siens	les siennes	his hers
le nôtre	la nôtre	les nôtres	les nôtres	ours
le vôtre	la vôtre	les vôtres	les vôtres	yours
le leur	la leur	les leurs	les leurs	theirs

Ces CD-là, ce sont <u>les miens</u>.	Those CDs are mine.
Heureusement que tu as tes clés. J'ai oublié <u>les miennes</u>.	It's lucky you've got your keys. I forgot mine.

> *Tip*
>
> In French, possessive pronouns agree with what they describe, <u>NOT</u> with the person who owns that thing. For example, **le sien** can mean *his* or *hers*, but can only be used to replace a masculine singular noun.
>
> | | |
> |---|---|
> | **'C'est <u>le vélo</u> de Paul?'** – **'Oui, c'est <u>le sien</u>.'** | 'Is that Paul's bike?' – 'Yes, it's <u>his</u>.' |
> | **'C'est <u>le vélo</u> d'Isabelle?'** – **'Oui, c'est <u>le sien</u>.'** | 'Is that Isabelle's bike?' – 'Yes, it's <u>hers</u>.' |

Grammar Extra!

Remember that **à** with the definite article **le** becomes **au**, and **à** with **les** becomes **aux**, so:

> **à + le mien → au mien**
> **à + les miens → aux miens**
> **à + les miennes → aux miennes**

> **Tu préfères ce manteau <u>au mien</u>?**   Do you prefer this coat to mine?

Remember that **de** with the definite article **le** becomes **du**, and **de** with **les** becomes **des,** so:

> **de + le mien → du mien**
> **de + les miens → des miens**
> **de + les miennes → des miennes**

> **J'ai oublié mes clés. J'ai besoin <u>des tiennes</u>.**   I've forgotten my keys. I need yours.

⇨ *For more information on **Articles**, see page 12.*

Key points

✔ The French possessive pronouns are **le mien**, **le tien**, **le sien** for singular subject pronouns, and **le nôtre**, **le vôtre** and **le leur** for plural subject pronouns. Their forms change in the feminine and the plural.

✔ In French, the pronoun you choose has to agree with the noun it replaces, and <u>not</u> with the person who owns that thing.

en and y

➤ **en** and **y** do not usually refer to people. How we translate them into English depends on where **en** and **y** are found in French.

1 en

➤ **en** is used with verbs and phrases normally followed by **de** to avoid repeating the same word.

Si tu as un problème, tu peux m'<u>en</u> parler.	If you've got a problem, you can talk to me about it. (**en** *replaces* **de** *in* **parler** <u>*de quelque chose*</u>)
Est-ce que tu peux me prêter ce livre? J'<u>en</u> ai besoin.	Can you lend me that book? I need it. (**en** *replaces* **de** *in* **avoir besoin** <u>*de quelque chose*</u>)
Il a un beau jardin et il <u>en</u> est très fier.	He's got a beautiful garden and is very proud of it. (**en** *replaces* **de** *in* **être fier** <u>*de quelque chose*</u>)

➤ **en** can also replace the <u>partitive article</u> (**du**, **de la**, **de l'**, **des**).

Je n'ai pas d'argent. Tu <u>en</u> as?	I haven't got any money. Have you got any?
'Tu peux me prêter des timbres?' – 'Non, je dois <u>en</u> acheter.'	'Can you lend me some stamps?' – 'No, I have to buy some.'

⇨ *For more information on the **Partitive article**, see page 22.*

➤ **en** is also used:
- as a preposition
- with the present participle of verbs

⇨ *For more information on **Prepositions** and the **Present participle**, see pages 162 and 125.*

➤ When **en** is used with **avoir**, with **il y a** or with numbers, it is often not translated in English but can <u>NEVER</u> be missed out in French.

'Est-ce que tu as un dictionnaire?' – 'Oui, j'<u>en</u> ai un.'	'Have you got a dictionary?' – 'Yes, I've got one.'
'Combien d'élèves y a-t-il dans ta classe?' – 'Il y <u>en</u> a trente.'	'How many pupils are there in your class?' – 'There are thirty.'
J'<u>en</u> veux deux.	I want two (of them).

2 y

➤ **y** is used with verbs and phrases normally followed by **à** to avoid repeating the same word.

'Je pensais à l'examen.' – 'Mais arrête d'y penser!'	'I was thinking about the exam.' – 'Well, stop thinking about it!' (**y** replaces **à** in **penser** **à quelque chose**)
'Je ne m'attendais pas à ça.' – 'Moi, je m'y attendais.'	'I wasn't expecting that.' – 'Well, I was expecting it.' (**y** replaces **à** in **s'attendre** **à quelque chose**)

➤ **y** can also mean *there*. It can be used to replace phrases that would use prepositions such as **dans** (meaning *in*) and **sur** (meaning *on*).

Elle y passe tout l'été.	She spends the whole summer there.
Regarde dans le tiroir. Je pense que les clés y sont.	Look in the drawer. I think the keys are in there.

3 Word order with en and y

➤ **en** and **y** usually come <u>BEFORE</u> the verb.

J'en veux.	I want some.
Elle en a parlé avec lui.	She talked to him about it.
En êtes-vous content?	Are you pleased with it/them?
Comment fait-on pour y aller?	How do you get there?
N'y pense plus.	Don't think about it any more.

➤ In orders and instructions telling someone to do something, **en** or **y** come <u>AFTER</u> the verb and are attached to it with a hyphen (-).

Prenez-en.	Take some.
Restez-y.	Stay there.

Tip

The final **-s** of **-er** verbs is usually dropped in the **tu** form used for orders and instructions. When an **-er** verb in the **tu** form is used before **en** or **y**, however, the **-s** is not dropped, to make it easier to say.

Donne des bonbons à ton frère.	Give some sweets to your brother.
Donnes-en à ton frère.	Give some to your brother.
Va dans ta chambre!	Go to your room!
Vas-y!	Go on!

➡ For more information on the **Imperative**, see page 85.

➤ **en** and **y** come <u>AFTER</u> other direct or indirect object pronouns.

Donnez-<u>leur-en</u>.	Give them some.
Il <u>m'en</u> a parlé.	He spoke to me about it.

⇨ *For more information on **Direct object pronouns** and **Indirect object pronouns**, see pages 47 and 49.*

Key points

- ✔ **en** is used with verbs and expressions normally followed by **de** to avoid repeating the same word.
- ✔ **en** can also replace the partitive article.
- ✔ When **en** is used with **avoir** and **il y a** or with numbers, it is often not translated in English but can never be missed out in French.
- ✔ **y** is used with verbs and expressions normally followed by **à** to avoid repeating the same word.
- ✔ **y** can also mean *there* and may replace expressions that would be used with **dans** and **sur** or some other preposition indicating a place.
- ✔ **en** and **y** usually come before the verb, except in orders and instructions telling someone to do something, when **en** or **y** follows the verb and is attached to it with a hyphen.
- ✔ **en** and **y** come after other direct or indirect object pronouns.

Using different types of pronoun together

➤ Sometimes you find a direct object pronoun and an indirect object pronoun in the same sentence.

> He gave me *(indirect object)* them *(direct object)*.
>
> He gave them *(direct object)* to me *(indirect object)*.

➤ When this happens in French, you have to put the indirect and direct object pronouns in a certain order.

Indirect	Direct	Indirect	
me	le	lui	en
te	la	leur	y
nous	les		
vous			

Dominique vous l'envoie demain.	Dominique's sending it to you tomorrow.
Il te les a montrés?	Has he shown them to you?
Je les lui ai lus.	I read them to him/her.
Ne la leur donne pas.	Don't give it to them.
Elle ne m'en a pas parlé.	She didn't speak to me about it.

Key points

✔ If a direct and an indirect object pronoun are used in the same sentence, you usually put the indirect object pronoun before the direct object pronoun.

✔ With **lui** and **leur**, this order is reversed and you put the direct object pronoun before the indirect object pronoun.

Indefinite pronouns

> **What is an indefinite pronoun?**
> An **indefinite pronoun** is one of a small group of pronouns such as *everything*, *nobody* and *something* which are used to refer to people or things in a general way without saying exactly who or what they are.

➤ Here are the most common French indefinite pronouns:

- **chacun** (*masculine singular*)/**chacune** (*feminine singular*) each, everyone

Nous avons <u>chacun</u> donné dix euros.	We each gave ten euros.
<u>Chacun</u> fait ce qu'il veut.	Everyone does what they like.
Toutes les villas ont <u>chacune</u> leur piscine.	Each villa has its own swimming pool.

- **personne** nobody/no one, anybody/anyone

Il <u>n'y</u> a <u>personne</u> à la maison.	There's no one at home.
Elle <u>ne</u> veut voir <u>personne</u>.	She doesn't want to see anybody.

⇨ *For more information on **Negatives**, see page 138.*

> ### Tip
> You can use **personne** on its own to answer a question.
> **Qui connaît la réponse? <u>Personne</u>.** Who knows the answer? No one.
> If the sentence contains a verb you have to use **ne** with it.
> **Personne <u>n'</u>est venu.** Nobody came.

- **quelque chose** something, anything

J'ai <u>quelque chose</u> pour toi.	I've got something for you.
Avez-vous <u>quelque chose</u> à déclarer?	Do you have anything to declare?

- **quelqu'un** somebody/someone, anybody/anyone

Il y a <u>quelqu'un</u> à la porte.	There's someone at the door.
<u>Quelqu'un</u> a vu mon parapluie?	Has anybody seen my umbrella?

- **rien** nothing, anything

Elle n'a <u>rien</u> dit.	She didn't say anything.
<u>Rien</u> n'a changé.	Nothing's changed.

⇨ *For more information on **Negatives**, see page 138.*

For further explanation of grammatical terms, please see pages viii–xii.

Tip

You can use **rien** on its own to answer a question.

'Qu'est-ce tu as acheté?' – **'Rien.'**	'What did you buy?' – 'Nothing.'

If the sentence contains a verb you have to use **ne** with it.

Il n'a rien mangé.	He's eaten nothing.

- **tout** everything

Il organise tout.	He's organizing everything.
Tout va bien?	Is everything OK?

- **tous** (*masculine plural*)/**toutes** (*feminine plural*) all

Je les connais tous.	I know them all.
Elles sont toutes arrivées?	Are they all here?

➤ You can use **quelque chose de/rien de** and **quelqu'un de/personne de** with adjectives if you want to say *nothing interesting*, *something new* and so on.

rien d'intéressant	nothing interesting

Key points

✔ **rien** and **personne** can be used on their own to answer questions, but need to be used with **ne** when there is a verb in the sentence.

✔ **quelque chose/rien** and **quelqu'un/personne** can be followed by **de** + adjective.

Relative pronouns: qui, que, lequel, auquel, duquel

> **What is a relative pronoun?**
> In English a **relative pronoun** is one of the words *who*, *which* and *that* (and the more formal *whom*) which can be used to introduce information that makes it clear which person or thing is being talked about, for example, *The man who has just come in is Ann's boyfriend; The vase that you broke was quite valuable.*
> Relative pronouns can also introduce further information about someone or something, for example, *Peter, who is a brilliant painter, wants to study art; Jane's house, which was built in 1890, needs a lot of repairs.*

➤ In French, the relative pronouns are **qui**, **que**, **lequel**, **auquel**, and **duquel**.

1 qui and que

➤ **qui** and **que** can both refer to people or things.

	Relative pronoun	Meaning
Subject	qui	who which that
Direct object	que	who, whom which that

Mon frère, <u>qui</u> a vingt ans, est à l'université.	My brother, who's twenty, is at university.
Est-ce qu'il y a un bus <u>qui</u> va au centre-ville?	Is there a bus that goes to the town centre?
Les amis <u>que</u> je vois le plus sont Léa et Mehdi.	The friends (that) I see most are Léa and Mehdi.
Voilà la maison <u>que</u> nous voulons acheter.	That's the house (which) we want to buy.

> *Tip*
>
> **que** changes to **qu'** in front of a word beginning with a vowel and most words beginning with **h**.

➤ **qui** is also used after a preposition such as **à**, **de** or **pour** to talk about <u>people</u>.

la personne <u>à qui</u> il parle	the person he is speaking to
les enfants <u>pour qui</u> j'ai acheté des bonbons	the children I bought sweets for

---

Tip

In English we often miss out the object pronouns *who*, *which* and *that*. For example, we can say both *the friends <u>that</u> I see most*, or *the friends I see most*, and *the house <u>which</u> we want to buy*, or *the house we want to buy*. In French you can <u>NEVER</u> miss out **que** or **qui** in this way.

---

2 lequel, laquelle, lesquels, lesquelles

➤ **lequel** (meaning *which*) is used after a preposition such as **à**, **de** or **pour** to talk about <u>things</u>. It has to agree with the noun it replaces.

	Masculine	Feminine	Meaning
Singular	lequel	laquelle	which
Plural	lesquels	lesquelles	which

le livre <u>pour lequel</u> elle est connue	the book she is famous for
la table <u>sur laquelle</u> j'ai mis mon sac	the table I put my bag on

➤ Remember that **à** and **de** combine with the definite article **le** to become **au** and **du**, and with **les** to become ~~aux~~ and ~~des~~. **lequel/lesquels/lesquelles** combine with **à** and **de** as shown in the table. **laquelle** doesn't change.

	+ lequel	+ laquelle	+ lesquels	+ lesquelles	Meaning
à	auquel	à laquelle	auxquels	auxquelles	to which
de	duquel	de laquelle	desquels	desquelles	of which

⇨ *For more information on **à** and **de**, see pages 14 and 15.*

Grammar Extra!

dont means *whose, of whom, of which, about which* and so on. It can refer to people or things, but its form <u>NEVER</u> changes.

la femme <u>dont</u> la voiture est en panne	the woman whose car has broken down
les films <u>dont</u> tu parles	the films you're talking about

Key points

- ✔ **qui** and **que** can both refer to people or things: **qui** is the subject of the part of the sentence it is found in; **que** is the object.

- ✔ In English we often miss out the object pronouns *who*, *which* and *that*, but in French you can <u>never</u> miss out **que** or **qui**.

- ✔ After a preposition you use **qui** if you are referring to people, and **lequel** if you are referring to things – **lequel** agrees with the noun it replaces.

- ✔ **à + lequel → auquel**
  à + lesquels → auxquels
  à + lesquelles → auxquelles

- ✔ **de + lequel → duquel**
  de + lesquels → desquels
  de + lesquelles → desquelles

Demonstrative pronouns: ce, cela/ça, ceci, celui

> **What is a demonstrative pronoun?**
> In English a **demonstrative pronoun** is one of the words *this*, *that*, *these*, and *those* used instead of a noun to point people or things out, for example, *That* looks fun.

1 | ce

➤ **ce** is usually used with the verb **être** (meaning *to be*) in the expressions **c'est** (meaning *it's, that's*), **c'était** (meaning *it was, that was*), **ce sont** (meaning *it's, that's*) and so on.

C'est moi.	It's me.
C'était mon frère.	That was my brother.
Ce sont eux.	It's them.

> ### Tip
>
> **ce** becomes **c'** when it is followed by a part of the verb that starts with **e** or **é**.
>
> **ce** becomes **ç'** when it is followed by a part of the verb that starts with **a**.
>
> | | |
> |---|---|
> | **Ç'a été difficile.** | It was difficult. |
>
> Note that after **c'est** and **ce sont** and so on you have to use the emphatic form of the pronoun, for example, **moi** instead of **je**, **eux** instead of **ils** and so on.
>
> | | |
> |---|---|
> | **C'est <u>moi</u>.** | It's me. |
>
> ⇨ *For more information on* **Emphatic pronouns**, *see page* 51.

➤ **ce** is used:

- with a noun or a question word to identify a person or thing

Qui est-<u>ce</u>?	Who is it?, Who's this/that?
<u>Ce</u> sont des professeurs.	They're teachers.
Qu'est-ce que <u>c</u>'est?	What's this/that?
<u>C</u>'est un ouvre-boîte.	It's a tin-opener.

- with an adjective to refer to a statement, idea and so on that cannot be classed as either masculine or feminine

<u>C'</u>est très intéressant.	That's/It's very interesting.
<u>C'</u>est dangereux.	That's/It's dangerous.
<u>Ce</u> n'est pas grave.	It doesn't matter.

- for emphasis

<u>C'</u>est moi qui ai téléphoné.	It was me who phoned.
<u>Ce</u> sont les enfants qui ont fait le gâteau.	It was the children who made the cake.

2 cela, ça and ceci

➤ **cela** and **ça** mean *it, this* or *that*. Both refer to a statement, an idea or an object. **ça** is used instead of **cela** in everyday, informal French.

<u>Ça</u> ne fait rien.	It doesn't matter.
Écoute-moi <u>ça</u>!	Listen to this!
<u>Cela</u> dépend.	That/It depends.
Je n'aime pas <u>cela</u>.	I don't like that.
Donne-moi <u>ça</u>!	Give me that!

Tip

ça and cela are used in a more general way than **il** and **elle**, which are usually linked to a noun that has already been mentioned.

Alors, <u>ma nouvelle voiture, elle</u> te plaît?	So, do you like my new car?
<u>Ça</u> te plaît d'aller à l'étranger?	Do you like going abroad?

➤ **ceci** means *this* and is not as common as **cela** and **ça**. It is used to talk about something that has not yet been mentioned.

Lisez <u>ceci</u>.	Read this.

➤ **ceci** is also used to hand or show someone something.

Prends <u>ceci</u>. Tu en auras besoin.	Take this. You'll need it.

3 celui, celle, ceux, celles

➤ **celui** and **celle** mean *the one*; **ceux** and **celles** mean *the ones*. The form you choose depends on whether the noun it is replacing is masculine or feminine, and singular or plural.

	Masculine	Feminine	Meaning
Singular	celui	celle	the one
Plural	ceux	celles	the ones

➤ **celui** and its other forms are used before:

- **qui, que** or **dont**

'Quelle robe préférez-vous?'	'Which dress do you like best?'
– **'Celle qui est en vitrine.'**	– 'The one in the window.'
Prends ceux que tu préfères.	Take the ones you like best.
celui dont je t'ai parlé	the one I told you about
celui qui est proche de la fontaine	the one near the fountain

➤ **celui** and its other forms can be used with **de** to show who something belongs to. In English, we would use **'s**.

Je n'ai pas d'appareil photo mais je peux emprunter celui de ma sœur.	I haven't got a camera but I can borrow my sister's.
Comparez vos réponses à celles de votre voisin.	Compare your answers with your neighbour's.

➤ You can add the endings **-ci** and **-là** to **celui** and its other forms to emphasize the difference between something that is close to you and something that is further away.

- use **-ci** for something that is closer to you
- use **-là** for something that is further away

	Masculine	Feminine	Meaning
Singular	celui-ci	celle-ci	this, this one
	celui-là	celle-là	that, that one
Plural	ceux-ci	celles-ci	these, these ones
	ceux-là	celles-là	those, those ones

On prend quel fromage? Celui-ci ou celui-là?	Which cheese shall we get? This one or that one?
Ces chemises ont deux poches mais celles-là n'en ont pas.	These shirts have two pockets but those have none.

Key points

✔ **ce** is often found in the expressions **c'est**, **ce sont** and so on.

✔ **ce** is also used:

- to identify a person or thing
- to refer to a statement, idea and so on that cannot be classed as either masculine or feminine
- for emphasis

✔ **cela** and **ça** mean *it*, *this* or *that*; **ceci** means *this*, but is not as common.

✔ **celui** and **celle** mean *the one*; **ceux** and **celles** mean *the ones*. They are often found with the endings **-ci** and **-là** and are used to distinguish between things which are close and things which are further away.

Verbs

> **What is a verb?**
> A **verb** is a 'doing' word which describes what someone or something does, what someone or something is, or what happens to them, for example, *be*, *sing*, *live*.

The three conjugations

➤ Verbs are usually used with a noun, with a pronoun such as *I*, *you* or *she*, or with somebody's name. They can relate to the present, the past and the future; this is called their <u>tense</u>.

⇨ *For more information on **Nouns** and **Pronouns**, see pages 1 and 42.*

➤ Verbs are either:
  ● <u>regular</u>; their forms follow the normal rules
  ● <u>irregular</u>; their forms do not follow the normal rules

➤ Regular English verbs have a <u>base form</u> (the form of the verb without any endings added to it, for example, *walk*). The base form can have *to* in front of it, for example, *to walk*. This is called the <u>infinitive</u>. You will find one of these forms when you look a verb up in your dictionary.

➤ French verbs also have an infinitive, which ends in **-er**, **-ir** or **-re**, for example, **donner** (meaning *to give*), **finir** (meaning *to finish*), **attendre** (meaning *to wait*). <u>Regular</u> French verbs belong to one of these three verb groups, which are called <u>conjugations</u>. We will look at each of these three conjugations in turn on the next few pages.

➤ English verbs have other forms apart from the base form and infinitive: a form ending in *-s* (*walks*), a form ending in *-ing* (*walking*), and a form ending in *-ed* (*walked*).

➤ French verbs have many more forms than this, which are made up of endings added to a <u>stem</u>. The stem of a verb can usually be worked out from the infinitive.

➤ French verb endings change, depending on who you are talking about: **je** (*I*), **tu** (*you*), **il/elle/on** (*he/she/one*) in the singular, or **nous** (*we*), **vous** (*you*) and **ils/elles** (*they*) in the plural. French verbs also have different forms depending on whether you are referring to the present, future or past.

➤ Some verbs in French do not follow the normal rules, and are called <u>irregular verbs</u>. These include some very common and important verbs like **avoir** (meaning *to have*), **être** (meaning *to be*), **faire** (meaning *to do, to make*) and **aller** (meaning *to go*). There is information on many of these irregular verbs in the following sections.

⇨ For **Verb tables**, *see supplement*.

Key points

✔ French verbs have different forms depending on what noun or pronoun they are used with, and on their tense.

✔ They are made up of a stem and an ending. The stem is usually based on the infinitive.

✔ Regular verbs fit into one of three patterns or conjugations: **-er**, **-ir**, or **-re** verbs.

✔ Irregular verbs do not follow the normal rules.

The present tense

> **What is the present tense?**
> The **present tense** is used to talk about what is true at the moment, what happens regularly and what is happening now, for example, *I'm a student, I travel to college by train, I'm studying languages*.

➤ You use a verb in the present tense to talk about:

- things that are happening now
  It's raining.
  The phone's ringing.

- things that happen all the time or at certain intervals, or things that you do as a habit
  It always snows in January.
  I play football on Saturdays.

- things that are true at the present time:
  She's not very well.
  It's a beautiful house.

➤ There is more than one way to express the present tense in English. For example, you can say either *I give, I am giving*, or occasionally *I do give*. In French you use the same form (**je donne**) for all of these.

➤ In English you can also use the present tense to talk about something that is going to happen in the near future. You can do the same in French.

Je vais en France le mois prochain.	I'm going to France next month.
Nous prenons le train de dix heures.	We're getting the ten o'clock train.

> *Tip*
>
> Although English sometimes uses parts of the verb *to be* to form the present tense of other verbs (for example, *I am listening, she's talking*), French NEVER uses the verb **être** in this way.

The present tense: regular -er (first conjugation) verbs

➤ If an infinitive in French ends in **-er**, it means the verb belongs to the <u>first conjugation</u>, for example, **donner**, **aimer**, **parler**.

➤ To know which form of the verb to use in French, you need to work out what the stem of the verb is and then add the correct ending. The stem of -**er** verbs in the present tense is formed by taking the <u>infinitive</u> and chopping off **-er**.

Infinitive	Stem (without -**er**)
donner (to give)	**donn-**
aimer (to like, to love)	**aim-**
parler (to speak, to talk)	**parl-**

➤ Now you know how to find the stem of a verb, you can add the correct ending. Which one you choose will depend on whether you are referring to **je**, **tu**, **il**, **elle**, **on**, **nous**, **vous**, **ils** or **elles**.

⇨ For more information on **Pronouns**, see page 42.

➤ Here are the present tense endings for -**er** verbs:

Pronoun	Ending	Add to stem, e.g. donn-	Meanings
je (j')	-e	**je donne**	I give I am giving
tu	-es	**tu donnes**	you give you are giving
il **elle** **on**	-e	**il donne** **elle donne** **on donne**	he/she/it/one gives he/she/it/one is giving
nous	-ons	**nous donnons**	we give we are giving
vous	-ez	**vous donnez**	you give you are giving
ils **elles**	-ent	**ils donnent** **elles donnent**	they give they are giving

Marie <u>regarde</u> la télé.	Marie is watching TV.
Le train <u>arrive</u> à deux heures.	The train arrives at 2 o'clock.

> **Tip**
>
> **je** changes to **j'** in front of a word starting with a vowel (*a, e, i, o* or *u*), most words starting with **h**, and the French word **y**.

i Note that there are a few regular **-er** verbs that are spelled slightly differently from the way you might expect.

⇨ *For more information on **Spelling changes in -er verbs**, see page 78.*

Key points

✔ Verbs ending in **-er** belong to the first conjugation and form their present tense stem by losing the **-er** from the infinitive.

✔ The present tense endings for **-er** verbs are:
-e, -es, -e, -ons, -ez, -ent.

The present tense: regular -ir (second conjugation) verbs

➤ If an infinitive ends in **-ir**, it means the verb belongs to the <u>second conjugation</u>, for example, **finir**, **choisir**, **remplir**.

➤ The stem of **-ir** verbs in the present tense is formed by taking the <u>infinitive</u> and chopping off **-ir**.

Infinitive	Stem (without **-ir**)
finir (*to finish*)	**fin-**
choisir (*to choose*)	**chois-**
remplir (*to fill, to fill in*)	**rempl-**

➤ Now add the correct ending, depending on whether you are referring to **je**, **tu**, **il**, **elle**, **on**, **nous**, **vous**, **ils** or **elles**.

⇨ *For more information on **Pronouns**, see page 42.*

➤ Here are the present tense endings for **-ir** verbs:

Pronoun	Ending	Add to stem, e.g. fin-	Meanings
je (j')	-is	je fin<u>is</u>	I finish I am finishing
tu	-is	tu fin<u>is</u>	you finish you are finishing
il elle on	-it	il fin<u>it</u> elle fin<u>it</u> on fin<u>it</u>	he/she/it/one finishes he/she/it/one is finishing
nous	-issons	nous fin<u>issons</u>	we finish we are finishing
vous	-issez	vous fin<u>issez</u>	you finish you are finishing
ils elles	-issent	ils fin<u>issent</u> elles fin<u>issent</u>	they finish they are finishing

Le cours <u>finit</u> à onze heures.   The lesson finishes at eleven o'clock.
Je <u>finis</u> mes devoirs.   I'm finishing my homework.

Tip

je changes to **j'** in front of a word starting with a vowel, most words starting with **h**, and the French word **y**.

➤ The **nous** and **vous** forms of **-ir** verbs have an extra syllable.

tu fi|nis	*(two syllables)*
vous fi|ni|ssez	*(three syllables)*

Key points

✔ Verbs ending in **-ir** belong to the second conjugation and form their present tense stem by losing the **-ir** from the infinitive.

✔ The present tense endings for **-ir** verbs are:
-is, -is, -it, -issons, -issez, -issent.

✔ Remember the extra syllable in the **nous** and **vous** forms.

The present tense: regular -re (third conjugation) verbs

➤ If an infinitive ends in **-re**, it means the verb belongs to the <u>third conjugation</u>, for example, **attendre**, **vendre**, **entendre**.

➤ The stem of **-re** verbs in the present tense is formed by taking the <u>infinitive</u> and chopping off **-re**.

Infinitive	Stem (without -re)
attendre (*to wait*)	**attend-**
vendre (*to sell*)	**vend-**
entendre (*to hear*)	**entend-**

➤ Now add the correct ending, depending on whether you are referring to **je**, **tu**, **il**, **elle**, **on**, **nous**, **vous**, **ils** or **elles**.

⇨ *For more information on **Pronouns**, see page 42.*

➤ Here are the present tense endings for **-re** verbs:

Pronoun	Ending	Add to stem, e.g. attend-	Meanings
je (j')	-s	j'attend<u>s</u>	I wait I am waiting
tu	-s	tu attend<u>s</u>	you wait you are waiting
il **elle** **on**	-	il attend elle attend on attend	he/she/it/one waits he/she/it/one is waiting
nous	-ons	nous attend<u>ons</u>	we wait we are waiting
vous	-ez	vous attend<u>ez</u>	you wait you are waiting
ils **elles**	-ent	ils attend<u>ent</u> elles attend<u>ent</u>	they wait they are waiting

J'<u>attends</u> ma sœur.	I'm waiting for my sister.
Chaque matin nous <u>attendons</u> le train ensemble.	Every morning we wait for the train together.

> ## *Tip*
> **je** changes to **j'** in front of a word starting with a vowel, most words starting with **h**, and the French word **y**.

Key points

✔ Verbs ending in **-re** belong to the third conjugation and form their present tense stem by losing the **-re** from the infinitive.

✔ The present tense endings for **-re** verbs are:
-s, **-s**, **-**, **-ons**, **-ez**, **-ent**.

The present tense: spelling changes in -er verbs

➤ Learning the patterns shown on pages 72–73 means you can now work out the forms of most **-er** verbs. A few verbs, though, involve a small spelling change. This is usually to do with how a word is pronounced. In the tables below the form(s) with the irregular spelling is/are <u>underlined</u>.

1 | **Verbs ending in -cer**

➤ With verbs such as **lancer** (meaning *to throw*), which end in **-cer**, **c** becomes **ç** before an **a** or an **o**. This is so the letter **c** is still pronounced as in the English word *ice*.

Pronoun	Example verb: lancer
je	lance
tu	lances
il elle on	lance
nous	<u>lançons</u>
vous	lancez
ils elles	lancent

2 | **Verbs ending in -ger**

➤ With verbs such as **manger** (meaning *to eat*), which end in **-ger**, **g** becomes **ge** before an **a** or an **o**. This is so the letter **g** is still pronounced like the **s** in the English word *leisure*.

Pronoun	Example verb: manger
je	mange
tu	manges
il elle on	mange
nous	<u>mangeons</u>
vous	mangez
ils elles	mangent

3 Verbs ending in -eler

➤ With verbs such as **appeler** (meaning *to call*), which end in **-eler**, the **l** doubles before **-e**, **-es** and **-ent**. The double consonant (**ll**) affects the pronunciation of the word. In **appeler**, the first **e** sounds like the vowel sound at the end of the English word *teacher*, but in **appelle** the first **e** sounds like the one in the English word *pet*.

Pronoun	Example verb: appeler
j'	<u>appelle</u>
tu	<u>appelles</u>
il elle on	<u>appelle</u>
nous	appelons
vous	appelez
ils elles	<u>appellent</u>

➤ The exceptions to this rule are **geler** (meaning *to freeze*) and **peler** (meaning *to peel*), which change in the same way as **lever** (*see page 80*).

➤ Verbs like this are sometimes called '1, 2, 3, 6 verbs' because they change in the first person singular (**je**), second person singular (**tu**), and third person singular and plural (**il/elle/on** and **ils/elles**).

4 Verbs ending in -eter

➤ With verbs such as **jeter** (meaning *to throw*), which end in **-eter**, the **t** doubles before **-e**, **-es** and **-ent**. The double consonant (**tt**) affects the pronunciation of the word. In **jeter**, the first **e** sounds like the vowel sound at the end of the English word *teacher*, but in **jette** the first **e** sounds like the one in the English word *pet*.

Pronoun	Example verb: jeter
je	<u>jette</u>
tu	<u>jettes</u>
il elle on	<u>jette</u>
nous	jetons
vous	jetez
ils elles	<u>jettent</u>

➤ The exceptions to this rule include **acheter** (meaning *to buy*), which changes in the same way as **lever**.

➤ Verbs like this are sometimes called '1, 2, 3, 6 verbs'.

5 Verbs ending in -yer

➤ With verbs such as **nettoyer** (meaning *to clean*), which end in **-yer**, the **y** changes to **i** before **-e**, **-es** and **-ent**.

Pronoun	Example verb: nettoyer
je	nettoie
tu	nettoies
il elle on	nettoie
nous	nettoyons
vous	nettoyez
ils elles	nettoient

➤ Verbs ending in **-ayer**, such as **payer** (meaning *to pay*) and **essayer** (meaning *to try*), can be spelled with either a **y** or an **i**. So **je paie** and **je paye**, for example, are both correct.

➤ Verbs like this are sometimes called '1, 2, 3, 6 verbs'.

6 Changes involving accents

➤ With verbs such as **lever** (meaning *to raise*), **peser** (meaning *to weigh*) and **acheter** (meaning *to buy*), **e** changes to **è** before the consonant + **-e**, **-es** and **-ent**. The accent changes the pronunciation too. In **lever** the first **e** sounds like the vowel sound at the end of the English word *teacher*, but in **lève** and so on the first **e** sounds like the one in the English word *pet*.

Pronoun	Example verb: lever
je	lève
tu	lèves
il elle on	lève
nous	levons
vous	levez
ils elles	lèvent

➤ With verbs such as **espérer** (meaning *to hope*), **régler** (meaning *to adjust*) and **préférer** (meaning *to prefer*), **é** changes to **è** before the consonant + **-e**, **-es** and **-ent**.

Pronoun	Example verb: espérer
j'	espère
tu	espères
il elle on	espère
nous	espérons
vous	espérez
ils elles	espèrent

➤ Verbs like this are sometimes called '1, 2, 3, 6 verbs'.

Key points

✔ In verbs ending in **-cer** and **-ger**:
  c → ç and g → ge in the **nous** form.
✔ In verbs ending in **-eler** and **-eter**:
  l → ll and t → tt in all but the **nous** and **vous** forms.
✔ In verbs ending in **-yer**:
  y → i in all but the **nous** and **vous** forms (optional in **-ayer** verbs).

The present tense: irregular verbs

➤ Some verbs in French do not follow the normal rules. These verbs include some very common and important verbs like **avoir** (meaning *to have*), **être** (meaning *to be*), **faire** (meaning *to do, to make*) and **aller** (meaning *to go*). The present tense of these four verbs is given in full below.

⇨ *For* **Verb tables**, *see supplement.*

1 The present tense of avoir

Pronoun	avoir	Meaning: *to have*
j'	ai	I have
tu	as	you have
il elle on	a	he/she/it/one has
nous	avons	we have
vous	avez	you have
ils elles	ont	they have

J'<u>ai</u> deux sœurs.	I have two sisters.
Il <u>a</u> les yeux bleus.	He has blue eyes.
Elle <u>a</u> trois ans.	She's three.
Qu'est-ce qu'il y <u>a</u>?	What's the matter?

2 The present tense of être

Pronoun	être	Meaning: *to be*
je	suis	I am
tu	es	you are
il elle on	est	he/she/it/one is
nous	sommes	we are
vous	êtes	you are
ils elles	sont	they are

Je <u>suis</u> heureux.	I'm happy.
Mon père <u>est</u> instituteur.	My father's a primary school teacher.
Il <u>est</u> deux heures.	It's two o'clock.

For further explanation of grammatical terms, please see pages viii–xii.

3 The present tense of faire

Pronoun	faire	Meaning: *to do, to make*
je	fais	I do/make I am doing/making
tu	fais	you do/make you are doing/making
il elle on	fait	he/she/it/one does/makes he/she/it/one is doing/making
nous	faisons	we do/make we are doing/making
vous	faites	you do/make you are doing/making
ils elles	font	they do/make they are doing/making

Je **fais** un gâteau.	I'm making a cake.
Qu'est-ce que tu **fais?**	What are you doing?
Il **fait** chaud.	It's hot.
Ça ne **fait** rien.	It doesn't matter.

4 The present tense of aller

Pronoun	aller	Meaning: *to go*
je	vais	I go I am going
tu	vas	you go you are going
il elle on	va	he/she/it/one goes he/she/it/one is going
nous	allons	we go we are going
vous	allez	you go you are going
ils elles	vont	they go they are going

Je **vais** à Londres.	I'm going to London.
'Comment **allez**-vous?' – 'Je **vais** bien.'	'How are you?' – 'I'm fine.'
'Comment ça **va**?' – 'Ça **va** bien.'	'How are you?' – 'I'm fine.'

5 Irregular -ir verbs

➤ Many irregular verbs that end in **-ir**, such as **partir** (meaning *to go*) and **tenir** (meaning *to hold*), have a common pattern in the singular. The **je** and **tu** forms often end in **-s**, and the **il/elle/on** form often ends in **-t**.

Pronoun	partir	tenir
je	par**s**	tien**s**
tu	par**s**	tien**s**
il/elle/on	par**t**	tien**t**

Je pars demain.	I'm leaving tomorrow.
Elle tient le bébé.	She is holding the baby.

⇨ For **Verb tables**, *see supplement*.

Key points

✔ Some very important French verbs are irregular, including **avoir**, **être**, **faire** and **aller**. They are worth learning in full.

✔ The **-s**, **-s**, **-t** pattern occurs frequently in irregular **-ir** verbs.

The imperative

> **What is the imperative?**
> An **imperative** is a form of the verb used when giving orders and
> instructions, for example, *Shut the door!; Sit down!; Don't go!*

1 Using the imperative

➤ In French, there are two forms of the imperative that are used to give
instructions or orders to someone. These correspond to **tu** and **vous**.

⇨ *For more information on the difference between **tu** and **vous**, see page 43.*

➤ There is also a form of the imperative that corresponds to **nous**. This means
the same as *let's* in English. It is not used as often as the **tu** and **vous** forms.

2 Forming the present tense imperative

➤ For regular verbs, the imperative is the same as the **tu**, **nous** and **vous** forms
of the present tense, except that you do not say the pronouns **tu**, **nous** and
vous. Also, in the **tu** form of **-er** verbs like **donner**, the final **-s** is dropped.

Pronoun	-er verbs: donner	Meaning	-ir verbs: finir	Meaning	-re verbs: attendre	Meaning
tu	donne	give	finis	finish	attends	wait
nous	donnons	let's give	finissons	let's finish	attendons	let's wait
vous	donnez	give	finissez	finish	attendez	wait

Donne-moi ça!	Give me that!
Finissez vos devoirs et allez vous coucher.	Finish your homework and go to bed.
Attendons le bus.	Let's wait for the bus.

> *Tip*
>
> When a **tu** imperative comes before **en** or **y**, the final **-s** is kept to
> make the words easier to pronounce. The **s** is pronounced like the z in
> the English word *zip*:
>
> **Vas-y!** Go on!
> **Donnes-en à ton frère.** Give some to your brother.

3 Where to put the object pronoun

➤ An object pronoun is a word like **la** (meaning *her/it*), **me/moi** (meaning *me*) or **leur** (meaning *to them*) that is used instead of a noun as the object of a sentence. In orders and instructions, the position of these object pronouns in the sentence changes depending on whether you are telling someone <u>TO DO</u> something or <u>NOT TO DO</u> something.

⇨ *For more information on **Object pronouns**, see page 47.*

➤ If you are telling someone <u>NOT TO DO</u> something, you put the object pronouns <u>BEFORE</u> the verb.

Ne <u>me</u> dérange pas.	Don't disturb me.
Ne <u>leur</u> parlons pas.	Let's not speak to them.
Ne <u>le</u> regardez pas.	Don't look at him/it.

➤ If you are telling someone <u>TO DO</u> something, you put the object pronouns <u>AFTER</u> the verb and join the two words with a hyphen. The word order is the same as in English.

Excusez-<u>moi</u>.	Excuse me.
Aide-<u>nous</u>.	Help us.
Attendons-<u>la</u>.	Let's wait for her/it.

➤ Orders and instructions telling someone to do something may contain <u>direct object</u> and <u>indirect object pronouns</u>. When this happens, the pronouns go in this order:

DIRECT		INDIRECT
le		**moi**
la	BEFORE	**toi**
les		**lui**
		nous
		vous
		leur

Prête-<u>les-moi</u>!	Lend them to me! *or* Lend me them!
Donnez-<u>la-nous</u>!	Give it to us! *or* Give us it!

⇨ *For imperatives using **Reflexive verbs**, see page 90.*

4 Imperative forms of irregular verbs

➤ **avoir** (meaning *to have*), **être** (meaning *to be*), **savoir** (meaning *to know*) and **vouloir** (meaning *to want*) have irregular imperative forms.

Pronoun	avoir	être	savoir	vouloir
tu	aie	sois	sache	veuille
nous	ayons	soyons	sachons	veuillons
vous	ayez	soyez	sachez	veuillez

<u>Sois</u> sage.	Be good.
<u>Veuillez</u> fermer la porte.	Please shut the door.

Key points

✔ The imperative has three forms: **tu**, **nous** and **vous**.

✔ The forms are the same as the **tu**, **nous** and **vous** forms of the present tense, except that the final **-s** is dropped in the **tu** form of **-er** verbs.

✔ Object pronouns go before the verb when you are telling someone not to do something, but after the verb with a hyphen when you are telling someone to do something.

✔ **avoir**, **être**, **savoir** and **vouloir** have irregular imperative forms.

Reflexive verbs

> **What is a reflexive verb?**
> A **reflexive verb** is one where the subject and object are the same, and where the action 'reflects back' on the subject. It is used with a reflexive pronoun such as *myself*, *yourself* and *herself* in English, for example, *I washed myself*; *He shaved himself*.

1 Using reflexive verbs

➤ In French, reflexive verbs are much more common than in English, and many are used in everyday French. They are shown in dictionaries as **se** plus the infinitive (**se** means *himself, herself, itself, themselves* or *oneself*). **se** is called a <u>reflexive pronoun</u>.

> *Tip*
>
> **se** changes to **s'** in front of a word starting with a vowel, most words starting with **h**, and the French word **y**.

➤ Reflexive verbs are often used to describe things you do (to yourself) every day or that involve a change of some sort (going to bed, sitting down, getting angry, going to sleep). Some of the most common French reflexive verbs are listed here:

s'amuser	to play, to enjoy oneself
s'appeler	to be called
s'arrêter	to stop
s'asseoir	to sit down
se baigner	to go swimming
se coucher	to go to bed
se dépêcher	to hurry
s'habiller	to get dressed
s'intéresser à quelque chose	to be interested in something
se laver	to wash, to have a wash
se lever	to get up, to rise, to stand up
se passer	to take place, to happen, to go
se promener	to go for a walk
se rappeler	to remember
se réveiller	to wake up
se trouver	to be (situated)

For further explanation of grammatical terms, please see pages viii–xii.

Qu'est-ce qui <u>se passe</u>?	What's happening?
Le soleil <u>se lève</u> à cinq heures.	The sun rises at five o'clock.
<u>Asseyez-vous</u>!	Sit down!

ⓘ Note that **se** and **s'** are very rarely translated as *himself* and so on in English.

➤ Some French verbs can be used with a reflexive pronoun or without a reflexive pronoun, for example, the verbs **appeler** and **s'appeler**, and **arrêter** and **s'arrêter**. Sometimes, however, their meaning may change.

<u>Appelle</u> le chien.	<u>Call</u> the dog.
Je <u>m'appelle</u> Jacques.	<u>I'm called</u> Jacques.
Il <u>arrête</u> le moteur.	He <u>switches off</u> the engine.
Elle <u>s'arrête</u> devant une vitrine.	She <u>stops</u> in front of a shop window.

2 Forming the present tense of reflexive verbs

➤ To use a reflexive verb in French, you need to decide which reflexive pronoun to use. The forms shown in brackets in the table are used before a word starting with a vowel, most words starting with **h**, or the French word **y**.

Subject pronoun	Reflexive pronoun	Meaning
je	me (m')	myself
tu	te (t')	yourself
il elle on	se (s')	himself herself itself oneself
nous	nous	ourselves
vous	vous	yourself (*singular*) yourselves (*plural*)
ils elles	se (s')	themselves

Je <u>me lève</u> tôt.	I get up early.
Elle <u>s'habille</u>.	She's getting dressed.
Ils <u>s'intéressent</u> beaucoup aux animaux.	They're very interested in animals.

➤ The present tense forms of a reflexive verb work in just the same way as an ordinary verb, except that the reflexive pronoun is used as well.

Reflexive forms	Meaning
je me lave	I wash (myself)
tu te laves	you wash (yourself)
il se lave elle se lave on se lave	he washes (himself) she washes (herself) it washes (itself) one washes (oneself)
nous nous lavons	we wash (ourselves)
vous vous lavez	you wash (yourself) (*singular*) you wash (yourselves) (*plural*)
ils se lavent elles se lavent	they wash (themselves)

➤ Some reflexive verbs, such as **s'asseoir** (meaning *to sit down*), are irregular. Some of these irregular verbs are shown in the **Verb tables**.

⇨ *For **Verb tables**, see supplement.*

3 Where to put the reflexive pronoun

➤ In the present tense, the reflexive pronoun almost always comes <u>BEFORE</u> the verb.

Je me couche tôt.	I go to bed early.
Comment t'appelles-tu?	What's your name?

➤ When telling someone <u>NOT TO DO</u> something, you put the reflexive pronoun <u>BEFORE</u> the verb as usual.

Ne te lève pas.	Don't get up.
Ne vous habillez pas.	Don't get dressed.

➤ When telling someone <u>TO DO</u> something, you put the reflexive pronoun <u>AFTER</u> the verb and join the two words with a hyphen.

Lève-toi!	Get up!
Dépêchez-vous!	Hurry up!
Habillons-nous.	Let's get dressed.

Tip

When you are telling someone <u>TO DO</u> something, **te** or **t'** changes to **toi**.

Assieds-<u>toi</u>. Sit down.

When you are telling someone <u>NOT TO DO</u> something, **te** or **t'** is used, not **toi**.

Ne te lève pas. Don't get up.

➪ *For more information on the **Imperative**, see page 85.*

---

4 *Each other* **and** *one another*

➤ We use *each other* in English when we are talking about two people, and *one another* when we are talking about three or more people. The French reflexive pronouns **nous**, **vous** and **se** can all mean two or more people.

Nous <u>nous</u> parlons tous les jours.	We speak to <u>each other</u> every day.
On <u>se</u> voit demain?	Shall we see <u>each other</u> tomorrow?
Les trois pays <u>se</u> ressemblent beaucoup.	The three countries are really like <u>one another</u>.

Key points

✔ A reflexive verb is made up of a reflexive pronoun and a verb.

✔ The reflexive pronouns are: **me**, **te**, **se**, **nous**, **vous**, **se** (**m'**, **t'**, **s'**, **nous**, **vous**, **s'** before a vowel, most words beginning with **h** and the French word **y**).

✔ The reflexive pronoun comes before the verb, except when you are telling someone to do something.

The imperfect tense

> **What is the imperfect tense?**
> The **imperfect tense** is one of the verb tenses used to talk about the past, especially in descriptions, and to say what used to happen, for example, I _used to walk_ to school; It _was_ sunny at the weekend.

1 Using the imperfect tense

➤ The imperfect tense is used:

- to describe what things were like and how people felt in the past

    I <u>was</u> very sad when she left.
    It <u>was pouring</u> with rain.

- to say what used to happen or what you used to do regularly in the past

    We <u>used to get up</u> very early in those days.
    I never <u>used to like</u> milk.

- to indicate things that were happening or something that was true when something else took place

    I <u>was watching</u> TV when the phone rang.
    As we <u>were looking</u> out of the window, we saw someone walk across the lawn.

[i] Note that if you want to talk about an event or action that took place and was completed in the past, you use the <u>perfect tense</u>.

⇨ _For more information on the **Perfect tense**, see page 111._

➤ You can often recognize an imperfect tense in English because it uses a form like _were looking_ or _was raining_. The words _used to_ also show an imperfect tense.

> _Tip_
>
> Remember that you <u>NEVER</u> use the verb **être** to translate _was_ or _were_ in forms like _was raining_ or _were looking_ and so on. You change the French verb ending instead.

2 Forming the imperfect tense of -er verbs

➤ To form the imperfect tense of **-er** verbs, you use the same stem of the verb as for the present tense. Then you add the correct ending, depending on whether you are referring to **je**, **tu**, **il**, **elle**, **on**, **nous**, **vous**, **ils** or **elles**.

Pronoun	Ending	Add to stem, e.g. donn-	Meanings
je (j')	-ais	je donn<u>ais</u>	I gave I was giving I used to give
tu	-ais	tu donn<u>ais</u>	you gave you were giving you used to give
il elle on	-ait	il donn<u>ait</u> elle donn<u>ait</u> on donn<u>ait</u>	he/she/it/one gave he/she/it/one was giving he/she/it/one used to give
nous	-ions	nous donn<u>ions</u>	we gave we were giving we used to give
vous	-iez	vous donn<u>iez</u>	you gave you were giving you used to give
ils elles	-aient	ils donn<u>aient</u> elles donn<u>aient</u>	they gave they were giving they used to give

Il <u>portait</u> toujours un grand chapeau noir.	He always wore a big black hat.
Nous <u>habitions</u> à Paris à cette époque.	We were living in Paris at that time.
Pour gagner un peu d'argent, je <u>donnais</u> des cours de français.	To earn a little money I used to give French lessons.

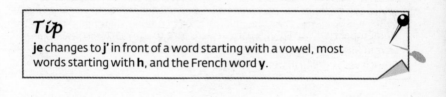

Tip

je changes to **j'** in front of a word starting with a vowel, most words starting with **h**, and the French word **y**.

3 Forming the imperfect tense of -ir verbs

➤ To form the imperfect tense of **-ir** verbs, you use the same stem of the verb as for the present tense. Then you add the correct ending, depending on whether you are referring to **je**, **tu**, **il**, **elle**, **on**, **nous**, **vous**, **ils** or **elles**.

Pronoun	Ending	Add to stem, e.g. fin-	Meanings
je (j')	-issais	je fin<u>issais</u>	I finished I was finishing I used to finish
tu	-issais	tu fin<u>issais</u>	you finished you were finishing you used to finish
il elle on	-issait	il fin<u>issait</u> elle fin<u>issait</u> on fin<u>issait</u>	he/she/it/one finished he/she/it/one was finishing he/she/it/one used to finish
nous	-issions	nous fin<u>issions</u>	we finished we were finishing we used to finish
vous	-issiez	vous fin<u>issiez</u>	you finished you were finishing you used to finish
ils elles	-issaient	ils fin<u>issaient</u> elles fin<u>issaient</u>	they finished they were finishing they used to finish

Il <u>finissait</u> souvent ses devoirs avant le dîner.	He often finished his homework before dinner.
Cet après-midi-là ils <u>choisissaient</u> une bague de fiançailles.	That afternoon they were choosing an engagement ring.

4 Forming the imperfect tense of -re verbs

➤ To form the imperfect tense of **-re** verbs, you use the same stem of the verb as for the present tense. Then you add the correct ending, depending on whether you are referring to **je**, **tu**, **il**, **elle**, **on**, **nous**, **vous**, **ils** or **elles**. These endings are the same as for **-er** verbs.

Pronoun	Ending	Add to stem, e.g. attend-	Meanings
je (j')	-ais	j'attend<u>ais</u>	I waited I was waiting I used to wait
tu	-ais	tu attend<u>ais</u>	you waited you were waiting you used to wait
il elle on	-ait	il attend<u>ait</u> elle attend<u>ait</u> on attend<u>ait</u>	he/she/it/one waited he/she/it/one was waiting he/she/it/one used to wait
nous	-ions	nous attend<u>ions</u>	we waited we were waiting we used to wait
vous	-iez	vous attend<u>iez</u>	you waited you were waiting you used to wait
ils elles	-aient	ils attend<u>aient</u> elles attend<u>aient</u>	they waited they were waiting they used to wait

Christine m'<u>attendait</u> tous les soirs à la sortie.	Christine used to wait for me every evening at the exit.
Je <u>vivais</u> seule après mon divorce.	I was living alone after my divorce.

5 Spelling changes in -er verbs

➤ As with the present tense, a few **-er** verbs change their spellings slightly when they are used in the imperfect tense. The forms with spelling changes have been <u>underlined</u> in the tables.

➤ With verbs such as **lancer** (meaning *to throw*), which end in **-cer**, **c** becomes **ç** before an **a** or an **o**. This is so that the letter **c** is still pronounced as in the English word *ice*.

Pronoun	Example verb: lancer
je	<u>lançais</u>
tu	<u>lançais</u>
il elle on	<u>lançait</u>
nous	lancions
vous	lanciez
ils elles	<u>lançaient</u>

➤ With verbs such as **manger** (meaning *to eat*), which end in **-ger**, **g** becomes **ge** before an **a** or an **o**. This is so the letter **g** is still pronounced like the *s* in the English word *leisure*.

Pronoun	Example verb: manger
je	<u>mangeais</u>
tu	<u>mangeais</u>
il elle on	<u>mangeait</u>
nous	mangions
vous	mangiez
ils elles	<u>mangeaient</u>

➤ These verbs follow the <u>1,2,3,6 pattern</u>. That is, they change in the first, second and third person singular, and in the third person plural.

6 Reflexive verbs in the imperfect tense

➤ The imperfect tense of reflexive verbs is formed just as for ordinary verbs, except that you add the reflexive pronoun (**me**, **te**, **se**, **nous**, **vous**, **se**).

Subject pronoun	Reflexive pronoun	Example with laver	Meaning
je	me (m')	lavais	I washed I was washing I used to wash
tu	te (t')	lavais	you washed you were washing you used to wash
il elle on	se (s')	lavait	he/she/it/one washed he/she/it/one was washing he/she/it/one used to wash
nous	nous	lavions	we washed we were washing we used to wash
vous	vous	laviez	you washed you were washing you used to wash
ils elles	se (s')	lavaient	they washed they were washing they used to wash

7 Irregular verbs in the imperfect tense

➤ The only verb that is irregular in the imperfect tense is **être**.

Pronoun	être	Meaning
j'	étais	I was
tu	étais	you were
il elle on	était	he/she/it/one was
nous	étions	we were
vous	étiez	you were
ils elles	étaient	they were

J'<u>étais</u> heureux.	I was happy.
Mon père <u>était</u> instituteur.	My father was a primary school teacher.

Key points

✔ The imperfect tense endings for **-er** and **-re** verbs are:
  -ais, -ais, -ait, -ions, -iez, -aient.

✔ The imperfect tense endings for **-ir** verbs are:
  -issais, -issais, -issait, -issions, -issiez, -issaient.

✔ In verbs ending in **-cer** and **-ger**:
  c → ç and g → ge in all but the **nous** and **vous** forms.

✔ **être** is irregular in the imperfect tense.

The future tense

> **What is the future tense?**
> The **future tense** is a verb tense used to talk about something that will happen or will be true.

1 Using the future tense

➤ In English the future tense is often shown by *will* or its shortened form *'ll*.

> What <u>will</u> you do?
> The weather <u>will</u> be warm and dry tomorrow.
> He<u>'ll</u> be here soon.
> I<u>'ll</u> give you a call.

➤ Just as in English, you can use the present tense in French to refer to something that is going to happen in the future.

> **Je <u>prends</u> le train de dix heures.**   I'm taking the ten o'clock train.
> **Nous <u>allons</u> à Paris la semaine**   We're going to Paris next week.
> **prochaine.**

➤ In English we often use *going to* followed by an infinitive to talk about something that will happen in the immediate future. You can use the French verb **aller** (meaning *to go*) followed by an infinitive in the same way.

> **Tu <u>vas tomber</u> si tu continues.**   You're going to fall if you carry on.
> **Il <u>va manquer</u> le train.**   He's going to miss the train.

> *Tip*
> Remember that French has no direct equivalent of the word *will* in verb forms like *will rain* or *will look* and so on. You change the French verb ending instead to form the future tense.

2 Forming the future tense

➤ To form the future tense in French, you use:
- the <u>infinitive</u> of **-er** and **-ir** verbs, for example, **donner**, **finir**
- the <u>infinitive without the final</u> **e** of **-re** verbs: for example, **attendr-**

➤ Then add the correct ending to the stem, depending on whether you are talking about **je**, **tu**, **il**, **elle**, **on**, **nous**, **vous**, **ils** or **elles**. The endings are the same for **-er**, **-ir** and **-re** verbs.

Verbs

[i] Note that apart from the **nous** and **vous** forms, the endings are the same as the present tense of **avoir**.

⇨ *For the present tense of **avoir**, see page 82.*

Pronoun	Ending	Add to stem, e.g. donner-, finir-, attendr-	Meanings
je (j')	-ai	je donner<u>ai</u> je finir<u>ai</u> j'attendr<u>ai</u>	I will give I will finish I will wait
tu	-as	tu donner<u>as</u> tu finir<u>as</u> tu attendr<u>as</u>	you will give you will finish you will wait
il elle on	-a	il/elle/on donner<u>a</u> il/elle/on finir<u>a</u> il/elle/on attendr<u>a</u>	he/she/it/one will give he/she/it/one will finish he/she/it/one will wait
nous	-ons	nous donner<u>ons</u> nous finir<u>ons</u> nous attendr<u>ons</u>	we will give we will finish we will wait
vous	-ez	vous donner<u>ez</u> vous finir<u>ez</u> vous attendr<u>ez</u>	you will give you will finish you will wait
ils elles	-ont	ils/elles donner<u>ont</u> ils/elles finir<u>ont</u> ils/elles attendr<u>ont</u>	they will give they will finish they will wait

Elle te <u>donnera</u> mon adresse.   She'll give you my address.
Le cours <u>finira</u> à onze heures.   The lesson will finish at eleven o'clock.

Nous t'<u>attendrons</u> devant le cinéma.   We'll wait for you in front of the cinema.

Tip
je changes to **j'** in front of a word starting with a vowel, most words starting with **h**, and the French word **y**.

3 Spelling changes in -er verbs

➤ As with the present and imperfect tenses, a few **-er** verbs change their spellings slightly in the future tense. The forms with spelling changes have been <u>underlined</u> in the tables.

➤ With verbs such as **appeler** (meaning *to call*), which end in **-eler**, the l doubles throughout the future tense. The double consonant (**ll**) affects the pronunciation of the word. In **appeler**, the first **e** sounds like the vowel sound at the end of the English word *teacher*, but in **appellerai** the first **e** sounds like the one in the English word *pet*.

Pronoun	Example verb: appeler
j'	appellerai
tu	appelleras
il elle on	appellera
nous	appellerons
vous	appellerez
ils elles	appelleront

➤ The exceptions to this rule are **geler** (meaning *to freeze*) and **peler** (meaning *to peel*), which change in the same way as **lever** (*see page* 101).

➤ With verbs such as **jeter** (meaning *to throw*), that end in **-eter**, the **t** doubles throughout the future tense. The double consonant (**tt**) affects the pronunciation of the word. In **jeter**, the first **e** sounds like the vowel sound at the end of the English word *teacher*, but in **jetterai** the first **e** sounds like the one in the English word *pet*.

Pronoun	Example verb: jeter
je	jetterai
tu	jetteras
il elle on	jettera
nous	jetterons
vous	jetterez
ils elles	jetteront

➤ The exceptions to this rule include **acheter** (meaning *to buy*), which changes in the same way as **lever** (*see page* 101).

➤ With verbs such as **nettoyer** (meaning *to clean*), that end in **-yer**, the **y** changes to **i** throughout the future tense.

Pronoun	Example verb: nettoyer
je	nettoierai
tu	nettoieras
il elle on	nettoiera
nous	nettoierons
vous	nettoierez
ils elles	nettoieront

➤ Verbs ending in **-ayer**, such as **payer** (meaning *to pay*) and **essayer** (meaning *to try*), can be spelled with either a **y** or an **i**. So **je paierai** and **je payerai**, for example, are both correct.

➤ With verbs such as **lever** (meaning *to raise*), **peser** (meaning *to weigh*) and **acheter** (meaning *to buy*), **e** changes to **è** throughout the future tense. In **lever** the first **e** sounds like the vowel sound at the end of the English word *teacher*, but in **lèverai** and so on the first **e** sounds like the one in the English word *pet*.

Pronoun	Example verb: lever
je	lèverai
tu	lèveras
il elle on	lèvera
nous	lèverons
vous	lèverez
ils elles	lèveront

4 Reflexive verbs in the future tense

➤ The future tense of reflexive verbs is formed in just the same way as for ordinary verbs, except that you have to remember to give the reflexive pronoun (**me**, **te**, **se**, **nous**, **vous**, **se**).

Subject pronoun	Reflexive pronoun	Example with laver	Meaning
je	me (m')	laverai	I will wash
tu	te (t')	laveras	you will wash
il elle on	se (s')	lavera	he/she/it/one will wash
nous	nous	laverons	we will wash
vous	vous	laverez	you will wash
ils elles	se (s')	laveront	they will wash

Tip

me changes to **m'**, **te** to **t'** and **se** to **s'** before a vowel, most words starting with **h** and the French word **y**.

5 Irregular verbs in the future tense

➤ There are some verbs that do not use their infinitives as the stem for the future tense, including **avoir**, **être**, **faire** and **aller**, which are shown in full on pages 103–104.

➤ Other irregular verbs include:

Verb	Meaning	je	tu	il/elle/on	nous	vous	ils/elles
devoir	to have to, must	devrai	devras	devra	devrons	devrez	devront
pouvoir	to be able to, can	pourrai	pourras	pourra	pourrons	pourrez	pourront
savoir	to know	saurai	sauras	saura	saurons	saurez	sauront
tenir	to hold	tiendrai	tiendras	tiendra	tiendrons	tiendrez	tiendront
venir	to come	viendrai	viendras	viendra	viendrons	viendrez	viendront
voir	to see	verrai	verras	verra	verrons	verrez	verront
vouloir	to want	voudrai	voudras	voudra	voudrons	voudrez	voudront

For further explanation of grammatical terms, please see pages viii–xii.

➤ **il faut** becomes **il faudra** (meaning *it will be necessary to*).

➤ **il pleut** becomes **il pleuvra** (meaning *it will rain*).

➤ This is the future tense of **avoir**:

Pronoun	avoir	Meaning: *to have*
j'	aurai	I will have
tu	auras	you will have
il elle on	aura	he/she/it/one will have
nous	aurons	we will have
vous	aurez	you will have
ils elles	auront	they will have

➤ This is the future tense of **être**:

Pronoun	être	Meaning: *to be*
je	serai	I will be
tu	seras	you will be
il elle on	sera	he/she/it/one will be
nous	serons	we will be
vous	serez	you will be
ils elles	seront	they will be

➤ This is the future tense of **faire**:

Pronoun	faire	Meaning: *to do, to make*
je	ferai	I will do/make
tu	feras	you will do/make
il elle on	fera	he/she/it/one will do/make
nous	ferons	we will do/make
vous	ferez	you will do/make
ils elles	feront	they will do/make

➤ This is the future tense of **aller**:

Pronoun	aller	Meaning: *to go*
j'	irai	I will go
tu	iras	you will go
il elle on	ira	he/she/it/one will go
nous	irons	we will go
vous	irez	you will go
ils elles	iront	they will go

⇨ For **Verb tables**, see supplement.

Key points

✔ You can use a present tense in French to talk about something that will happen or be true in the future, just as in English.

✔ You can use **aller** with an infinitive to refer to things that will happen in the immediate future.

✔ The stem is the same as the infinitive for **-er**, **-ir** and **-re** verbs, except that the final **-e** of **-re** verbs is lost.

✔ The future tense endings are the same for **-er**, **-ir** and **-re** verbs: **-ai**, **-as**, **-a**, **-ons**, **-ez**, **-ont**.

✔ In verbs ending in **-eler** and **-eter**:
l → **ll** and **t** → **tt** throughout the future tense.

✔ In verbs ending in **-yer**:
y → **i** throughout the future tense (optional in **-ayer** verbs).

✔ Some verbs are irregular in the future tense. It is worth learning these in full.

The conditional

> **What is the conditional?**
> The **conditional** is a verb form used to talk about things that would happen or that would be true under certain conditions, for example, I _would_ help you _if I could_.
> It is also used to say what you would like or need, for example, _Could you give me the bill?_

1 Using the conditional

➤ You can often recognize a conditional in English by the word _would_ or its shortened form _'d_.

> I <u>would</u> be sad if you left.
> If you asked him, he'<u>d</u> help you.

➤ You use the conditional for:

- asking for something formally and politely, especially in shops
  I'<u>d</u> like a kilo of pears, please.
- saying what you would like
  I'<u>d</u> like to go to the United States.
- making a suggestion
  I <u>could</u> come and pick you up.
- giving advice
  You <u>should</u> say you're sorry.

> **Tip**
> There is no direct French translation of _would_ in verb forms like _would be_, _would like_, _would help_ and so on. You change the French verb ending instead.

2 Forming the conditional

➤ To form the conditional in French, you have to use:

- the infinitive of **-er** and **-ir** verbs, for example, **donner-**, **finir-**
- the infinitive without the final **e** of **-re** verbs, for example, **attendr-**

➤ Then add the correct ending to the stem, depending on whether you are talking about **je**, **tu**, **il**, **elle**, **on**, **nous**, **vous**, **ils** or **elles**. The endings are the same for all verbs. In fact, they are the same as the **-er** and **-re** endings for the <u>IMPERFECT TENSE</u>, but the stem is the same as the <u>FUTURE TENSE</u>.

➡ _For more information on the **Imperfect tense** and the **Future tense**, see pages 92 and 98._

Pronoun	Ending	Add to stem, e.g. donner-, finir-, attendr-	Meanings
je (j')	-ais	je donner<u>ais</u> je finir<u>ais</u> j'attendr<u>ais</u>	I would give I would finish I would wait
tu	-ais	tu donner<u>ais</u> tu finir<u>ais</u> tu attendr<u>ais</u>	you would give you would finish you would wait
il elle on	-ait	il/elle/on donner<u>ait</u> il/elle/on finir<u>ait</u> il/elle/on attendr<u>ait</u>	he/she/it/one would give he/she/it/one would finish he/she/it/one would wait
nous	-ions	nous donner<u>ions</u> nous finir<u>ions</u> nous attendr<u>ions</u>	we would give we would finish we would wait
vous	-iez	vous donner<u>iez</u> vous finir<u>iez</u> vous attendr<u>iez</u>	you would give you would finish you would wait
ils elles	-aient	ils/elles donner<u>aient</u> ils/elles finir<u>aient</u> ils/elles attendr<u>aient</u>	they would give they would finish they would wait

J'<u>aimerais</u> aller aux États-Unis.   I'd like to go to the United States.

> ### Tip
> **je** changes to **j'** in front of a word starting with a vowel, most words starting with **h**, and the French word **y**.

i Note that you have to be careful not to mix up the future tense and the conditional. They look very similar.

FUTURE	CONDITIONAL
je donnerai	je donnerais
je finirai	je finirais
j'attendrai	j'attendrais
j'aimerai	j'aimerais
je voudrai	je voudrais
je viendrai	je viendrais
je serai	je serais

3 Spelling changes in -er verbs

➤ As with the future tense, a few **-er** verbs change their spellings slightly in the conditional. The forms with spelling changes have been <u>underlined</u> in the tables below.

➤ With verbs such as **appeler** (meaning *to call*), which end in **-eler**, the **l** doubles throughout the conditional. The double consonant (**ll**) affects the pronunciation of the word. In **appeler**, the first **e** sounds like the vowel sound at the end of the English word *teacher*, but in **appellerais** the first **e** sounds like the one in the English word *pet*.

Pronoun	Example verb: appeler
j'	<u>appellerais</u>
tu	<u>appellerais</u>
il elle on	<u>appellerait</u>
nous	<u>appellerions</u>
vous	<u>appelleriez</u>
ils elles	<u>appelleraient</u>

➤ The exceptions to this rule are **geler** (meaning *to freeze*) and **peler** (meaning *to peel*), which change in the same way as **lever** (*see page 108*).

➤ With verbs such as **jeter** (meaning *to throw*), which end in **-eter**, the **t** doubles throughout the conditional. The double consonant (**tt**) affects the pronunciation of the word. In **jeter**, the first **e** sounds like the vowel sound at the end of the English word *teacher*, but in **jetterais** the first **e** sounds like the one in the English word *pet*.

Pronoun	Example verb: jeter
je	<u>jetterais</u>
tu	<u>jetterais</u>
il elle on	<u>jetterait</u>
nous	<u>jetterions</u>
vous	<u>jetteriez</u>
ils elles	<u>jetteraient</u>

➤ The exceptions to this rule include **acheter** (meaning *to buy*), which changes in the same way as **lever** (*see page 108*).

➤ With verbs such as **nettoyer** (meaning *to clean*), that end in **-yer**, the **y** changes to **i** throughout the conditional.

Pronoun	Example verb: nettoyer
je	nettoierais
tu	nettoierais
il elle on	nettoierait
nous	nettoierions
vous	nettoieriez
ils elles	nettoieraient

➤ Verbs ending in **-ayer**, such as **payer** (meaning *to pay*) and **essayer** (meaning *to try*), can be spelled with either a **y** or an **i**. So **je paierais** and **je payerais**, for example, are both correct.

➤ With verbs such as **lever** (meaning *to raise*), **peser** (meaning *to weigh*) and **acheter** (meaning *to buy*), **e** changes to **è** throughout the conditional. In **lever** the first **e** sounds like the vowel sound at the end of the English word *teacher*, but in **lèverais** and so on the first **e** sounds like the one in the English word *pet*.

Pronoun	Example verb: lever
je	lèverais
tu	lèverais
il elle on	lèverait
nous	lèverions
vous	lèveriez
ils elles	lèveraient

4 Reflexive verbs in the conditional

➤ The conditional of reflexive verbs is formed in just the same way as for ordinary verbs, except that you have to remember to give the reflexive pronoun (**me**, **te**, **se**, **nous**, **vous**, **se**).

Subject pronoun	Reflexive pronoun	Example with laver	Meaning
je	me (m')	laverais	I would wash
tu	te (t')	laverais	you would wash
il elle on	se (s')	laverait	he/she/it would wash
nous	nous	laverions	we would wash
vous	vous	laveriez	you would wash
ils elles	se (s')	laveraient	they would wash

Tip

me changes to **m'**, **te** to **t'** and **se** to **s'** before a vowel, most words starting with **h** and the French word **y**.

5 Irregular verbs in the conditional

➤ The same verbs that are irregular in the future tense are irregular in the conditional, including: **avoir**, **être**, **faire**, **aller**, **devoir**, **pouvoir**, **savoir**, **tenir**, **venir**, **voir**, **vouloir**.

➡ For more information on **Irregular verbs in the future tense**, see page 102.

➤ To form the conditional of an irregular verb, use the same stem as for the future tense, for example:

    avoir → aur-
    être → ser-

➤ Then add the usual endings for the conditional.

Infinitive	Future stem	Conditional endings	Conditional form
avoir	aur-	-ais, -ais, -ait, -ions, -iez, -aient	j'aur<u>ais</u>, tu aur<u>ais</u>, il/elle/on aur<u>ait</u>, nous aur<u>ions</u>, vous aur<u>iez</u>, ils/elles aur<u>aient</u>
être	ser-	-ais, -ais, -ait, -ions, -iez, -aient	je ser<u>ais</u>, tu ser<u>ais</u>, il/elle/on ser<u>ait</u>, nous ser<u>ions</u>, vous ser<u>iez</u>, ils/elles ser<u>aient</u>
faire	fer-	-ais, -ais, -ait, -ions, -iez, -aient	je fer<u>ais</u>, tu fer<u>ais</u>, il/elle/on fer<u>ait</u>, nous fer<u>ions</u>, vous fer<u>iez</u>, ils/elles fer<u>aient</u>
aller	ir-	-ais, -ais, -ait, -ions, -iez, -aient	j'ir<u>ais</u>, tu ir<u>ais</u>, il/elle/on ir<u>ait</u>, nous ir<u>ions</u>, vous ir<u>iez</u>, ils/elles ir<u>aient</u>

J'<u>irais</u> si j'avais le temps.	I would go if I had time.
Je <u>voudrais</u> un kilo de poires, s'il vous plaît.	I'd like a kilo of pears, please.
Tu <u>devrais</u> t'excuser.	You should say you're sorry.

Key points

✔ The conditional endings are the same for **-er**, **-ir** and **-re** verbs: **-ais**, **-ais**, **-ait**, **-ions**, **-iez**, **-aient**.

✔ The conditional endings are the same as the endings for the imperfect tense of **-er** and **-re** verbs, but the stem is the same as the stem of the future tense.

✔ In verbs ending in **-eler** and **-eter**:
l → ll and t → tt throughout the conditional.

✔ In verbs ending in **-yer**:
y → i throughout the conditional (optional in **-ayer** verbs).

✔ The same verbs that are irregular in the future are irregular in the conditional. It is worth learning these in full.

The perfect tense

What is the perfect tense?
The **perfect** is one of the verb tenses used to talk about the past, especially about actions that took place and were completed in the past.

1 Using the perfect tense

➤ You can often recognize a perfect tense in English by a form like *I gave*, *I have finished*.

> I <u>gave</u> her my phone number.
> I <u>have finished</u> my soup.

> *Tip*
>
> The perfect tense is the tense you will need most to talk about things that have happened or were true in the past. It is used to talk about actions that took place and <u>WERE COMPLETED</u> in the past.
> Use the <u>imperfect tense</u> for regular events and in most descriptions.
>
> ⟹ *For more information on the* **Imperfect tense**, *see page 92.*

2 Forming the perfect tense

➤ The present, imperfect, future and conditional tenses in French are made up of just <u>one</u> word, for example, **je donne**, **tu finissais**, **il attendra** or **j'aimerais**. The perfect tense has <u>TWO</u> parts to it:

- the <u>present</u> tense of the verb **avoir** (meaning *to have*) or **être** (meaning *to be*)

- a part of the main verb called the <u>past participle</u>, like *given*, *finished* and *done* in English

➤ In other words, the perfect tense in French is like the form *I have done* in English.

⟹ *For more information on forming the present tense of* **avoir** *and* **être**, *see page 82.*

3 Forming the past participle

➤ To form the past participle of regular verbs, you use the <u>infinitive</u> of the verb:

- For **-er** verbs, you replace the **-er** at the end of the infinitive with **é**.

Infinitive	Take off -er	Add -é
donner (to give)	**donn-**	**donn<u>é</u>**
tomber (to fall)	**tomb-**	**tomb<u>é</u>**

- For **-ir** verbs, you replace the **-ir** at the end of the infinitive with **-i**.

Infinitive	Take off -ir	Add -i
finir (to finish)	**fin-**	**fin<u>i</u>**
partir (to leave, to go)	**part-**	**part<u>i</u>**

- For **-re** verbs, you replace the **-re** at the end of the infinitive with **-u**.

Infinitive	Take off -re	Add -u
attendre (to wait)	**attend-**	**attend<u>u</u>**
descendre (to go down, to come down, to get off)	**descend-**	**descend<u>u</u>**

4 Verbs that form their perfect tense with avoir

➤ Most verbs form their perfect tense with **avoir**, for example **donner**:

Pronoun	avoir	Past participle	Meaning
j'	**ai**	**donné**	I gave / I have given
tu	**as**	**donné**	you gave / you have given
il **elle** **on**	**a**	**donné**	he/she/it/one gave / he/she/it/one has given
nous	**avons**	**donné**	we gave / we have given
vous	**avez**	**donné**	you gave / you have given
ils **elles**	**ont**	**donné**	they gave / they have given

Elle <u>a donné</u> son numéro de téléphone à Claude. — She gave Claude her phone number.

Il <u>a acheté</u> un ordinateur. — He's bought a computer.

Je n'<u>ai</u> pas <u>regardé</u> la télé hier. — I didn't watch TV yesterday.

> ### Tip
> **je** changes to **j'** in front of a word starting with a vowel, most words starting with **h**, and the French word **y**.

➤ The perfect tense of **-ir** verbs like **finir** is formed in the same way, except for the past participle: **j'ai fini**, **tu as fini** and so on.

➤ The perfect tense of **-re** verbs like **attendre** is formed in the same way, except for the past participle: **j'ai attendu**, **tu as attendu** and so on.

5 avoir or être?

➤ MOST verbs form their perfect tense with **avoir**; these include **donner** as shown on page 112.

➤ There are two main groups of verbs which form their perfect tense with **être** instead of **avoir**:

- all reflexive verbs

⇨ *For more information on **Reflexive verbs**, see page 88.*

- a group of verbs that are mainly used to talk about movement or a change of some kind, including these ones:

aller	to go
venir	to come
arriver	to arrive, to happen
partir	to leave, to go
descendre	to go down, to come down, to get off
monter	to go up, to come up
entrer	to go in, to come in
sortir	to go out, to come out
mourir	to die
naître	to be born
devenir	to become
rester	to stay
tomber	to fall

Je <u>suis allé</u> au match de football hier.	I went to the football match yesterday.
Il <u>est sorti</u> acheter un journal.	He's gone out to buy a newspaper.
Vous <u>êtes descendu</u> à quelle station?	Which station did you get off at?

Grammar Extra!

Some of the verbs on the previous page take **avoir** when they are used with a direct object, for example:

descendre quelque chose	to get something down, to bring something down, to take something down
monter quelque chose	to go up something, to come up something
sortir quelque chose	to take something out
Est-ce que tu <u>as descendu</u> les bagages?	Did you bring the bags down?
Elle <u>a monté</u> les escaliers.	She went up the stairs.
Elle <u>a sorti</u> son porte-monnaie de son sac.	She took her purse out of her handbag.

⇨ *For more information on **Direct objects**, see page 47.*

---

6 Verbs that form their perfect tense with être

➤ When a verb takes **être**, the past participle <u>ALWAYS</u> agrees with the subject of the verb; that is, the endings change in the feminine and plural forms.

	Masculine endings	Examples	Feminine endings	Examples
Singular	-	tombé parti descendu	-e	tombé<u>e</u> parti<u>e</u> descendu<u>e</u>
Plural	-s	tombé<u>s</u> parti<u>s</u> descendu<u>s</u>	-es	tombé<u>es</u> parti<u>es</u> descendu<u>es</u>

Est-ce ton frère est <u>allé</u> à l'étranger?	Did your brother go abroad?
Elle est <u>venue</u> avec nous.	She came with us.
Ils sont <u>partis</u> à six heures.	They left at six o'clock.
Mes cousines sont <u>arrivées</u> hier.	My cousins arrived yesterday. (*The cousins are female.*)

➤ Here are the perfect tense forms of **tomber** in full:

Pronoun	avoir	Past participle	Meaning
je	suis	**tombé** (*masculine*) **tombée** (*feminine*)	I fell/I have fallen
tu	es	**tombé** (*masculine*) **tombée** (*feminine*)	you fell/you have fallen
il	est	**tombé**	he/it fell, he/it has fallen
elle	est	**tombée**	she/it fell, she/it has fallen
on	est	**tombé** (*singular*) **tombés** (*masculine plural*) **tombées** (*feminine plural*)	one fell/one has fallen, we fell/we have fallen
nous	sommes	**tombés** (*masculine*) **tombées** (*feminine*)	we fell/we have fallen
vous	êtes	**tombé** (*masculine singular*) **tombée** (*feminine singular*) **tombés** (*masculine plural*) **tombées** (*feminine plural*)	you fell/you have fallen
ils	sont	**tombés**	they fell/they have fallen
elles	sont	**tombées**	they fell/they have fallen

Grammar Extra!

When **on** means *we*, the past participle can agree with the subject of the sentence, but it is optional.

On est <u>arrivés</u> en retard.	We arrived late. (*masculine*)
On est <u>rentrées</u> toutes les deux à la même heure.	We both came in at the same time. (*feminine*)

➤ The perfect tense of **-ir** verbs like **partir** is formed in the same way, except for the past participle: **je suis parti(e)**, **tu es parti(e)** and so on.

➤ The perfect tense of **-re** verbs like **descendre** is formed in the same way, except for the past participle: **je suis descendu(e)**, **tu es descendu(e)** and so on.

Grammar Extra!

When a verb takes **avoir**, the past participle usually stays in the masculine singular form, as shown in the table for **donner**, and does not change for the feminine or plural forms.

Il a <u>fini</u> sa dissertation.	He's finished his essay.
Elles ont <u>fini</u> leur dissertation.	They've finished their essay.

In one particular case, however, the past participle of verbs with **avoir** does change in the feminine and plural forms. In the sentences above, **dissertation** is the direct object of the verb **finir.** When the direct object comes <u>AFTER</u> the verb, as it does in the examples above, then the past participle doesn't change. If the direct object comes <u>BEFORE</u> the verb, however, the past participle has to change to agree with that direct object.

<u>la</u> dissertation qu'il a **fini<u>e</u>** hier	the essay that he finished yesterday
<u>la</u> dissertation qu'elles ont **fini<u>e</u>** hier	the essay that they finished yesterday

Since object pronouns usually come BEFORE the verb, the past participle changes to agree with the pronoun.

Il a bu son thé? – Oui, il <u>l'a</u> bu.	Did he drink his tea? – Yes, he's drunk it.
Il a bu sa limonade? – Oui, il <u>l'a</u> <u>bue</u>.	Did he drink his lemonade? – Yes, he's drunk it.

Tip

Remember that with verbs taking **être**, it is the <u>subject</u> of the verb that tells you what ending to add to the past participle. Compare this with the rule for verbs taking **avoir** that have a direct object; in their case, it is the <u>direct object</u> coming before the verb that tells you what ending to add to the past participle.

---

7 | The perfect tense of reflexive verbs

➤ Here is the perfect tense of the reflexive verb **se laver** (meaning *to wash (oneself)*, *to have a wash, to get washed*) in full. Remember that all reflexive verbs take **être**, and so the past participle of reflexive verbs usually agrees with the subject of the sentence.

Subject pronoun	Reflexive pronoun	Present tense of être	Past participle	Meaning
je	me	suis	**lavé** (*masculine*) **lavée** (*feminine*)	I washed myself
tu	t'	es	**lavé** (*masculine*) **lavée** (*feminine*)	you washed yourself
il	s'	est	**lavé**	he washed himself one washed oneself
elle	s'	est	**lavée**	she washed herself
on	s'	est	**lavé** (*singular*) **lavés** (*masculine plural*) **lavées** (*feminine plural*)	one washed oneself we washed ourselves
nous	nous	sommes	**lavés** (*masculine*) **lavées** (*feminine*)	we washed ourselves
vous	vous	êtes	**lavé** (*masculine singular*) **lavée** (*feminine singular*) **lavés** (*masculine plural*) **lavées** (*feminine plural*)	you washed yourself (*singular*) you washed yourselves (*plural*)
ils	se	sont	**lavés**	they washed themselves
elles	se	sont	**lavées**	they washed themselves

Tip

When **on** means *we*, the past participle can agree with the subject of the sentence, but it is optional.

On s'est <u>lavées</u> l'une après l'autre.   We washed ourselves one after the other. (*feminine*)

Grammar Extra!

The past participle of reflexive verbs <u>DOES NOT</u> change if the direct object (**la jambe** in the example below) <u>FOLLOWS</u> the verb.

Elle s'<u>est cassé</u> la jambe.   She's broken her leg.

---

8 | Irregular verbs in the perfect tense

➤ Some past participles are irregular. There aren't too many, so try to learn them.

avoir (meaning *to have*)	→ **eu**
devoir (meaning *to have to, must*)	→ **dû**
dire (meaning *to say, to tell*)	→ **dit**
être (meaning *to be*)	→ **été**
faire (meaning *to do, to make*)	→ **fait**
mettre (meaning *to put*)	→ **mis**
pouvoir (meaning *to be able to, can*)	→ **pu**
prendre (meaning *to take*)	→ **pris**
savoir (meaning *to know*)	→ **su**
tenir (meaning *to hold*)	→ **tenu**
venir (meaning *to come*)	→ **venu**
voir (meaning *to see*)	→ **vu**
vouloir (meaning *to want*)	→ **voulu**

➤ **il pleut** becomes **il a plu** (*it rained*).

➤ **il faut** becomes **il a fallu** (*it was necessary*).

> #### Key points
> ✔ The perfect tense describes things that happened and were completed in the past. It is not used for things that happened regularly or in descriptions.
> ✔ The perfect tense is formed with the present tense of **avoir** or **être** and a past participle.
> ✔ Most verbs take **avoir** in the perfect tense. All reflexive verbs and a small group of verbs referring to movement or change take **être**.
> ✔ The past participle ends in **-é** for **-er** verbs, in **-i** for **-ir** verbs, and in **-u** for **-re** verbs.
> ✔ With verbs that take **avoir**, the past participle does not usually change. With verbs that take **être**, including reflexive verbs, the past participle changes in the feminine and plural.

For further explanation of grammatical terms, please see pages viii–xii.

The pluperfect tense

> **What is the pluperfect tense?**
> The **pluperfect** is a verb tense which describes something that <u>had</u> happened or <u>had</u> been true at a point in the past, for example, *I'd forgotten to finish my homework.*

1 Using the pluperfect tense

➤ You can often recognize a pluperfect tense in English by a form like *I had arrived*, *you'd fallen*.

Elle <u>avait essayé</u> des dizaines de pulls.	She <u>had tried on</u> dozens of jumpers.
Nous <u>avions</u> déjà <u>commencé</u> à manger quand il est arrivé.	We'd already <u>started</u> eating when he arrived.
J'<u>étais arrivée</u> la première.	I <u>had arrived</u> first.
Mes parents <u>s'étaient couchés</u> tôt.	My parents <u>had gone</u> to bed early.

2 Forming the pluperfect tense

➤ Like the perfect tense, the pluperfect tense in French has <u>two</u> parts to it:

• the <u>imperfect</u> tense of the verb **avoir** (meaning *to have*) or **être** (meaning *to be*)
• the past participle

➤ If a verb takes **avoir** in the perfect tense, then it will take **avoir** in the pluperfect too. If a verb takes **être** in the perfect, then it will take **être** in the pluperfect too.

⇨ *For more information on the **Imperfect tense** and the **Perfect tense**, see pages 92 and 111.*

3 Verbs taking avoir

➤ Here are the pluperfect tense forms of **donner** (meaning *to give*) in full.

Pronoun	avoir	Past participle	Meaning
j'	avais	donné	I had given
tu	avais	donné	you had given
il elle on	avait	donné	he/she/it/one had given
nous	avions	donné	we had given
vous	aviez	donné	you had given
ils elles	avaient	donné	they had given

➤ The pluperfect tense of **-ir** verbs like **finir** (meaning *to finish*) is formed in the same way, except for the past participle: **j'avais fini**, **tu avais fini** and so on.

➤ The pluperfect tense of **-re** verbs like **attendre** (meaning *to wait*) is formed in the same way, except for the past participle: **j'avais attendu**, **tu avais attendu** and so on.

4 | Verbs taking être

➤ Here are the pluperfect tense forms of **tomber** (meaning *to fall*) in full. When a verb takes **être** in the pluperfect tense, the past participle <u>always</u> agrees with the subject of the verb; that is, the endings change in the feminine and plural forms.

Pronoun	être	Past participle	Meaning
j'	étais	tombé (*masculine*) tombée (*feminine*)	I had fallen
tu	étais	tombé (*masculine*) tombée (*feminine*)	you had fallen
il	était	tombé	he/it had fallen
elle	était	tombée	she/it had fallen
on	était	tombé (*singular*) tombés (*masculine plural*) tombées (*feminine plural*)	one had fallen we had fallen
nous	étions	tombés (*masculine*) tombées (*feminine*)	we had fallen
vous	étiez	tombé (*masculine singular*) tombée (*feminine singular*) tombés (*masculine plural*) tombées (*feminine plural*)	you had fallen
ils	étaient	tombés	they had fallen
elles	étaient	tombées	they had fallen

➤ The pluperfect tense of **-ir** verbs like **partir** (meaning *to leave, to go*) is formed in the same way, except for the past participle: **j'étais parti(e), tu étais parti(e)** and so on.

➤ The pluperfect tense of **-re** verbs like **descendre** (meaning *to come down, to go down, to get off*) is formed in the same way, except for the past participle: **j'étais descendu(e), tu étais descendu(e)** and so on.

> ## Tip
> When **on** means *we*, the past participle can agree with the subject of the sentence, but it is optional.
>
> **On était <u>tombées</u>.**   We had fallen. (*feminine*)

5 | Reflexive verbs in the pluperfect tense

➤ Reflexive verbs in the pluperfect tense are formed in the same way as in the perfect tense, but with the imperfect tense of the verb **être** (*see page 97*).

⇨ *For more information on the **Perfect tense of reflexive verbs**, see page 117.*

6 Irregular verbs in the pluperfect tense

➤ Irregular past participles are the same as for the perfect tense (*see page 118*).

> **Key points**
> ✔ The pluperfect tense describes things that had happened or were true at a point in the past before something else happened.
> ✔ It is formed with the imperfect tense of **avoir** or **être** and the past participle.
> ✔ The rules for agreement of the past participle are the same as for the perfect tense.

The passive

> **What is the passive?**
> The **passive** is a form of the verb that is used when the subject of the verb is the person or thing that is affected by the action, for example, *I was given, we were told, it had been made.*

1 Using the passive

➤ In a normal, or *active* sentence, the 'subject' of the verb is the person or thing that carries out the action described by the verb. The 'object' of the verb is the person or thing that the verb 'happens' to.

> Ryan *(subject)* hit *(active verb)* me *(object)*.

➤ In English, as in French, you can turn an <u>active</u> sentence round to make a <u>passive</u> sentence.

> I *(subject)* was hit *(passive verb)* by Ryan *(agent)*.

➤ Very often, however, you cannot identify who is carrying out the action indicated by the verb.

> I was hit in the face.
> The trees will be chopped down.
> I've been chosen to represent the school.

Tip

There is a very important difference between French and English in sentences containing an <u>indirect object</u>. In English we can quite easily turn a normal (active) sentence with an indirect object into a passive sentence.

Active

Someone *(subject)* gave *(active verb)* me *(indirect object)* a book *(direct object)*.

Passive

I *(subject)* was given *(passive verb)* a book *(direct object)*.

In French, an indirect object can <u>NEVER</u> become the subject of a passive verb.

⇨ *For more information on* **Direct** *and* **Indirect objects**, *see pages 47 and 49.*

For further explanation of grammatical terms, please see pages viii–xii.

2 Forming the passive

➤ In English we use the verb *to be* with the past participle (*was hit, was given*) to form the passive. In French the passive is formed in exactly the same way, using **être** and the past participle. The past participle agrees with the subject of the passive verb; that is, the endings change in the feminine and plural forms.

Elle <u>est encouragée</u> par ses parents.	She is encouraged by her parents.
Vous <u>êtes</u> tous bien <u>payés</u>.	You are all well paid. (*'you' refers to more than one person here*)
Les portes <u>ont été fermées</u>.	The doors have been closed.

⟹ *For more information on the **Past participle**, see page 111.*

➤ Here is the present tense of the **-er** verb **aimer** (meaning *to like, to love*) in its passive form.

Pronoun	Present tense of être	Past participle	Meaning
je	suis	**aimé** (*masculine*) **aimée** (*feminine*)	I am loved
tu	es	**aimé** (*masculine*) **aimée** (*feminine*)	you are loved
il	est	**aimé**	he/it is loved
elle	est	**aimée**	she/it is loved
on	est	**aimé** (*singular*) **aimés** (*masculine plural*) **aimées** (*feminine plural*)	~~one is loved~~ we are loved
nous	sommes	**aimés** (*masculine*) **aimées** (*feminine*)	we are loved
vous	êtes	**aimé** (*masculine singular*) **aimée** (*feminine singular*) **aimés** (*masculine plural*) **aimées** (*feminine plural*)	you are loved
ils	sont	**aimés**	they are loved
elles	sont	**aimées**	they are loved

➤ The passive of **-ir** verbs is formed in the same way, except that the past participle is different. For example, **elle est remplie** (meaning *it is full*).

➤ The passive of **-re** verbs is formed in the same way, except that the past participle is different. For example, **il est défendu** (meaning *it is forbidden*).

Grammar Extra!

When **on** means *we*, the past participle can agree with the subject of the sentence, but it is optional.

On est <u>aimés</u> de tout le monde.   We're loved by everyone. (*masculine*)

➤ You can form other tenses of the passive by changing the tense of the verb **être**.

     Imperfect: **j'étais aimé(e)** I was loved
     Future: **tu seras aimé(e)** you will be loved
     Perfect: **il a été aimé** he has been loved

⇨ *For more information on the **Imperfect**, **future** and **perfect tenses**, see pages 92, 98 and 111.*

➤ Irregular past participles are the same as for the perfect tense (*see page 118*).

3 <u>Avoiding the passive</u>

➤ Passives are not as common in French as in English. There are <u>two</u> main ways that French speakers express the same idea.

- by using the pronoun **on** (meaning *someone* or *they*) with a normal, active verb

<u>On</u> leur a envoyé une lettre.	They were sent a letter. (*literally: Someone sent them a letter.*)
<u>On</u> m'a dit que tu ne venais pas.	I was told that you weren't coming. (*literally: They told me you weren't coming.*)

⇨ *For more information on **Pronouns**, see page 42.*

- by using a reflexive verb

     Les melons <u>se vendent</u> 2 euros la pièce.   Melons are sold for 2 euros each.

⇨ *For more information on **Reflexive verbs**, see page 88.*

> **Key points**
> ✔ The present tense of the passive is formed by using the present tense of **être** with the past participle.
> ✔ The past participle always agrees with the <u>subject</u> of the passive verb.
> ✔ You can sometimes avoid a passive construction by using a reflexive verb or the pronoun **on**.

The present participle

> **What is a present participle?**
> The **present participle** is a verb form ending in *-ing* which is used in English to form verb tenses, and which may be used as an adjective and a noun, for example, *What are you doing?*; the *setting* sun; *Swimming* is easy!

1 Using the present participle

➤ Present participles are not as common in French as in English, because they are not used to form tenses. The main uses of the present participle in French are:

- as a verb, on its own, corresponding to the English *-ing* form. It <u>DOES NOT</u> agree with the subject of the verb when it is used in this way.

Habitant près de Paris, je vais assez souvent en ville.	Living close to Paris, I go into town quite often.
les voyageurs **descendant** à Périgueux	travellers getting off at Périgueux

- as a verb, after the preposition **en**. The present participle <u>DOES NOT</u> agree with the subject of the verb when it is used in this way. The subject of the two parts of the sentence is always the same. **en** can be translated in a number of different ways.

En attendant sa sœur, Richard s'est endormi.	While waiting for his sister, Richard fell asleep.
Appelle-nous **en arrivant** chez toi.	Call us when you get home.
En appuyant sur ce bouton, on peut imprimer ses documents.	By pressing this button, you can print your documents.
Il s'est blessé **en essayant** de sauver un chat.	He hurt himself trying to rescue a cat.

⇨ *For more information on the preposition **en**, see page 168.*

- as an adjective, like in English. As with all adjectives in French, the ending <u>DOES</u> change in the feminine and plural forms.

le soleil **couchant**	the setting sun
l'année **suivante**	the following year
Ces enfants sont **énervants**.	Those children are annoying.
des chaises **pliantes**	folding chairs

> *Tip*
>
> The French present participle is <u>NEVER</u> used to translate English verb forms like *I was walking*, *we are leaving*.
>
> ➪ *For more information on the* **Imperfect tense** *and the* **Present tense**, *see pages 92 and 71.*

➤ English verbs describing movement that are followed by an adverb such as *out* or *down*, or a preposition such as *across* or *up* are often translated by a verb + **en** + present participle.

Il **est sorti en courant**.	He ran out. (*literally: He came out running*.)
J'**ai traversé** la rue **en boîtant**.	I limped across the street. (*literally: I crossed the street limping*.)

2 Forming the present participle

➤ To form the present participle of regular **-er**, **-ir** and **-re** verbs, you use the **nous** form of the present tense and replace the **-ons** ending with **-ant**.

nous form of present tense	Take off -ons	Add -ant
donnons	donn-	donnant
lançons	lanç-	lançant
mangeons	mange-	mangeant
finissons	finiss-	finissant
partons	part-	partant
attendons	attend-	attendant
descendons	descend-	descendant

3 Irregular verbs

➤ Three verbs have an irregular present participle:

avoir (meaning *to have*) → **ayant**
être (meaning *to be*) → **étant**
savoir (meaning *to know*) → **sachant**

> ### Key points
> ✔ Present participles are never used to form tenses in French, but they can be used as verbs, either on their own or after **en**.
> ✔ They can also be used as adjectives, in which case they agree with the noun they describe.
> ✔ They are formed by taking the **nous** form of the present tense and replacing the **-ons** ending with **-ant**. The exceptions are **avoir, être** and **savoir**.

Impersonal verbs

> **What is an impersonal verb?**
> An **impersonal verb** is one that does not refer to a real person or thing and where the subject is represented by *it*, for example, *It's going to rain; It's ten o'clock.*

➤ Impersonal verbs are only used with **il** (meaning *it*) and in the infinitive. They are called impersonal verbs because **il** does not really refer to a real person, animal or thing, just like *it* and *there* in English in the examples below.

Il pleut.	It's raining.
Il va pleuvoir.	It's going to rain.
Il y a un problème.	There's a problem.
Il pourrait y avoir un problème.	There could be a problem.

➤ There are also some very common verbs that can be used in this way in addition to their normal meanings, for example, **avoir**, **être** and **faire**.

Infinitive	Expression	Meaning
avoir + noun	**il y a**	there is (*singular*) there are (*plural*)
être + time	**il est**	it is
faire + noun	**il fait jour** **il fait nuit**	it's daylight it's dark
falloir + noun	**il faut**	we/you *etc*. need it takes
falloir + infinitive	**il faut**	we/you *etc*. have to
manquer	**il manque**	there is ... missing (*singular*) there are ... missing (*plural*)
paraître	**il paraît que**	it appears that it seems that
rester + noun	**il reste**	there is ... left (*singular*) there are ... left (*plural*)
sembler	**il semble que**	it appears that it seems that
valoir mieux + infinitive	**il vaut mieux**	it would be better to

Il y a quelqu'un à la porte.	There's somebody at the door.
Il est deux heures.	It's two o'clock.
Il faut partir.	I've/We've *etc*. got to go.
Il manque cent euros.	100 euros are missing.
Il reste du pain.	There's some bread left.
Il vaut mieux ne rien dire.	It would be better to say nothing.

128 Verbs

➤ Several impersonal verbs relate to the weather.

Infinitive	Expression	Meaning
faire + adjective	**il fait beau** **il fait mauvais**	the weather's lovely the weather's bad
faire + noun	**il fait du vent** **il fait du soleil**	it's windy it's sunny
geler	**il gèle**	it's freezing
neiger	**il neige**	it's snowing
pleuvoir	**il pleut**	it's raining

Grammar Extra!

There is another group of useful expressions that start with an impersonal **il**. These are followed by a form of the verb called the <u>subjunctive</u>.

il faut que
Il faut que je <u>parte</u>.　　　　　I've got to go.

il est nécessaire que
Il est nécessaire que le comité　　The committee has to take a
<u>prenne</u> une décision rapidement.　decision quickly.

il est possible que
Il est possible qu'il <u>vienne</u>.　　He might come.

il est dommage que
Il est dommage que tu ne　　　　It's a shame you didn't see him.
l'<u>aies</u> pas vu.

⇨　*For more information on the **Subjunctive**, see page 129.*

Key points
- ✔ Impersonal verbs can only be used in the infinitive and the **il** form.
- ✔ **il faut**, **il y a**, **il est** and **il fait** with expressions relating to the weather are very common.

The subjunctive

> **What is the subjunctive?**
> The **subjunctive** is a verb form that is used in certain circumstances to express some sort of feeling, or to show there is doubt about whether something will happen or whether something is true. It is only used occasionally in modern English, for example, *If I _were_ you, I wouldn't bother.; So _be_ it.*

1 | Using the subjunctive

➤ In French the subjunctive is used after certain verbs and conjunctions when two parts of a sentence have different subjects.

I'm afraid <u>he</u> won't come back.
(The subject of the first part of the sentence is 'I'; the subject of the second part of the sentence is 'he'.)

➤ Sometimes, in a sentence like *We want her to be happy*, you use the infinitive of the verb in English (*to be*). This is <u>NOT</u> possible in French when there is a different subject in the two parts of the sentence (*we* and *her*). You have to use a subjunctive for the second verb.

Nous voulons être heureux. We want to be happy.
(No change of subject, so you can just use an infinitive – être – in French.)

Nous voulons qu'elle soit heureuse. We want her to be happy.
*(Subject changes from **nous** to **elle**, so you have to use a subjunctive – **soit** – in French.)*

➤ You can only use the infinitive instead of the subjunctive in French with impersonal verbs.

Il faut que tu <u>viennes</u> à l'heure.   →   **Il faut <u>venir</u> à l'heure.**
   (using subjunctive)   *(using infinitive)*
You have to come on time.

Il vaut mieux que tu <u>restes</u> chez toi.   →   **Il vaut mieux <u>rester</u> chez toi.**
   (using subjunctive)   *(using infinitive)*
It's better that you stay at home.

2 | Coming across the subjunctive

➤ The subjunctive has several tenses but you are only likely to come across the present subjunctive.

➤ You may see a subjunctive after certain verbs that you use when you are:

- wishing something: **vouloir que** and **désirer que** (meaning *to wish that, to want*), **aimer que** (meaning *to like that*), **aimer mieux que** and **préférer que** (meaning *to prefer that*)
- fearing something: **avoir peur que** (meaning *to be afraid that*)
- giving your opinion: **croire que** (meaning *to think that*)

- saying how you feel: **regretter que** (meaning *to be sorry that*), **être content que** (meaning *to be pleased that*), **être surpris que** (meaning *to be surprised that*) and so on

> **Je suis content que vous les <u>aimiez</u>.** | I'm pleased you like them.
>
> **J'ai peur qu'il ne <u>revienne</u> pas.** | I'm afraid he won't come back.

➤ You may see a subjunctive after certain verbal expressions starting with **il**, such as **il faut que** (meaning *it is necessary that*) and **il vaut mieux que** (meaning *it is better that*).

> **Il faut que je vous <u>parle</u>.** | I need to speak to you.

⇨ *For a list of some expressions requiring the subjunctive, see page 128.*

3 | Forming the present subjunctive of -er verbs

➤ To form the stem of the present subjunctive you take the <u>infinitive</u> and chop off **-er**, just as for the present tense. Then you add the correct ending, depending on whether you are referring to **je, tu, il, elle, on, nous, vous, ils** or **elles**.

➤ For **-er** verbs the endings are the same as for the ordinary present tense, apart from the **nous** and **vous** forms, which have an extra **i**, as in the imperfect tense.

Pronoun	Ending	Add to stem, e.g. donn-	Meanings
je (j')	-e	je donn<u>e</u>	I give
tu	-es	tu donn<u>es</u>	you give
il elle on	-e	il donn<u>e</u> elle donn<u>e</u> on donn<u>e</u>	he/she/it/one gives
nous	-ions	nous donn<u>ions</u>	we give
vous	-iez	vous donn<u>iez</u>	you give
ils elles	-ent	ils donn<u>ent</u> elles donn<u>ent</u>	they give

---

Tip

je changes to **j'** in front of a word starting with a vowel, most words starting with **h**, and the French word **y**.

Verbs

Forming the present subjunctive of -ir verbs

➤ To form the stem of the present subjunctive you take the <u>infinitive</u> and chop off **-ir**, just as for the present tense. Then you add the correct ending, depending on whether you are referring to to **je, tu, il, elle, on, nous, vous, ils** or **elles**.

Pronoun	Ending	Add to stem, e.g. fin-	Meanings
je (j')	-isse	je fin<u>isse</u>	I finish
tu	-isses	tu fin<u>isses</u>	you finish
il elle on	-isse	il fin<u>isse</u> elle fin<u>isse</u> on fin<u>isse</u>	he/she/it/one finishes
nous	-issions	nous fin<u>issions</u>	we finish
vous	-issiez	vous fin<u>issiez</u>	you finish
ils elles	-issent	ils fin<u>issent</u> elles fin<u>issent</u>	they finish

> *Tip*
>
> **je** changes to **j'** in front of a word starting with a vowel, most words starting with **h**, and the French word **y**.

Forming the present subjunctive of -re verbs

➤ To form the stem of the present subjunctive you take the <u>infinitive</u> and chop off **-re**, just as for the present tense. Then you add the correct ending, depending on whether you are referring to to **je, tu, il, elle, on, nous, vous, ils** or **elles**.

Pronoun	Ending	Add to stem, e.g. attend-	Meanings
je (j')	-e	j'attend<u>e</u>	I wait
tu	-es	tu attend<u>es</u>	you wait
il elle on	-e	il attend<u>e</u> elle attend<u>e</u> on attend<u>e</u>	he/she/it/one waits
nous	-ions	nous attend<u>ions</u>	we wait
vous	-iez	vous attend<u>iez</u>	you wait
ils elles	-ent	ils attend<u>ent</u> elles attend<u>ent</u>	they wait

> *Tip*
>
> **je** changes to **j'** in front of a word starting with a vowel, most words starting with **h**, and the French word **y**.

6 Irregular verbs in the subjunctive

➤ Some important verbs have irregular subjunctive forms.

Verb	Meaning	je (j')	tu	il/elle/on	nous	vous	ils/elles
aller	*to go*	aille	ailles	aille	allions	alliez	aillent
avoir	*to have*	aie	aies	ait	ayons	ayez	aient
devoir	*to have to, must*	doive	doives	doive	devions	deviez	doivent
dire	*to say, to tell*	dise	dises	dise	disions	disiez	disent
être	*to be*	sois	sois	soit	soyons	soyez	soient
faire	*to do, to make*	fasse	fasses	fasse	fassions	fassiez	fassent
pouvoir	*to be able to, can*	puisse	puisses	puisse	puissions	puissiez	puissent
prendre	*to take*	prenne	prennes	prenne	prenions	preniez	prennent
(**apprendre** and **comprendre** also behave like this – **j'apprenne, tu apprennes** and so on)							
savoir	*to know*	sache	saches	sache	sachions	sachiez	sachent
venir	*to come*	vienne	viennes	vienne	venions	veniez	viennent
vouloir	*to want to*	veuille	veuilles	veuille	voulions	vouliez	veuillent

Key points

✔ After certain verbs you have to use a subjunctive in French when there is a different subject in the two clauses. These verbs mostly relate to wishing, fearing, and saying what you think, what you feel and that you are uncertain. A subjunctive is also found after certain verbal expressions that start with **il**.

✔ The stem of the present tense subjunctive is the same as the stem used for the ordinary present tense.

✔ The present tense subjunctive endings for **-er** and **-re** verbs are: **-e, -es, -e, -ions, -iez** and **-ent**.

✔ The present tense subjunctive endings for **-ir** verbs are: **-isse, -isses, -isse, -issions, -issiez** and **-issent**.

Verbs followed by an infinitive

1 Linking two verbs together

➤ Many verbs in French can be followed by another verb in the infinitive. The infinitive is the form of the verb that is found in the dictionary, such as **donner** (meaning *to give*), **finir** (meaning *to finish*) and **attendre** (meaning *to wait*).

➤ There are three main ways that verbs can be linked together:

- with no linking word

Vous voulez attendre?	Would you like to wait?

- with the preposition **à**

J'apprends <u>à</u> nager.	I'm learning to swim.

- with the preposition **de**

Essayez <u>de</u> venir.	Try to come.

⇨ *For more information on **Prepositions after adjectives**, and on **Prepositions after verbs**, see pages 183 and 178.*

2 Verbs followed by an infinitive with no preposition

➤ A number of verbs and groups of verbs can be followed by an infinitive with no preposition. The following important group of verbs are all very irregular, but they crop up so frequently that they are worth learning in full:

- **devoir** (*to have to, must, to be due to*)

Tu <u>dois être</u> fatiguée.	You must be tired.
Elle <u>doit partir</u>.	She has to leave.
Le nouveau centre commercial <u>doit ouvrir</u> en mai.	The new shopping centre is due to open in May.

- **pouvoir** (*can, may*)

Je <u>peux t'aider</u>, si tu veux.	I can help you, if you like.
Puis-je <u>venir</u> vous voir samedi?	May I come and see you on Saturday?

- **savoir** (*to know how to, can*)

Tu <u>sais conduire</u>?	Can you drive?
Je <u>sais faire</u> les omelettes.	I know how to make omelettes.

- **vouloir** (*to want*)

Élise <u>veut rester</u> un jour de plus.	Élise wants to stay one more day.
Ma voiture ne <u>veut</u> pas <u>démarrer</u>.	My car won't start.
Voulez-vous <u>boire</u> quelque chose?	Would you like something to drink?
Je <u>voudrais acheter</u> un ordinateur.	I'd like to buy a computer.

➤ **falloir** (meaning *to be necessary*) and **valoir mieux** (meaning *to be better*) are only used in the infinitive and with **il**.

Il faut prendre une décision.	We/you *etc*. have to make a decision.
Il vaut mieux téléphoner avant.	It's better to ring first.

⇨ *For more information on **Impersonal verbs**, see page 127.*

➤ The following common verbs can also be followed by an infinitive <u>without</u> a preposition:

adorer	to love
aimer	to like, to love
aimer mieux	to prefer
désirer	to want
détester	to hate
envoyer	to send
espérer	to hope
faire	to make
laisser	to let
préférer	to prefer
sembler	to seem

J'<u>espère</u> te <u>voir</u> la semaine prochaine.	I hope to see you next week.
Ne me <u>fais</u> pas <u>rire</u>!	Don't make me laugh!
Je <u>préfère manger</u> à la cantine.	I prefer to eat in the canteen.

➤ Some of these verbs combine with infinitives to make set phrases with a special meaning.

aller chercher quelque chose	to go and get something
laisser tomber quelque chose	to drop something
vouloir dire quelque chose	to mean something

<u>Va chercher</u> ton papa!	Go and get your dad!
Paul <u>a laissé tomber</u> le vase.	Paul dropped the vase.
Qu'est-ce que ça <u>veut dire</u>?	What does that mean?

➤ Verbs that relate to seeing or hearing, such as **voir** (meaning *to see*), **regarder** (meaning *to watch, to look at*), **écouter** (meaning *to listen to*) and **entendre** (meaning *to hear*) can be followed by an infinitive.

Il nous <u>a vus arriver</u>.	He saw us arrive.
On <u>entend chanter</u> les oiseaux.	You can hear the birds singing.

➤ Verbs that relate to movement of some kind and do not have a direct object, such as **aller** (meaning *to go*) and **venir** (meaning *to come*), can be followed by an infinitive.

Je <u>vais voir</u> Nicolas ce soir.	I'm going to see Nicolas tonight.
<u>Viens voir</u>!	Come and see!

3 | Verbs followed by à + infinitive

➤ There are some common verbs that can be followed by **à** and an infinitive.

s'amuser <u>à</u> faire quelque chose	to have fun doing something
apprendre <u>à</u> faire quelque chose	to learn to do something
commencer <u>à</u> faire quelque chose	to begin to do something
continuer <u>à</u> faire quelque chose	to go on doing something
s'habituer <u>à</u> faire quelque chose	to get used to doing something
J'apprends <u>à</u> skier.	I'm learning to ski.
Il a commencé <u>à</u> pleuvoir.	It began to rain.

➤ Some verbs can be followed by a person's name or by a noun relating to a person, and then by **à** and an infinitive. Sometimes you need to put **à** in front of the person too.

aider quelqu'un <u>à</u> faire quelque chose	to help someone do something
apprendre <u>à</u> quelqu'un <u>à</u> faire quelque chose	to teach someone to do something
inviter quelqu'un <u>à</u> faire quelque chose	to invite someone to do something

4 | Verbs followed by de + infinitive

➤ There are some common verbs that can be followed by **de** and an infinitive.

arrêter <u>de</u> faire quelque chose, s'arrêter <u>de</u> faire quelque chose	to stop doing something
continuer <u>de</u> faire quelque chose	to go on doing something
décider <u>de</u> faire quelque chose	to decide to do something
se dépêcher <u>de</u> faire quelque chose	to hurry to do something
essayer <u>de</u> faire quelque chose	to try to do something
s'excuser <u>de</u> faire quelque chose	to apologize for doing something
finir <u>de</u> faire quelque chose	to finish doing something
oublier <u>de</u> faire quelque chose	to forget to do something
proposer <u>de</u> faire quelque chose	to suggest doing something
refuser <u>de</u> faire quelque chose	to refuse to do something
suggérer <u>de</u> faire quelque chose	to suggest doing something

| **J'ai décidé de lui écrire.** | I decided to write to her. |
| **Je leur ai suggéré de partir de bonne heure.** | I suggested that they set off early. |

➤ The following verbs meaning asking or telling are also followed by **de** and an infinitive. Sometimes you need to put **à** in front of the person you are asking or telling.

commander à quelqu'un de faire quelque chose	to order someone to do something
demander à quelqu'un de faire quelque chose	to ask someone to do something
dire à quelqu'un de faire quelque chose	to tell someone to do something
empêcher quelqu'un de faire quelque chose	to prevent someone from doing something
interdire à quelqu'un de faire quelque chose	to forbid someone to do something
remercier quelqu'un de faire quelque chose	to thank someone for doing something

Grammar Extra!

If it is important to emphasize that something is going on at a particular time, you can use the phrase **être en train de faire quelque chose**.

| **Il est en train de travailler. Est-ce que vous pouvez rappeler plus tard?** | He's working. Can you call back later? |

If you want to say you have just done something, you can use the phrase **venir de faire quelque chose**. In English you use the PAST tense, but in French you use the PRESENT tense.

| **Élisabeth vient de partir.** | Élisabeth has just left. |

Key points
✔ Many French verbs can be followed by another verb in the infinitive.
✔ The two verbs may be linked by nothing at all, or by the preposition **à** or **de**.
✔ The construction in French does not always match the English exactly. It's best to learn these constructions when you learn a new verb.

Other uses of the infinitive

➤ The infinitive can be used in many other ways:

- after certain adjectives

  content de happy to
  prêt à ready to

Il est toujours <u>prêt à rendre</u> service.	He's always ready to help.

- after certain prepositions

<u>Pour aller</u> à la gare?	How do you get to the station?
Il est parti <u>sans dire</u> au revoir.	He left without saying goodbye.

- after certain set phrases involving a verb plus a noun

avoir envie de faire quelque chose	to feel like doing something
avoir besoin de faire quelque chose	to need to do something
avoir peur de faire quelque chose	to be frightened of doing something
J'ai besoin de <u>changer</u> de l'argent.	I need to change some money.

- in instructions that are aimed at the general public – for example, on signs or in cookery books

<u>Ajouter</u> le sel et le poivre, et bien <u>mélanger</u>.	Add the salt and pepper, and mix well.
<u>Conserver</u> au frais.	Keep refrigerated.

- as the subject or object of a sentence, when the infinitive corresponds to the *-ing* form in English used as a noun

<u>Fumer</u> n'est pas bon pour la santé.	Smoking isn't good for your health.
J'adore <u>lire</u>.	I love reading.

Tip

You can use the verb **faire** with an infinitive to refer to something you are having done by someone else.

Je dois <u>faire réparer</u> ma voiture.	I have to get my car repaired.

Key points

✔ Infinitives are found after certain adjectives, prepositions and set phrases, and in instructions to the general public.

✔ They can also function like nouns, as the subject or object of another verb.

Negatives

> **What is a negative?**
> A **negative** question or statement is one which contains a word such as *not*, *no*, *never* or *nothing* and is used to say that something is not happening, is not true or is absent.

1 Using negatives

➤ In English we use words like *not*, *no*, *nothing* and *never* to show a negative.

> I'm <u>not</u> very pleased.
> Dan <u>never</u> rang me.
> <u>Nothing</u> ever happens here!
> There's <u>no</u> milk left.

➤ *Not* is often combined with certain English verbs – for example, *can't*, *won't*, *didn't*, *hasn't*.

> He <u>isn't</u> joking.
> She <u>didn't</u> say.

➤ In French, if you want to make something negative, you generally use a pair of words, for example, **ne ... pas** (meaning *not*). The verb goes in the middle.

ne ... pas	not
ne ... rien	nothing, not ... anything
ne ... personne	nobody, no one, not ... anybody, not ... anyone
ne ... jamais	never, not ... ever
ne ... plus	no longer, no more, not ... any longer, not ... any more

Je <u>ne</u> fume <u>pas</u>.	I don't smoke.
<u>Ne</u> changez <u>rien</u>.	Don't change anything.
Je <u>ne</u> vois <u>personne</u>.	I can't see anybody.
Elle <u>n'</u>arrive <u>jamais</u> à l'heure.	She never arrives on time.
Il <u>ne</u> travaille <u>plus</u> ici.	He's no longer working here.

> ### Tip
> **ne** changes to **n'** in front of a word that starts with a vowel, most words beginning with **h** and the French word **y**.

➤ In English, *did* is often used to make a statement negative.

> I went to his party. → I did<u>n't</u> go to his party.
>
> We saw David at the weekend. → We did<u>n't</u> see David at the weekend.

[*i*] Note that the French verb **faire** is <u>NEVER</u> used in this way.

➤ **non plus** is the equivalent of English *neither* in phrases like *me neither, neither do I* and so on.

'Je n'aime pas les hamburgers.' – 'Moi <u>non plus</u>.'	'I don't like hamburgers.' – 'Me neither.'
Il n'y va pas et moi <u>non plus</u>.	He isn't going and neither am I.

➤ The French word **ne** is missed out when negatives are used without a verb to answer a question.

'Qui a téléphoné?' – '<u>Personne</u>.'	'Who rang?' – 'Nobody.'
'Qu'est-ce que tu fais cet après-midi?' – '<u>Rien</u>.'	'What are you doing this afternoon?' – 'Nothing.'

Tip

In everyday conversation French native speakers often miss out the word **ne**. Be careful about doing this yourself in formal situations.

Je peux pas venir ce soir.	I can't come tonight.
Il me l'a pas dit.	He didn't tell me.

Grammar Extra!

Sometimes you will find two of these negative expressions combined.

~~Ils ne font jamais rien d'intéressant.~~	They never do anything interesting.
Je ne connais plus personne à Nice.	I don't know anyone in Nice any more.

---

2 Word order with negatives

➤ Negative expressions in French 'sandwich' the verb in the present tense and in other tenses that consist of just one word. **ne** goes before the verb and the other half of the expression comes after the verb.

Il <u>ne</u> boit <u>jamais</u> d'alcool.	He never drinks alcohol.
Il <u>ne</u> pleuvait <u>pas</u>.	It wasn't raining.

➤ In the perfect tense and other tenses that consist of two or more words such as the pluperfect, there are two possibilities:

- **ne ... pas**, **ne ... rien**, **ne ... plus** and **ne ... jamais** follow the pattern: **ne (n')** + **avoir** or **être** + **pas/rien/plus/jamais** + past participle

Elle n'a pas fait ses devoirs.	She hasn't done her homework.
Je n'ai rien dit.	I didn't say anything.
Pierre n'est pas encore arrivé.	Pierre isn't here yet.

- **ne ... personne** follows the pattern: **ne (n')** + **avoir** + past participle + **personne**

Je n'ai vu personne.	I didn't see anybody.

➪ *For more information on the **Perfect tense**, see page 111.*

➤ A negative sentence may also contain a pronoun such as **te**, **le**, **lui** and so on that is the direct or indirect object of the verb, or a reflexive pronoun. If so, **ne** comes before the pronoun.

Je ne t'entends pas.	I can't hear you.
Ne lui parle pas!	Don't speak to him/her!
Tu ne te souviens pas de lui?	Don't you remember him?
Il ne se lève jamais avant midi.	He never gets up before midday.

➪ *For more information on **Direct** and **Indirect object pronouns** and on **Reflexive pronouns**, see pages 47, 49 and 89.*

➤ When a verb is in the infinitive, **ne ... pas**, **ne ... rien**, **ne ... plus** and **ne ... jamais** come together before the infinitive.

Il essayait de ne pas rire.	He was trying not to laugh.
J'ai peur de ne pas réussir.	I'm afraid of not succeeding.

Tip

After these negative expressions, **un**, **une** and **des** (the indefinite article) and **du**, **de la**, **de l'** and **des** (the partitive article) change to **de**.

Il ne reste plus de biscuits.	There aren't any biscuits left.

➪ *For more information on the **Indefinite article** and the **Partitive article**, see pages 19 and 22.*

3 | non and pas

➤ **non** (meaning *no*) is the usual negative answer to a question. It can also correspond to *not* in English.

'Tu veux nous accompagner?' **– 'Non, merci.'**	'Do you want to come with us?' – '<u>No</u> thanks.'
Tu viens ou <u>non</u>?	Are you coming or <u>not</u>?
J'espère que <u>non</u>.	I hope <u>not</u>.

➤ **pas** is generally used when a distinction is being made, or for emphasis. It, too, often corresponds to *not* in English.

'Qui veut m'aider?' – 'Pas moi!'	'Who wants to help me?' – '<u>Not</u> me!'
'Est-il de retour?' – 'Pas encore.'	'Is he back?' – '<u>Not</u> yet.'
'Tu as froid?' – 'Pas du tout.'	'Are you cold?' – '<u>Not</u> at all.'
Pas question!	<u>No</u> way!

Key points

✔ Negatives indicate when something is not happening or is not true. French uses set expressions or word pairs to indicate this.

✔ The two parts of these negative expressions 'sandwich' the verb in tenses consisting of only one word.

✔ **ne** comes before any object pronouns or reflexive pronouns.

✔ Before infinitives, **ne ... pas**, **ne ... rien**, **ne ... plus** and **ne ... jamais** come together.

✔ The articles **un**, **une**, **des**, **du**, **de la** and **de l'** change to **de** after negatives.

Questions

> **What is a question?**
> A **question** is a sentence which is used to ask someone about something and which normally has the verb in front of the subject. A question word such as *why, where, who, which* or *how* is used to ask a question.

How to ask a question in French

1 The basic rules

➤ There are four ways of asking questions in French:
- by making your voice go up at the end of the sentence
- by using the phrase **est-ce que**
- by changing round the order of words in a sentence
- by using a question word

2 Asking a question by making your voice go up

➤ If you are expecting the answer *yes* or *no*, there is a very straightforward way of asking a question. You can keep word order just as it would be in a normal sentence (subject then verb), but turn it into a question by making your voice go up at the end of the sentence. So to turn the sentence **Vous aimez la France** (meaning *You like France*) into a question, all you need to do is to add a question mark and make your voice go up at the end.

Vous (*subject*) **aimez** (*verb*) **la France?**	Do you like France?
On part tout de suite.	We're leaving right away.
On part tout de suite?	Are we leaving right away?
C'est vrai.	That's true.
C'est vrai?	Is that true?
Tes parents sont en vacances.	Your parents on holiday.
Tes parents sont en vacances?	Are your parents on holiday?

> *Tip*
> French speakers use this way of asking a question in ordinary, everyday conversations.

3 Asking a question by using est-ce que

➤ The phrase **est-ce que** is used to ask a question. Word order stays just the same as it would in an ordinary sentence. **Est-ce que** comes before the subject, and the verb comes after the subject. So to turn the sentence **Tu connais Marie** (meaning *You know Marie*) into a question, all you need to do is to add **est-ce que**.

Est-ce que tu (*subject*) **connais** (*verb*) **Marie?**	Do you know Marie?
Est-ce que vous allez en ville?	Are you going into town?
Est-ce que ta sœur est vraiment heureuse?	Is your sister really happy?

4 Asking a question by changing word order

➤ In ordinary sentences, the verb comes <u>AFTER</u> its subject. In this type of question, the verb is put <u>BEFORE</u> the subject. This change to normal word order is called <u>inversion</u>. You can do this when the subject is a pronoun such as **vous** or **il**. When you change the word order (or <u>invert</u>) in this way, you add a hyphen (-) between the verb and the pronoun.

Vous (*subject*) **aimez** (*verb*) **la France.**	You like France.
Aimez (*verb*)**-vous** (*subject*) **la France?**	Do you like France?
Il écrit bien.	He writes well.
<u>**Écrit-il**</u> **bien?**	Does he write well?
On part tout de suite.	We're leaving right away.
~~**Partez-vous** tout de suite?~~	Are you leaving right away?

➡ For more information on **Pronouns**, see page 42.

> *Tip*
> This is quite a formal way of asking a question.

➤ In the perfect tense and other tenses that consist of two or more words such as the pluperfect, the part of the verb that comes from **avoir** or **être** is the one that goes before the pronoun.

<u>**As**</u>**-tu vu mon sac?**	Have you seen my bag?
<u>**Est**</u>**-elle restée longtemps?**	Did she stay long?

➡ For more information on the **Perfect tense**, see page 111.

➤ When the verb ends in a vowel in the **il/elle** form, **-t-** is inserted before the pronoun to make the words easier to say.

Aime-t-il les chiens?	Does he like dogs?
A-t-elle assez d'argent?	Does she have enough money?

> ## *Tip*
>
> Unlike English there are two ways in French of answering *yes* to a question or statement. **oui** is the word you use to reply to an ordinary question.
>
> | | |
> |---|---|
> | **'Tu l'as fait?' – 'Oui.'** | 'Have you done it?' – 'Yes.' |
> | **'Elle est belle, n'est-ce pas?'**
 – 'Oui.' | 'She's beautiful, isn't she?'
 – 'Yes.' |
>
> **si** is the word you use to reply to a question or statement that contains a negative expression like **ne ... pas**.
>
> | | |
> |---|---|
> | **'Tu ne l'as pas fait?' – 'Si.'** | 'Haven't you done it?' – 'Yes (I have).' |
> | **'Elle n'est pas très belle.'**
 – 'Mais si!' | 'She isn't very beautiful.'
 – 'Yes, she is!' |

Grammar Extra!

You can also form a question in this way with a noun or a person's name. If you do this, the noun or name comes first, then you add an extra pronoun after the verb and link them with a hyphen.

Jean-Pierre *(subject)* **est***(verb)***-il** *(pronoun)* **là?**	Is Jean-Pierre there?
La pièce dure-t-elle longtemps?	Does the play last long?

In less formal French, the pronoun may come before the verb, and the noun or name may come at the end of the sentence.

Il est là, Jean-Pierre?	Is Jean-Pierre there?
Elle dure longtemps, la pièce?	Does the play last long?

---

5 Asking a question by using a question word

➤ A question word is a word like *when* or *how* that is used to ask for information. The most common French question words are listed on pages 146–150.

➤ You can use a question word with one of the methods described above:

● you can make your voice go up at the end of the sentence. If you do this, the question word goes at the <u>END</u> of the sentence.

- you can use **est-ce que**. If you do this, the question word goes at the <u>START</u> of the sentence.
- you can change word order so that the verb comes before the subject. If you do this, the question word goes at the <u>START</u> of the sentence.

Vous arrivez <u>quand</u>?	
<u>Quand</u> est-ce que vous arrivez?	<u>When</u> do you arrive?
<u>Quand</u> arrivez-vous?	
Tu prends <u>quel</u> train?	
<u>Quel</u> train est-ce que tu prends?	<u>What</u> train are you getting?
<u>Quel</u> train prends-tu?	
Ils vont <u>où</u>?	
<u>Où</u> est-ce qu'ils vont?	<u>Where</u> are they going?
<u>Où</u> vont-ils?	

➡ *For more information on **Negatives**, see page 138.*

Key points

✔ You ask a question in French by making your voice go up at the end of the sentence, by using **est-ce que**, by changing normal word order, or by using a question word.

✔ When you put the verb in front of the subject, you join the two words with a hyphen. A **-t-** is used in the **il/elle** form if the verb ends in a vowel.

✔ You use **oui** to answer *yes* to an ordinary question, but **si** if there is a negative in the question or statement.

Question words

1 Common question words

➤ Listed below are some very common question words. **que**, **quel**, **qui**, **quoi** and **lequel** are explained on pages 147–150.

- **combien** + *verb*? how much?, how many?
  combien de + *noun*? how much?, how many?

Combien coûte cet ordinateur?	How much does this computer cost?
C'est **combien**, ce pantalon?	How much are these trousers?
Tu en veux **combien**? Deux?	How many do you want? Two?
Combien de personnes vas-tu inviter?	How many people are you going to invite?

- **comment?** how?

Comment va-t-elle?	How is she?
Comment tu t'appelles?	What's your name?

> **Tip**
>
> **pardon** and **comment** are also used to ask someone to repeat something, and are the same as *Pardon?* in English. **quoi** can mean the same thing, but is informal, and is the same as *What?* in English.

- **où?** where?

Où allez-vous?	Where are you going?
D'où viens-tu?	Where are you from?

> **Tip**
>
> Be careful not to mix up **où**, which means *where*, and **ou** (without an accent), which means *or*.

- **pourquoi?** why?

Pourquoi est-ce qu'il ne vient pas avec nous?	Why isn't he coming with us?

- **quand?** when?

Quand est-ce que tu pars en vacances?	When are you going on holiday?
Depuis quand est-ce que vous le connaissez?	How long have you known him?

2 | qui?, que? and quoi?

➤ In questions, **qui**, **que** and **quoi** are all pronouns. Which of them you choose depends on:

- whether you are referring to people or to things
- whether you are referring to the subject or object of the verb (the subject is the person or thing that is carrying out the action described by the verb; the object is the person or thing that 'receives' the action)
- whether the word you use will come after a preposition such as **à**, **de** or **en**

⇨ *For more information on **Pronouns** and **Prepositions**, see pages 42 and 62.*

➤ **qui?** and **que?** have longer forms, as shown in the table below. There is a difference in word order between the longer and shorter forms.

➤ **qui?** is used for talking about people, and means *who?* or *whom?* in English. You can use *whom?* in formal English to refer to the object of verb, though most people use *who?*. **qui?** can be used after a preposition.

Who? Whom?	Referring to people	Meaning	Examples	Meaning
Subject	qui? qui est-ce qui?	who?	Qui vient? Qui est-ce qui vient?	Who's coming?
Object	qui? qui est-ce que?	who? whom?	Qui vois-tu? Qui est-ce que tu vois?	Who/Whom can you see?
After prepositions	qui? qui est-ce que?	who? whom?	De qui est-ce qu'il parle? Pour qui est ce livre? À qui avez-vous écrit?	Who's he talking about? Who's this book for? Who did you write to?, To whom did you write?

Tip

que changes to **qu'** before a vowel, most words beginning with **h**, and the French word **y**.

⇨ *For more information on **que** and **qui**, see page 62.*

➤ **à qui** is the usual way of saying *whose* in questions.

> **À qui est ce sac?**   Whose is this bag?

⇨   *For more information on using à to show possession, see page 165.*

➤ **que?** and **quoi?** are used for talking about things, and mean *what?* in English. **que?** <u>cannot</u> be used after a preposition; you have to use **quoi?** instead.

What?	Referring to things	Meaning	Examples	Meaning
Subject	qu'est-ce qui?	what?	Qu'est-ce qui se passe? Qu'est-ce qui t'inquiète?	What's happening? What's worrying you?
Object	qu'est-ce que? que?	what?	Qu'est-ce que vous faites? Que faites-vous?	What are you doing?
After prepositions	quoi?	what?	À quoi penses-tu? De quoi parlez-vous?	What are you thinking about? What are you talking about?

> ## Tip
> It is possible to finish an English sentence with a preposition such as *about* or *of*, even though some people think this is not good grammar.
> *Who did you write <u>to</u>?*
> *What are you talking <u>about</u>?*
> It is <u>NEVER</u> possible to end a French sentence with a preposition.

3 quel?, quelle?, quels? and quelles?

➤ **quel?** (meaning *who?*, *which?* or *what?*) can be used with a noun (as an <u>adjective</u>) or can replace a noun (as a <u>pronoun</u>). Compare this with **que?** (and its longer forms) and **quoi?**, which also mean *what?*, but are <u>NEVER</u> used with nouns.

⇨   *For more information on **Adjectives** and **Pronouns**, see pages 25 and 42.*

➤ **quel**, **quelle**, **quels** and **quelles** are all forms of the same word. The form that you choose depends on whether you are referring to something that is masculine or feminine, singular or plural.

	Masculine	Feminine	Meaning
Singular	quel?	quelle?	who? what? which?
Plural	quels?	quelles?	who? what? which?

Quel est ton chanteur préféré?	Who's your favourite singer?
Quel vin recommandez-vous?	Which wine do you recommend?
Quelle est ta couleur préférée?	What's your favourite colour?
Quelle heure est-il?	What time is it?
Quels sont tes chanteurs préférés?	Who are your favourite singers?
Vous jouez de quels instruments?	What instruments do you play?
Quelles sont tes couleurs préférées?	What are your favourite colours?
Quelles chaussures te plaisent le plus?	Which shoes do you like best?

➪ *For more information on how **quel** in used in exclamations, see page 21.*

4 lequel?, laquelle?, lesquels? and lesquelles?

➤ In questions **lequel**, **laquelle**, **lesquels** and **lesquelles** (meaning *which one/ ones?*) are all forms of the same pronoun, and are used to replace nouns. The form that you choose depends on whether you are referring to something that is masculine or feminine, singular or plural.

	Masculine	Feminine	Meaning
Singular	lequel?	laquelle?	which? which one?
Plural	lesquels?	lesquelles?	which? which ones?

'J'ai choisi un livre.' – 'Lequel?'	'I've chosen a book.' – 'Which one?'
Laquelle de ces valises est à Bruno?	Which of these cases is Bruno's?

'Tu te souviens de mes amis?' – **'Lesquels?'**	'Do you remember my friends?' – 'Which ones?'
Lesquelles de vos sœurs sont mariées?	Which of your sisters are married?

⇨ *For more information on **lequel**, see page 63.*

5 n'est-ce pas? and non?

➤ English speakers often use an expression like *isn't it?*, *don't they?*, *weren't we?* or *will you?* tagged on to the end of a sentence to turn it into a question. French uses **n'est-ce pas?** instead. This useful little phrase never changes, so is very easy to use. You use it in questions when you expect the person you are talking to to agree with you.

Il fait chaud, <u>n'est-ce pas?</u>	It's warm, <u>isn't it</u>?
Tu parles français, <u>n'est-ce pas?</u>	You speak French, <u>don't you</u>?
Vous n'oublierez pas, <u>n'est-ce pas?</u>	You won't forget, <u>will you</u>?

➤ It is very common to use **non** (meaning *no*) in the same way in spoken French. **hein?** means the same as *eh?* in English, and is only used in very informal conversations.

Il fait chaud, <u>non?</u>	It's warm, isn't it?
Il fait chaud, <u>hein?</u>	It's warm, eh?

Key points

✔ In questions **qui?** means *who?*; **que?** and **quoi?** mean *what?*

✔ **qui est-ce qui?** (*subject*) and **qui est-ce que?** (*object*) are longer forms of **qui?** Both mean *who?* The word order is different from **qui**.

✔ **qu'est-ce qui?** (*subject*) and **qu'est-ce que?** (*object*) are longer forms of **que?** Both mean *what?* The word order is different from **que**.

✔ **qui?** (for people) and **quoi?** (for things) can be used after prepositions.

✔ **quel?** is both an adjective and a pronoun. It means *who?*, *what?* or *which?* in questions, and is used with a noun or replaces a noun.

✔ **lequel?** is a pronoun; it means *which?* or *which one?* in questions.

✔ **n'est-ce pas?** or **non?** can be tagged on to the end of sentences to turn them into questions.

Grammar Extra!

All the questions in the previous section are the actual words that someone uses when they are asking a question, and so they all end with a question mark. These are called <u>direct</u> questions. When you are telling someone else about a question that is being asked, you use an <u>indirect</u> question. Indirect questions never end with a question mark, and they are always introduced by a verb such as *to ask*, *to tell*, *to wonder*, *to know* and so on.

> He asked me what the time was. (His actual question was *What is the time?*)
>
> Tell me which way to go. (Your actual question was *Which way do I go?*)

Word order in indirect questions is generally the same as in English:
question word + subject + verb.

Dites-moi quel *(question word)* **autobus** *(subject)* **va** *(verb)* **à la gare.**	Tell me which bus goes to the station.
Il m'a demandé combien d'argent j'avais.	He asked me how much money I had.
Je me demande s'il viendra ou pas.	I wonder if he'll come or not.

When the subject of the question is a noun and <u>NOT</u> a pronoun like **je** or **il**, the subject and verb that come after the question word are often swapped round.

Je me demande où *(question word)* **sont** *(verb)* **mes clés** *(subject).*	I wonder where my keys are.
Demande-lui qui est venu.	Ask him who came.

Adverbs

What is an adverb?
An **adverb** is a word usually used with verbs, adjectives or other adverbs that gives more information about when, how, where, or in what circumstances something happens, for example, *quickly, happily, now*.

How adverbs are used

➤ In general, adverbs are used together with:

- verbs (*act <u>quickly</u>, speak <u>strangely</u>, smile <u>cheerfully</u>*)
- adjectives (*<u>rather</u> ill, <u>a lot</u> better, <u>deeply</u> sorry*)
- other adverbs (*<u>really</u> fast, <u>too</u> quickly, <u>very</u> well*)

➤ Adverbs can also relate to the whole sentence; they often tell you what the speaker is thinking or feeling.

> <u>Fortunately</u>, Jan had already left.
> <u>Actually</u>, I don't think I'll come.

How adverbs are formed

1 The basic rules

➤ Adverbs in French <u>NEVER</u> change their form, no matter what they refer to.

Il est <u>très</u> beau.	He's very handsome.
Elles sont <u>très</u> belles.	They're very beautiful.
J'y vais <u>souvent</u>.	I often go there.
Nous y allons <u>souvent</u>.	We often go there.

i Note that there is one exception to this rule. The word **tout** changes in certain phrases, for example, **tout seul** (meaning *all alone*).

Il est arrivé <u>tout seul</u>.	He arrived on his own.
Elle est souvent <u>toute seule</u>.	She's often on her own.

➤ Many English adverbs end in -ly, which is added to the end of the adjective (*quick → quickly; sad → sadly; frequent → frequently*). In French, many adverbs end in **-ment**. This is usually added to the end of the <u>feminine singular</u> form of the adjective.

Masculine adjective	Feminine adjective	Adverb	Meaning
heureux	heureuse	heureusement	fortunately
doux	douce	doucement	gently, slowly
seul	seule	seulement	only

➤ The adverb ending **-ment** is added to the <u>masculine</u> not the feminine form of the adjective if the masculine ends in **-é**, **-i** or **-u**.

Masculine adjective	Feminine adjective	Adverb	Meaning
désespéré	désespérée	désespérément	desperately
vrai	vraie	vraiment	truly
absolu	absolue	absolument	absolutely

➤ If the adjective ends in **-ant**, the adverb ends in **-amment**. If the adjective ends in **-ent**, the adverb ends in **-emment**. The first vowel in the **-emment** and **-amment** endings is pronounced in the same way in both – like the *a* in the English word *cat*.

    courant → **couramment** (*fluently*)
    récent → **récemment** (*recently*)

[*i*] Note that an exception to this rule is the adverb **lentement** (meaning *slowly*), which comes from the adjective **lent** (meaning *slow*).

2 Irregular adverbs

➤ There are a number of common irregular adverbs.

Adjective	Meaning	Adverb	Meaning
bon	good	bien	well
gentil	nice, kind	gentiment	nicely, kindly
mauvais	bad	mal	badly
meilleur	better, best	mieux	better
petit	small	peu	little
pire	worse	pis	worse

    Elle travaille <u>bien</u>.   She works well.
    C'est un emploi très <u>mal</u> payé.   It's a very badly paid job.

3 Adjectives used as adverbs

➤ Certain adjectives are used as adverbs, mostly in set phrases:
    • **bon** good
    sentir bon to smell nice

- **cher** expensive
  coûter cher to be expensive
  payer cher to pay a lot

- **droit** straight
  aller tout droit to go straight on

- **dur** hard
  travailler dur to work hard

- **fort** loud
  parler plus fort to speak up

- **mauvais** bad
  sentir mauvais to smell

4 Adverbs made up of more than one word

➤ Adverbs can be made up of several words instead of just one. Here are some common ones:

bien sûr	of course
c'est-à-dire	that is
d'abord	first
d'habitude	usually
de temps en temps	from time to time
en général	usually
en retard	late
tout de suite	straight away

Key points

✔ With the exception of **tout**, French adverbs do not change their form.

✔ The ending **-ment** is usually added to the feminine singular form of the corresponding adjective.

✔ If the masculine singular adjective ends in **-é**, **-i** or **-u**, the **-ment** ending is added to that.

✔ If the adjective ends in **-ant** or **-ent**, the adverb ends in **-amment** or **-emment** (apart from **lentement**).

Comparatives and superlatives of adverbs

1 Comparative adverbs

What is a comparative adverb?
A **comparative adverb** is one which, in English, has -er on the end of it or
more or *less* in front of it, for example, *earlier, later, sooner, more/less frequently*.

➤ Adverbs can be used to make comparisons in French, just as they can in
English. The comparative (*more often, faster*) of adverbs is formed using the
same phrases as for adjectives.

- **plus ... (que)**   more ... (than)
  Tu marches <u>plus</u> vite <u>que</u> moi.   You walk faster than me.
  Elle chante <u>plus</u> fort <u>que</u> les **autres.**   She's singing louder than the others.

- **moins ... (que)**   less ... (than)
  Parle <u>moins</u> vite!   Don't speak so fast! (*literally: Speak less fast!*)
  Nous nous voyons <u>moins</u> **souvent <u>qu'</u>avant.**   We see each other less often than before.

- **aussi ... que**   as ... as
  Je parle français <u>aussi</u> bien <u>que</u> **toi!**   I can speak French as well as you!
  Viens <u>aussi</u> vite <u>que</u> possible.   Come as quickly as possible.

⇨ *For more information on **Comparative adjectives**, see page 34.*

2 Superlative adverbs

What is a superlative adverb?
A **superlative adverb** is one which, in English, has -est on the end of it or *most*
or *least* in front of it, for example, *soonest, fastest, most/least frequently*.

➤ The superlative of adverbs (*the most, the fastest*) is formed using the same
phrases as for adjectives, except that **le** <u>NEVER</u> changes to **la** or **les** in the
feminine and plural with adverbs as it does with adjectives.

- **le plus ... (que)** the most ... (that)
  Marianne parle <u>le plus</u> vite.   Marianne speaks fastest.
- **le moins ... (que)** the least ... (that)
  C'est Gordon qui a mangé <u>le moins</u>.   Gordon ate the least.

⇨ *For more information on **Superlative adjectives**, see page 34.*

3 Adverbs with irregular comparatives and superlatives

➤ Some of the most common adverbs have irregular comparative and superlative forms.

Adverb	Meaning	Comparative	Meaning	Superlative	Meaning
beaucoup	a lot	plus	more	le plus	(the) most
bien	well	mieux	better	le mieux	(the) best
mal	badly	pis plus mal	worse	le pis le plus mal	(the) worst
peu	little	moins	less	le moins	(the) least

C'est lui qui danse <u>le mieux</u>.   He dances best.

> ### Key points
> ✔ Comparatives of adverbs are formed in the same way as comparatives of adjectives, using **plus ... (que)**, **moins ... (que)** and **aussi ... que**.
> ✔ Superlatives of adverbs are formed in the same way as superlatives of adjectives, using **le plus ... (que)** and **le moins ... (que)**. **le** never changes in the feminine and plural.
> ✔ Unlike adjectives, adverbs do not change their form to agree with the verb, adjective or other adverb they relate to.

Some common adverbs

➤ Here are some common adverbs that do not end in **-ment**:

alors	then, so, at that time
après	afterwards
après-demain	the day after tomorrow
aujourd'hui	today
assez	enough, quite
aussi	also, too, as
avant-hier	the day before yesterday
beaucoup	a lot, much
bientôt	soon
cependant	however
dedans	inside
dehors	outside
déjà	already, before
demain	tomorrow
depuis	since
derrière	behind
devant	in front
encore	still, even, again
enfin	at last
ensemble	together
ensuite	then
environ	about
hier	yesterday
ici	here
jamais	never, ever

Tip

jamais can sometimes be used without **ne** to mean *never* or *ever*.

'Est-ce que tu vas souvent au cinéma?' – 'Non, <u>jamais</u>.'	'Do you go to the cinema a lot?' – 'No, <u>never</u>.'
As-tu <u>jamais</u> revu ton père?	Did you <u>ever</u> see your father again?

➪ *For more information on* **Negatives**, *see page 138.*

---

là	there, here
là-bas	over there
loin	far, far off, a long time ago

longtemps	a long time
maintenant	now, nowadays
même	even
moins	less
où	where
parfois	sometimes
partout	everywhere
peu	not much, not very

Tip

Be careful not to confuse **peu**, which means *not much* or *not very*, with **un peu**, which means *a little* or *a bit*.

Il voyage <u>peu</u>.	He does<u>n't</u> travel <u>much</u>.
Elle est <u>un peu</u> timide.	She's <u>a bit</u> shy.

---

peut-être	perhaps
plus	more
presque	nearly
puis	then
quelquefois	sometimes
si	so
soudain	suddenly
souvent	often
surtout	especially, above all
tard	late
tôt	early
toujours	always, still
tout	all, very
très	very
trop	too much, too
vite	quick, fast, soon

Tip

vite and **rapide** can both mean *fast* or *quick*. Remember, though, that **vite** is an <u>adverb</u> and **rapide** is an <u>adjective</u>.

une voiture <u>rapide</u>	a fast car
Il roule trop <u>vite</u>.	He drives too fast.

For further explanation of grammatical terms, please see pages viii–xii.

➤ Some of the adverbs listed on pages 157 and 158 can be followed by **de** and used in front of a noun to talk about quantities or numbers of things or people:

- **assez de** enough

  Nous n'avons pas <u>assez de</u> temps.   We don't have enough time.

- **beaucoup de** a lot of

  Elle fait <u>beaucoup de</u> fautes.   She makes a lot of mistakes.

- **trop de** too much, too many

  J'ai mangé <u>trop de</u> fromage.   I've eaten too much cheese.

➤ Several of the adverbs listed on pages 157 and 158 can also be used as prepositions: **après**, **avant**, **devant**, **derrière** and **depuis**.

⇨ *For more information on **Prepositions**, see page 162.*

➤ The question words **combien** (meaning *how much*, *how many*), **comment** (meaning *how*), **pourquoi** (meaning *why*) and **quand** (meaning *when*) are described on page 146.

➤ **pas**, **plus** and **jamais** are used in negative word pairs.

⇨ *For more information on **Negatives**, see page 138.*

Key points

✔ Many very common adverbs do not end in **-ment**. They are worth learning.

✔ Several adverbs can be followed by **de** + noun and used to talk about quantities and numbers.

Word order with adverbs

1 | Adverbs with verbs

➤ In English, adverbs can come in different places in a sentence.

I'm <u>never</u> coming back.

See you <u>soon</u>!

<u>Suddenly</u> the phone rang.

I'd <u>really</u> like to come.

➤ In French, the rules are more fixed. When an adverb goes with a verb that consists of just one word, such as a verb in the <u>present tense</u> or the <u>imperfect tense</u>, it generally goes <u>AFTER</u> that verb.

Il neige <u>toujours</u> en janvier.	It always snows in January.
Je pensais <u>souvent</u> à toi.	I often used to think about you.

➤ When an adverb goes with a verb that consists of more than one word, such as a verb in the <u>perfect tense</u>, it generally comes <u>BETWEEN</u> the part of the verb that comes from **avoir** or **être** and the past participle.

Il a <u>trop</u> mangé.	He's eaten too much.
Ils sont <u>déjà</u> partis.	They've already gone.

⇨ *For more information on the **Perfect tense**, see page 111.*

➤ The rule above covers most adverbs that tell you about quantity or time (apart from a few listed later), and some very common ones telling you how something is done.

beaucoup	a lot, much
bien	well
bientôt	soon
déjà	already, before
encore	still, even, again
enfin	at last
mal	badly
mieux	better
peu	not much, not very
rarement	rarely
souvent	often
toujours	always, still
trop	too much, too
vraiment	really

➤ Some adverbs <u>FOLLOW</u> the past participle of verbs that consist of more than one word. This rule covers most adverbs that tell you how or where something is done, and a few adverbs that tell you about time.

aujourd'hui	today
demain	tomorrow
hier	yesterday
loin	far, far off, a long time ago
longtemps	a long time
partout	everywhere
quelquefois	sometimes
tôt	early
tard	late
vite	quick, fast, soon

On les a vus <u>partout</u>.	We saw them everywhere.
Elle est revenue <u>hier</u>.	She came back yesterday.

2 Adverbs with adjectives and other adverbs

➤ When an adverb goes with an <u>adjective</u>, it generally comes just <u>BEFORE</u> that adjective.

Ils ont une <u>très</u> belle maison.	They have a very nice house.
une femme <u>bien</u> habillée	a well-dressed woman

➤ When an adverb goes with another <u>adverb</u>, it generally comes just <u>BEFORE</u> that adverb.

C'est <u>trop</u> tard.	It's too late.
Fatima travaille <u>beaucoup plus</u> vite.	Fatima works much faster.

Key points
✔ Adverbs follow verbs that consist of just one word.
✔ They generally go before the past participle of verbs that consist of two words when they relate to quantity or time.
✔ They generally go after the past participle of verbs that consist of two words when they relate to how or where something is done.
✔ When used with an adjective or another adverb, they generally come just before it.

Prepositions

What is a preposition?
A **preposition** is a word such as *at*, *for*, *with*, *into* or *from*, which is
usually followed by a noun, pronoun or, in English, a word ending in *-ing*.
Prepositions show how people and things relate to the rest of the sentence,
for example, *She's at home.*; *a tool for cutting grass*; *it's from David.*

Using prepositions

➤ Prepositions are used in front of nouns and pronouns (such as *me*, *him*, *the man*
and so on), and show the relationship between the noun or pronoun and the
rest of the sentence. Some prepositions can be used before verb forms ending
in *-ing* in English.

> I showed my ticket to the inspector.
> Come with me.
> This brush is really good for cleaning shoes.

⇨ *For more information on **Nouns** and **Pronouns**, see pages 1 and 42.*

➤ Prepositions are also used after certain adjectives and verbs and link them
to the rest of the sentence.

Je suis très contente de te voir.	I'm very happy to see you.
Tu aimes jouer au tennis?	Do you like playing tennis?

➤ In English it is possible to finish a sentence with a preposition such as *for*, *about*
or *on*, even though some people think this is not good grammar.
You can <u>NEVER</u> end a French sentence with a preposition.

Le café au lait, c'est pour qui?	Who's the white coffee for?
De quoi parlez-vous?	What are you talking about?

> *Tip*
> The French preposition is not always the direct equivalent of the
> preposition that is used in English. It is often difficult to give just one
> English equivalent for French prepositions, as the way they are used
> varies so much between the two languages.

à, de and en

1 **à**

➤ Be careful not to confuse the preposition **à** with the **il/elle/on** form of the verb **avoir: il a** (meaning *he has*) and so on.

> **Tip**
>
> When **à** is followed by **le**, the two words become **au**. Similarly, when **à** is followed by **les**, the two words become **aux**.
>
> ⇨ For more information on **Articles**, see page 12.

➤ **à** can mean *at*.

Les melons se vendent à 2 euros pièce.	Melons are selling <u>at</u> 2 euros each.
Nous roulions à 100 km à l'heure.	We were driving <u>at</u> 100 km an hour
J'ai lancé une pierre à Chantal.	I threw a stone <u>at</u> Chantal.
Je suis à la maison.	I'm <u>at</u> home.

📖 Note that **à la maison** can also mean *to the house*.

Je rentre à la maison.	I'm going back to the house *or* back home.

➤ **à** can mean *in*.

Nous habitons à la campagne.	We live <u>in</u> the country.
Mon père est à Londres.	My father is <u>in</u> London.
Restez au lit.	Stay <u>in</u> bed.
Jean est entré, un livre à la main.	Jean came in with a book <u>in</u> his hand.

> **Tip**
>
> **à** is used to mean *in* with the names of towns and cities, and **au** (*singular*) or **aux** (*plural*) with the names of countries that are masculine in French.
>
> | | |
> |---|---|
> | **J'habite au Mexique.** | I live <u>in</u> Mexico. |
> | **Elle est aux États-Unis.** | She's <u>in</u> the States. |

➤ **à** can mean *to*.

Je vais au cinéma ce soir.	I'm going <u>to</u> the cinema tonight.
Donne le ballon à ton frère.	Give the ball <u>to</u> your brother.

> **Tip**
>
> à is used to mean *to* with the names of towns and cities, and **au** (*singular*) or **aux** (*plural*) with the names of countries that are masculine in French.
>
> | | |
> |---|---|
> | **Je vais assez souvent <u>à</u> Paris.** | I go <u>to</u> Paris quite often. |
> | **Il va <u>aux</u> États-Unis la semaine prochaine.** | He's going <u>to</u> the States next week. |

➤ à is also used with **de** to mean *from ... to ...*

le trajet <u>de</u> Londres <u>à</u> Paris	the journey <u>from</u> London <u>to</u> Paris
La banque est ouverte <u>de</u> 9 heures <u>à</u> midi.	The bank is open <u>from</u> 9 <u>to</u> 12.
Je suis en vacances <u>du</u> 21 juin <u>au</u> 5 juillet.	I'm on holiday <u>from</u> 21 June <u>to</u> 5 July.

➤ à can mean *on*.

Il y a deux beaux tableaux <u>au</u> mur.	There are two beautiful paintings <u>on</u> the wall.
Le bureau se trouve <u>au</u> premier étage.	The office is <u>on</u> the first floor.
Qu'est-ce qu'il y a <u>à la</u> télé ce soir?	What's <u>on</u> TV tonight?

ℹ️ Note that à and **sur** can both mean *on* in English. **sur** usually means on the top of something. **sur la télé** means *on top of the TV set*, but **à la télé** means *broadcast on TV*. Both can be translated as *on the TV* in English. **sur le mur** means *on top of the wall*, but **au mur** means *hanging on the wall*.

➤ à is often used to describe:

- what someone looks like or is wearing

la femme <u>au</u> chapeau vert	the woman with the green hat
un garçon <u>aux</u> yeux bleus	a boy with blue eyes

- how something is done

fait <u>à</u> la main	hand-made
laver <u>à</u> la machine	to machine-wash

- what a type of food is made of

une tarte <u>aux</u> poires	a pear tart
un sandwich <u>au</u> jambon	a ham sandwich

- how you travel

On y va <u>à</u> pied?	Shall we walk?
Il est venu <u>à</u> vélo.	He came on his bike.

> *Tip*
>
> Apart from **à vélo** and **à cheval** (meaning *on horseback*), the prepositions **en** and **par** are used with most other means of transport.

➤ **à** can also show what something is used for.

une boîte <u>aux</u> lettres	a letter box
une machine <u>à</u> laver	a washing machine
une tasse <u>à</u> café	a coffee cup

[i] Note that **une tasse <u>à</u> café** means a *coffee cup*, but **une tasse <u>de</u> café** means *a cup of coffee*. In the same way, **un verre <u>à</u> vin** means *a wine glass* but **un verre <u>de</u> vin** means *a glass of wine*.

➤ **à** is used with times, centuries and the names of festivals.

<u>à</u> trois heures	at three o'clock
<u>au</u> vingtième siècle	in the twentieth century
<u>à</u> Noël	at Christmas
<u>à</u> Pâques	at Easter

➤ **à** is used to talk about distances and rates.

La maison est <u>à</u> 6 kilomètres d'ici.	The house is 6 kilometres from here.
C'est <u>à</u> deux minutes de chez moi.	It's two minutes from my place.
Je suis payé <u>à</u> l'heure.	I'm paid by the hour.

➤ **à** shows who owns something, or whose turn it is.

Ce cahier est <u>à</u> Paul.	This notebook is Paul's.
C'est <u>à</u> toi?	Is this yours?
C'est <u>à</u> qui de nettoyer la salle de bains?	Whose turn is it to clean the bathroom?

➤ If you want to say where something hurts, you use **à**.

J'ai mal <u>à</u> la tête.	I've got a headache.
J'ai mal <u>aux</u> jambes.	My legs ache.
J'ai mal <u>à</u> la gorge.	I've got a sore throat.

➤ **à** is used with certain adjectives.

Son écriture est difficile à lire.	His/Her writing is difficult to read.
Je suis prêt à tout.	I'm ready for anything.

⇨ *For more information about **Prepositions after adjectives**, see page 183.*

➤ **à** is used with certain verbs.

s'intéresser à quelque chose	to be interested in something
penser à quelque chose	to think about something

⇨ *For more information about **Prepositions after verbs**, see page 178.*

➤ Finally, some common ways of saying goodbye contain **à**.

À bientôt!	See you soon!
À demain!	See you tomorrow!
À samedi!	See you Saturday!
À tout à l'heure!	See you later!

2 de

➤ **de** is used as part of the partitive article, which is usually the equivalent of *some* or *any* in English.

⇨ *For more information on the **Partitive article**, see page 22.*

> ### Tip
> When **de** is followed by **le**, the two words become **du**. Similarly, when **de** is followed by **les**, the two words become **des**.
>
> ⇨ *For more information on **Articles**, see page 12.*

➤ **de** can mean *from*.

Je viens d'Édimbourg.	I'm <u>from</u> Edinburgh.
une lettre de Rachid	a letter <u>from</u> Rachid
Je la vois de temps en temps.	I see her <u>from</u> time to time.

> ### Tip
> **de** changes to **d'** in front of a word starting with a vowel, most words starting with **h**, and the French word **y**.

For further explanation of grammatical terms, please see pages viii–xii.

➤ **de** is also used with **à** to mean *from ... to ...*

le trajet <u>de</u> Londres <u>à</u> Paris	the journey <u>from</u> London <u>to</u> Paris
La banque est ouverte <u>de</u> 9 heures <u>à</u> midi.	The bank is open <u>from</u> 9 <u>to</u> 12.
Je suis en vacances <u>du</u> 21 juin <u>au</u> 5 juillet.	I'm on holiday <u>from</u> 21 June <u>to</u> 5 July.

➤ **de** often shows who or what something belongs to.

un ami <u>de</u> la famille	a friend of the family
les fenêtres <u>de</u> la maison	the windows of the house
la voiture <u>de</u> Marie-Pierre	Marie-Pierre's car

➤ **de** can indicate what something contains, when it usually corresponds to *of* in English.

une boîte <u>d'</u>allumettes	a box <u>of</u> matches
deux bouteilles <u>de</u> vin	two bottles <u>of</u> wine
une tasse <u>de</u> café	a cup <u>of</u> coffee

> [i] Note that **une tasse <u>de</u> café** means *a cup of coffee* but **une tasse <u>à</u> café** means *a coffee cup*. In the same way, **un verre <u>à</u> vin** means *a wine glass* but **un verre <u>de</u> vin** means *a glass of wine*.

➤ **de** can describe what material something is made of.

une robe <u>de</u> coton	a cotton dress
une porte <u>de</u> bois	a wooden door

Tip

en can also be used to say what something is made of, and is used when it is important to stress the material.

un bracelet <u>en</u> or	a gold bracelet

➤ You can use **de** to say what something is used for.

un sac <u>de</u> couchage	a sleeping bag
un terrain <u>de</u> foot	a football pitch
un arrêt <u>de</u> bus	a bus stop

➤ **de** is found after superlatives (*the most..., the biggest, the least ...* and so on).

la plus belle ville <u>du</u> monde	the most beautiful city in the world
le film le moins intéressant <u>du</u> festival	the least interesting film in the festival

⇨ *For more information on **Superlative adjectives**, see page 34.*

➤ **de** is used in phrases to talk about quantities.

Elle fait <u>beaucoup de</u> fautes.	She makes a lot of mistakes.
<u>Combien de</u> personnes as-tu invitées?	How many people have you invited?

➤ **de** is used with certain adjectives.

Je suis très surpris <u>de</u> te voir.	I'm very surprised to see you.
Il est triste <u>de</u> partir.	He's sad to be leaving.

⇨ *For more information on **Prepositions after adjectives**, see page 183.*

Grammar Extra!

If you want to use an adjective after **quelque chose**, **rien**, **quelqu'un** and **personne**, you link the words with **de**.

quelqu'un <u>d'</u>important	someone important
quelque chose <u>d'</u>intéressant	something interesting
rien <u>d'</u>amusant	nothing funny

➤ **de** is found after certain verbs.

dépendre <u>de</u> quelque chose	to depend on something
parler <u>de</u> quelque chose	to talk about something

⇨ *For more information on **Prepositions after verbs**, see page 178.*

3 en

ℹ️ Note that **en** is never followed by an article such as **le**, **du** or **des**.

➤ **en** is used to talk about a place. It can be the equivalent of the English *to* or *in*.

Je vais <u>en</u> ville.	I'm going <u>to</u> town.
Il a un appartement <u>en</u> ville.	He has a flat <u>in</u> town.
Nous allons <u>en</u> France cet été.	We're going <u>to</u> France this summer.
Nous habitons <u>en</u> France.	We live <u>in</u> France.

> *Tip*
>
> **en** is used with the names of countries that are feminine in French. Use **à** with the names of towns and cities, and **au** or **aux** with masculine countries.

➤ **en** is used to talk about years and months, and to say how long something will take, when it is the equivalent of *in/within*:

en 1923	in 1923
en janvier	in January
Je le ferai en trois jours.	I'll do it in three days.

Grammar Extra!

en and **dans** can both be used in French to talk about a length of time, but the meaning is very different.

Je le ferai dans trois jours.	I'll do it in three days.
Je le ferai en trois jours.	I'll do it in three days.

Though both can be translated in the same way, the first sentence means that you'll do it in three days' time; the second means that it will take three days for you to do it.

➤ **en** is used with the names of the seasons, except for spring.

en été	in summer
en automne	in autumn
en hiver	in winter
BUT: **au printemps**	in spring

➤ **en** is used for most means of transport.

Je suis venu en voiture.	I came by car.
C'est plus rapide en train.	It's quicker by train.
Il est allé en Italie en avion.	He flew to Italy.

Tip

The prepositions **à** and **par** are also used with means of transport.

➤ Use **en** to say what language something is in.

une lettre écrite en espagnol	a letter written in Spanish
Dis-le en anglais.	Say it in English.

➤ **en** can be used to say what something is made of when you particularly want to stress the material.

un bracelet en or	a bracelet made of gold, a gold bracelet
un manteau en cuir	a coat made of leather, a leather coat

> *Tip*
>
> **de** can also be used to say what something is made of.
>
> **une porte _de_ bois**   a wooden door

➤ **en** often describes the situation or state that something or someone is in.

Je suis _en_ vacances.	I'm on holiday.
La voiture est _en_ panne.	The car's broken down.
Tu es toujours _en_ retard!	You're always late!

➤ **en** is found before <u>present participles</u>, the form of the verb that ends in -*ing* in English and **-ant** in French.

Je fais mes devoirs _en_ <u>regardant</u> la télé.	I do my homework while watching TV.
Il m'a vu <u>en passant</u> devant la porte.	He saw me as he came past the door.

⇨ *For more information on the **Present participle**, see page 125.*

> **Key points**
> ✔ **à**, **de** and **en** are very frequent prepositions which you will use all the time.
> ✔ Each of them has several possible meanings, which depend on the context they are used in.

Some other common prepositions

[*i*] Note that some of these words are also adverbs, for example, **avant**, **depuis**.

⟹ *For more information on the **Adverbs**, see page 152.*

➤ The following prepositions are also frequently used in French:

- **après** after

après le déjeuner	after lunch
après son départ	after he had left
la troisième maison après la mairie	the third house after the town hall
Après vous!	After you!

[*i*] Note that where English uses a verb in the perfect tense following *after*, French uses the infinitive **avoir** or **être** and a past participle.

Nous viendrons après avoir fait la vaisselle.	We'll come after we've done the dishes.

- **avant** before

Il est arrivé avant toi.	He arrived before you.
Tournez à gauche avant la poste.	Turn left before the post office.

[*i*] Note that where English uses a verb ending in *-ing* after *before*, French uses **de** followed by the infinitive.

Je préfère finir mes devoirs avant de manger.	I prefer to finish my homework before eating.

- **avec** with

avec mon père	with my father
une chambre avec salle de bain	a room with its own bathroom
Ouvre-la avec un couteau.	Open it with a knife.

- **chez**

Elle est chez Pierre.	She's at Pierre's house.
Elle va chez Pierre.	She's going to Pierre's house.
Je reste chez moi ce week-end.	I'm staying at home this weekend.
Je vais rentrer chez moi.	I'm going home.
Ils habitent près de chez moi.	They live near my house.

172 Prepositions

> ## Tip
> **chez** is also used with the name of jobs or professions to indicate a shop or place of business.
>
> | | |
> |---|---|
> | **Je vais chez le médecin.** | I'm going to the doctor's. |

- **contre** against

Ne mets pas ton vélo contre le mur.	Don't put your bike against the wall.

- **dans** in, into

Il est dans sa chambre.	He's in his bedroom.
Nous passons une semaine dans les Alpes.	We're spending a week in the Alps.
dans deux mois	in two months' time
Il est entré dans mon bureau.	He came into my office.

Grammar Extra!

dans and **en** can both be used in French to talk about a length of time, but the meaning is very different.

Je le ferai dans trois jours.	I'll do it in three days.
Je le ferai en trois jours.	I'll do it in three days.

Though both can be translated in the same way, the first sentence means that you'll do it in three days' time; the second means that it will take three days for you to do it.

- **depuis** since, for

Elle habite Paris depuis 1998.	She's been living in Paris since 1998.
Elle habite Paris depuis cinq ans.	She's been living in Paris for five years.

  Note that French uses the present tense with **depuis** to talk about actions that started in the past and are still going on.

Il est en France depuis le mois de septembre.	He's been in France since September. (and he is still there)

  If you are saying how long something has NOT happened for, you use the perfect tense with **depuis**.

Nous ne l'avons pas vu depuis un mois.	We haven't seen him for a month.

  ➪ For more information on the **Present tense** and the **Perfect tense**, see pages 71 and 111.

For further explanation of grammatical terms, please see pages viii–xii.

- **derrière** behind

<u>derrière</u> la porte	behind the door

- **devant** in front of

Il est assis <u>devant</u> moi.	He's sitting in front of me.

- **entre ... et** between ... and

Il est assis <u>entre</u> son père <u>et</u> son oncle.	He's sitting between his father and his uncle.
Le bureau est fermé <u>entre</u> 13 <u>et</u> 14 heures.	The office is closed between 1 and 2 p.m.

- **jusque** as far as, until

Je te raccompagne <u>jusque</u> chez toi.	I'll go with you as far as your house.
<u>Jusqu'</u>où vas-tu?	How far are you going?
<u>Jusqu'</u>ici nous n'avons pas eu de problèmes.	Up to now we've had no problems.
Je reste <u>jusqu'</u>à la fin du mois.	I'm staying until the end of the month.

> *Tip*
>
> **jusque** changes to **jusqu'** before a word beginning with a vowel, most words starting with **h**, and the French word **y**.

- **par** by, with, per

deux <u>par</u> deux	two by two
<u>par</u> le train	by train
<u>par</u> la poste	by post
<u>par</u> e-mail	by email
Son nom commence <u>par</u> un H.	His name begins with H.
Prenez trois cachets <u>par</u> jour.	Take three tablets per day.
Le voyage coûte quatre cents euros <u>par</u> personne.	The trip costs four hundred euros per person.
Nous nous voyons une fois <u>par</u> mois.	We see each other once a month.
Il est tombé <u>par</u> terre.	He fell down.
Il y a beaucoup de touristes <u>par</u> ici.	There are a lot of tourists around here.

> ## Tip
> The prepositions **à** and **en** are also used with means of transport.

- **pendant** during, for

Ça s'est passé <u>pendant</u> l'été.	It happened during the summer.
Il n'a pas pu travailler <u>pendant</u> plusieurs mois.	He couldn't work for several months.

> ## Tip
> French uses the <u>perfect tense</u> with **pendant** to talk about actions in the past that are completed.
>
> | | |
> |---|---|
> | **Nous <u>avons habité pendant</u> dix ans en Écosse.** | We lived in Scotland for ten years. (*but don't any more*) |
>
> You can also miss out **pendant**.
>
> | | |
> |---|---|
> | **Nous avons habité dix ans en Écosse.** | We lived in Scotland for ten years. |
>
> **pendant** is also used to talk about something that will happen in the future.
>
> | | |
> |---|---|
> | **Je <u>serai</u> à New York <u>pendant</u> un mois.** | I'll be in New York for a month. |
>
> ⇨ *For more information on the **Perfect tense**, see page 111.*

- **pour** for (*who or what something is for, and where something or someone is going*)

C'est un cadeau <u>pour</u> toi.	It's a present for you.
Nous voudrions une chambre <u>pour</u> deux nuits.	We'd like a room for two nights.
le train <u>pour</u> Bordeaux	the train for Bordeaux

[*i*] Note that **pour** can also be used with infinitives, when it has the meaning of *in order to*.

Elle téléphone <u>pour savoir</u> à quelle heure on arrivera.	She's ringing to find out what time we'll get there.
<u>Pour aller</u> à Nice, s'il vous plaît?	Which way is it to Nice, please?

- **sans** without

Elle est venue <u>sans</u> son frère.	She came without her brother.
un café <u>sans</u> sucre	a coffee without sugar
un pull <u>sans</u> manches	a sleeveless sweater

[*i*] Note that **sans** can also be used before infinitives in French. In English a verb form ending in *-ing* is used after *without*.

Elle est partie <u>sans dire</u> au revoir.	She left <u>without saying</u> goodbye.

- **sauf** except

Tout le monde vient <u>sauf</u> lui.	Everyone's coming except him.

- **sous** under

<u>sous</u> la table	under the table
<u>sous</u> terre	underground

- **sur** on

Pose-le <u>sur</u> le bureau.	Put it down on the desk.
Ton sac est <u>sur</u> la table.	Your bag is on the table.
Vous verrez l'hôpital <u>sur</u> votre gauche.	You'll see the hospital on your left.
un livre <u>sur</u> la politique	a book on politics

[*i*] Note that **à** and **sur** can both mean *on* in English. **sur** usually means on the top of something. **sur la télé** means *on top of the TV set*, but **à la télé** means *broadcast on TV*. Both can be translated as *on the TV* in English. **sur le mur** means *on top of the wall*, but **au mur** means *hanging on the wall*.

> ### Tip
> With numbers and measurements **sur** can also mean *in*, *out of* and *by*.
>
> | | |
> |---|---|
> | une personne <u>sur</u> dix | one person <u>in</u> ten |
> | J'ai eu quatorze <u>sur</u> vingt en maths. | I got 14 <u>out of</u> 20 in maths. |
> | La pièce fait quatre mètres <u>sur</u> deux. | The room measures four metres <u>by</u> two. |

- **vers** towards (*a place*), at about

Il allait <u>vers</u> la gare.	He was going towards the station.
Je rentre chez moi <u>vers</u> cinq heures.	I go home at about 5 o'clock.

➤ **voici** (meaning *this is, here is*) and **voilà** (meaning *there is, that is*) are two very useful prepositions that French speakers often use to point things out.

<u>Voici</u> mon frère et <u>voilà</u> ma sœur.	This is my brother and that's my sister.
<u>Voici</u> ton sac.	Here's your bag.
Le <u>voici</u>!	Here he/it is!
Tiens! <u>Voilà</u> Paul.	Look! There's Paul.
Tu as perdu ton stylo? En <u>voilà</u> un autre.	Have you lost your pen? Here's another one.
Les <u>voilà</u>!	There they are!

Prepositions consisting of more than one word

➤ Prepositions can also be made up of several words instead of just one.

au bord de	at the edge of, at the side of
au bout de	after
à cause de	because of
au-dessous de	below
au-dessus de	above
au fond de	at the bottom of, at the end of
au milieu de	in the middle of

<u>Au bout d</u>'un moment, il s'est endormi.	After a while, he fell asleep.
Nous ne pouvons pas sortir <u>à cause du</u> mauvais temps.	We can't go out because of the bad weather.
J'ai garé la voiture <u>au bord de</u> la route.	I parked the car by the side of the road.
Mon porte-monnaie est <u>au fond de</u> mon sac.	My purse is at the bottom of my bag.
Place le vase <u>au milieu de</u> la table.	Put the vase in the middle of the table.

Prepositions after verbs

➤ Some French verbs can be followed by an <u>infinitive</u> (the *to* form of the verb) and linked to it by either **de** or **à**, or no preposition at all. This is also true of verbs and their <u>objects</u>: the person or thing that the verb 'happens' to.

⇨ *For more information on **Verbs followed by an infinitive**, see page 133.*

> *Tip*
>
> The preposition that is used in French is not always the same as the one that is used in English. Whenever you learn a new verb, try to learn which preposition can be used after it too.

➤ The lists in this section concentrate on those French verbs that involve a different construction from the one that is used in English.

1 Verbs that are followed by à + object

➤ **à** is often the equivalent of the English word *to* when it is used with an indirect object after verbs like *send*, *give* and *say*.

dire quelque chose <u>à</u> quelqu'un	to say something <u>to</u> someone
donner quelque chose <u>à</u> quelqu'un	to give something <u>to</u> someone
écrire quelque chose <u>à</u> quelqu'un	to write something <u>to</u> someone
envoyer quelque chose <u>à</u> quelqu'un	to send something <u>to</u> someone
montrer quelque chose <u>à</u> quelqu'un	to show something <u>to</u> someone

⇨ *For more information on **Indirect objects**, see page 49.*

> *Tip*
>
> There is an important difference between French and English with this type of verb. In English, you can say either *to give something <u>to</u> someone* or *to give someone something*; *to show something <u>to</u> someone* or *to show someone something*.
> You can <u>NEVER</u> miss out **à** in French in the way that you can sometimes miss out *to* in English.

➤ Here are some verbs taking **à** in French that have a different construction in English.

croire **à** quelque chose	to believe <u>in</u> something
s'intéresser **à** quelqu'un/quelque chose	to be interested <u>in</u> someone/something
jouer **à** quelque chose	to play something (*sports, games*)
obéir **à** quelqu'un	to obey someone
penser **à** quelqu'un/quelque chose	to think <u>about</u> someone/something
répondre **à** quelqu'un	to answer someone
téléphoner **à** quelqu'un	to phone someone

> ## Tip
>
> When you are using **jouer** to talk about sports and games, you use **à**. When you are using **jouer** to talk about musical instruments, you use **de**.
>
> | | |
> |---|---|
> | jouer <u>au</u> tennis | to play tennis |
> | jouer <u>aux</u> échecs | to play chess |
> | jouer <u>de</u> la guitare | to play the guitar |
> | jouer <u>du</u> piano | to play the piano |

➤ **plaire** followed by **à** is a common way of saying you like something.

plaire **à** quelqu'un	to please someone (*literally*)
Ton cadeau me plaît beaucoup.	I like your present a lot.
Ce film plaît beaucoup aux jeunes.	This film is very popular with young people.

Grammar Extra!

manquer à works quite differently from its English equivalent, *to miss*. The English object is the French subject, and the English subject is the French object.

manquer **à** quelqu'un	to be missed by someone (*literally*)
Tu (*subject*) me (*object*) **manques**.	I (*subject*) miss you (*object*).
Mon pays (*subject*) me (*object*) **manque beaucoup**.	I (*subject*) miss my country (*object*) very much.

➤ There are also some verbs where you can put a direct object before **à**. The verb **demander** is the most common.

demander quelque chose **à** quelqu'un	to ask someone something, to ask someone for something

➪ *For more information on **Direct objects**, see page 47.*

[*i*] Note that **demander** in French does <u>NOT</u> mean *to demand*. It means *to ask something* or *to ask for something*. If you want to say *demand* in French, use **exiger**.

Nous avons demandé notre chemin à un chauffeur de taxi.	We asked a taxi driver the way.
J'exige des excuses!	I demand an apology!

2 Verbs that are followed by de + object

➤ Here are some verbs taking **de** in French that have a different construction in English.

changer <u>de</u> quelque chose	to change something (*one's shoes and so on*)
dépendre <u>de</u> quelqu'un/ quelque chose	to depend <u>on</u> someone/something
s'excuser <u>de</u> quelque chose	to apologize <u>for</u> something
jouer <u>de</u> quelque chose	to play something
parler <u>de</u> quelque chose	to talk <u>about</u> something
se servir <u>de</u> quelque chose	to use something
se souvenir <u>de</u> quelqu'un/ quelque chose	to remember someone/something

> ### Tip
>
> When you are using **jouer** to talk about sports and games, you use **à**. When you are using **jouer** to talk about musical instruments, you use **de**.
>
> | | |
> |---|---|
> | **jouer <u>au</u> tennis** | to play tennis |
> | **jouer <u>aux</u> échecs** | to play chess |
> | **jouer <u>de</u> la guitare** | to play the guitar |
> | **jouer <u>du</u> piano** | to play the piano |

➤ Some common phrases using **avoir** also contain **de**.

<u>avoir</u> besoin <u>de</u> quelque chose	to need something
<u>avoir</u> envie <u>de</u> quelque chose	to want something
<u>avoir</u> peur <u>de</u> quelque chose	to be afraid of something

➤ There are also some verbs where you can put a direct object before **de**. **remercier** is the most common.

remercier quelqu'un <u>de</u> quelque chose to thank someone for something

⇨ *For more information on **Direct objects**, see page 47.*

Grammar Extra!

The verb **se tromper de quelque chose** is often the equivalent of *to get the wrong ...*

Je me suis trompé de numéro.	I got the wrong number.
Je me suis trompé de maison.	I got the wrong house.

---

3 Verbs taking a direct object in French but not in English

➤ In English there are a few verbs that are followed by *for, on, in, to* or *at* which, in French, are not followed by a preposition such as **à** or **de**. Here are the most common:

attendre quelqu'un/quelque chose	to wait <u>for</u> sb/sth
chercher quelqu'un/quelque chose	to look <u>for</u> sb/sth
demander quelqu'un/quelque chose	to ask <u>for</u> sb/sth
écouter quelqu'un/quelque chose	to listen <u>to</u> sb/sth
espérer quelque chose	to hope <u>for</u> sth
payer quelque chose	to pay <u>for</u> sth
regarder quelqu'un/quelque chose	to look <u>at</u> sb/sth

i Note that **attendre** does <u>NOT</u> mean *to attend* in English. It means *to wait for*. If you want to say that you attend something, use **assister à quelque chose**.

Je t'attends devant la gare.	I'll wait for you in front of the station.
Vous allez assister au concert?	Are you going to attend the concert?

➤ **habiter** can be used with or without a preposition:

- **habiter** is mostly used <u>without a preposition</u> when you are talking about living in a house, a flat and so on

Nous habitons un petit appartement en ville.	We live in a small flat in town.

- use **habiter** <u>with à</u> when you are talking about a town or city, and **au** (*singular*) or **aux** (*plural*) with the names of countries that are masculine in French

Nous habitons <u>à</u> Liverpool.	We live in Liverpool.
Nous habitons <u>aux</u> États-Unis.	We live in the United States.

- use **habiter** <u>with en</u> when you are talking about feminine countries

Nous habitons <u>en</u> Espagne.	We live in Spain.

Key points

✔ French prepositions after verbs are often not the ones that are used in English. French verbs often have a different construction from English verbs.

✔ French verbs are usually linked to their objects by **de**, **à** or nothing at all.

✔ You can never miss out **à** in French in the way that you can miss out *to* in English constructions like *to give someone something*.

Prepositions after adjectives

➤ Just like verbs, some French adjectives can be linked to what follows by either **à** or **de**.

➤ An adjective followed by **de** or **à** can be followed by a noun, a pronoun or an infinitive.

➤ Some adjectives that can be followed by **de** are used to say how you feel, that you are certain about something, or that it is necessary or important to do something. These are the most common:

certain	certain
content	happy
désolé	sorry
enchanté	delighted
heureux	happy
important	important
malheureux	unhappy
nécessaire	necessary
sûr	sure
triste	sad

Tu es <u>sûr de</u> pouvoir venir?	Are you sure you can come?
<u>Enchanté de</u> faire votre connaissance.	Delighted to meet you.
Il est <u>nécessaire de</u> réserver.	You have to book.

Grammar Extra!

➤ Some adjectives, such as **facile** (meaning *easy*), **intéressant** (meaning *interesting*) or **impossible** (meaning *impossible*), can be followed by either **à** or **de**. **de** tends to be used when you are saying something that is generally true. **à** tends to be used when you are saying something about someone or something in particular.

Il est difficile <u>de</u> prendre une décision.	It's difficult to make a decision.
Il est difficile <u>à</u> connaître.	He's difficult to get to know.
Son accent est difficile <u>à</u> comprendre.	His accent is difficult to understand.

Conjunctions

What is a conjunction?
A **conjunction** is a word such as *and*, *but*, *or*, *so*, *if* and *because*, that links two
words or phrases of a similar type, or two parts of a sentence, for example,
Diane <u>and</u> I have been friends for years; I left <u>because</u> I was bored.

et, mais, ou, parce que and si

➤ **et**, **mais**, **ou**, **parce que** and **si** are the most common conjunctions that you
  need to know in French.

- **et** and

toi <u>et</u> moi	you <u>and</u> me
Il pleut <u>et</u> il fait très froid.	It's raining <u>and</u> it's very cold.

- **mais** but

C'est cher <u>mais</u> de très bonne qualité.	It's expensive, <u>but</u> very good quality.

  i Note that **mais** is also commonly found in front of **oui** and **si**.

'Tu viens ce soir?' – '<u>Mais oui!</u>'	'Are you coming tonight?' – 'Definitely!'
'Il n'a pas encore fini?' – '<u>Mais si!</u>'	'Hasn't he finished yet?' – 'He certainly has!'

- **ou** or

Tu préfères le vert <u>ou</u> le bleu?	Do you like the green one <u>or</u> the blue one?
Donne-moi ça <u>ou</u> je me fâche!	Give me that <u>or</u> I'll get cross!

> ### Tip
> Be careful not to confuse **ou** (meaning *or*) with **où** (meaning *where*).

- **parce que** because

Je ne peux pas sortir <u>parce que</u> j'ai encore du travail à faire.	I can't go out <u>because</u> I've still got work to do.

> ### Tip
> **parce que** changes to **parce qu'** before a word beginning with a vowel, most words starting with **h**, and the French word **y**.
>
> | | |
> |---|---|
> | **Il ne vient pas <u>parce qu</u>'il n'a pas de voiture.** | He isn't coming <u>because</u> he doesn't have a car. |

- **si** if

Je me demande <u>si</u> elle ment.	I wonder <u>if</u> she's lying.
<u>Si</u> j'étais à ta place, je ne l'inviterais pas.	<u>If</u> I were you, I wouldn't invite him.

> ### Tip
> **si** changes to **s'** before **il** or **ils**.
>
> | | |
> |---|---|
> | **<u>S</u>'il ne pleut pas, on mangera dehors.** | <u>If</u> it doesn't rain, we'll eat outside. |

Some other common conjunctions

➤ Here are some other common French conjunctions:

- **car** because

  Il faut prendre un bus pour y accéder <u>car</u> il est interdit d'y monter en voiture.   You need to take a bus to get there because cars are prohibited.

[i] Note that **car** is used in formal language or in writing. The normal way of saying *because* is **parce que**.

- **comme** as

  <u>Comme</u> il pleut, je prends la voiture.   <u>As</u> it's raining, I'm taking the car.

- **donc** so

  J'ai raté le train, <u>donc</u> je serai en retard.   I missed the train, <u>so</u> I'll be late.

- **lorsque** when

  J'allais composer ton numéro <u>lorsque</u> tu as appelé.   I was about to dial your number <u>when</u> you called.

- **quand** when

  Je ne sors pas <u>quand</u> il pleut.   I don't go out <u>when</u> it rains.

[i] Note that when **quand** and **lorsque** are used to talk about something that will happen in the future, the French verb has to be in the <u>future tense</u> even though English uses a verb in the <u>present tense</u>.

   Quand je <u>serai</u> riche, j'achèterai une belle maison.   When I'<u>m</u> rich, I'll buy a nice house.

⇨ *For more information on the **Present tense** and the **Future tense**, see pages 71 and 98.*

➤ French, like English, also has conjunctions which have more than one part. Here are the most common:

- **ne ... ni ... ni** neither ... nor

  Je <u>n'</u>aime <u>ni</u> les lentilles <u>ni</u> les épinards.   I like <u>neither</u> lentils <u>nor</u> spinach.

[i] Note that the **ne** part of this expression goes just before the verb.

- **ou ... ou, ou bien ... ou bien** either ... or

  <u>Ou</u> il est malade <u>ou</u> il ment.   <u>Either</u> he's sick <u>or</u> he's lying.
  <u>Ou bien</u> il m'évite <u>ou bien</u> il ne me reconnaît pas.   <u>Either</u> he's avoiding me <u>or</u> else he doesn't recognize me.

The conjunction que

➤ When **que** is used to join two parts of a sentence, it means *that*.

Il dit qu'il m'aime.	He says <u>that</u> he loves me.
Elle sait que vous êtes là.	She knows <u>that</u> you're here.

> ### Tip
>
> In English you could say both *He says he loves me* and *He says that he loves me*, or *She knows you're here* and *She knows that you're here*. You can <u>NEVER</u> leave out **que** in French in the same way.

➤ **que** is also used when you are comparing two things or two people. In this case, it means *as* or *than*.

Ils n'y vont pas aussi souvent que nous.	They don't go as often <u>as</u> us.
Les melons sont plus chers que les bananes.	Melons are more expensive <u>than</u> bananas.

⇨ *For more information on **Comparative adjectives**, see page 34.*

➤ Some words which give you information about when something happens, can also be conjunctions if you put **que** after them. **pendant que** (meaning *while*) is the most common of these.

Christian a téléphoné pendant que Chantal prenait son bain.	Christian phoned <u>while</u> Chantal was in the bath.

ℹ️ Note that when **pendant que** (meaning *while*), **quand** (meaning *when*) and **lorsque** (meaning *when*) are used to talk about something that will happen in the future, the French verb has to be in the <u>future tense</u> even though English uses a verb in the <u>present tense</u>.

Pendant que je serai en France, j'irai les voir.	I'll go and visit them while I'<u>m</u> in France.

⇨ *For more information on the **Present tense** and the **Future tense**, see pages 71 and 98.*

Grammar Extra!

que can replace another conjunction to avoid having to repeat it.

Quand tu seras plus grand et que tu auras une maison à toi, ...	When you're older and you have a house of your own, ...
Comme il pleut et que je n'ai pas de parapluie, ...	As it's raining and I don't have an umbrella, ...

Numbers

1	un (une)
2	deux
3	trois
4	quatre
5	cinq
6	six
7	sept
8	huit
9	neuf
10	dix
11	onze
12	douze
13	treize
14	quatorze
15	quinze
16	seize
17	dix-sept
18	dix-huit
19	dix-neuf
20	vingt
21	vingt et un (une)
22	vingt-deux
30	trente
40	quarante
50	cinquante
60	soixante
70	soixante-dix
71	soixante et onze
72	soixante-douze
80	quatre-vingts
81	quatre-vingt-un (-une)
90	quatre-vingt-dix
91	quatre-vingt-onze
100	cent
101	cent un (une)
300	trois cents
301	trois cent un (une)
1000	mille
2000	deux mille
1,000,000	un million

1st	premier (1er), première (1re)
2nd	deuxième (2e or 2ème) or second(e) ($2^{nd(e)}$)
3rd	troisième (3e or 3ème)
4th	quatrième (4e or 4ème)
5th	cinquième (5e or 5ème)
6th	sixième (6e or 6ème)
7th	septième (7e or 7ème)
8th	huitième (8e or 8ème)
9th	neuvième (9e or 9ème)
10th	dixième (10e or 10ème)
11th	onzième (11e or 11ème)
12th	douzième (12e or 12ème)
13th	treizième (13e or 13ème)
14th	quatorzième (14e or 14ème)
15th	quinzième (15e or 15ème)
16th	seizième (16e or 16ème)
17th	dix-septième (17e or 17ème)
18th	dix-huitième (18e or 18ème)
19th	dix-neuvième (19e or 19ème)
20th	vingtième (20e or 20ème)
21st	vingt et unième (21e or 21ème)
22nd	vingt-deuxième (22e or 22ème)
30th	trentième (30e or 30ème)
100th	centième (100e or 100ème)
101st	cent unième (101e or 101ème)
1000th	millième (1000e or 1000ème)

1/2	un demi
1/3	un tiers
2/3	deux tiers
1/4	un quart
1/5	un cinquième
0.5	zéro virgule cinq (0,5)
3.4	trois virgule quatre (3,4)
10%	dix pour cent
100%	cent pour cent

EXEMPLES

EXAMPLES

Il habite au dix.	He lives at number ten.
à la page dix-neuf	on page nineteen
au chapitre sept	in chapter seven
Il habite au cinquième (étage).	He lives on the fifth floor.
Il est arrivé troisième.	He came in third.
échelle au vingt-cinq millième	scale one to twenty-five thousand

Time and Date

L'HEURE	THE TIME
Quelle heure est-il?	What time is it?
Il est...	It's...
une heure	one o'clock
une heure dix	ten past one
une heure et quart	quarter past one
une heure et demie	half past one
deux heures moins vingt	twenty to two
deux heures moins le quart	quarter to two
À quelle heure?	At what time?
à minuit	at midnight
à midi	at midday, at noon
à une heure (de l'après-midi)	at one o'clock (in the afternoon)
à huit heures (du soir)	at eight o'clock (in the evening)
à 11h15 *or*	at 11.15 *or* eleven fifteen
onze heures quinze	
à 20h45 *or*	at 20.45 *or* twenty forty-five
vingt heures quarante-cinq	

LA DATE	THE DATE
LES JOURS DE LA SEMAINE	**DAYS OF THE WEEK**
lundi	Monday
mardi	Tuesday
mercredi	Wednesday
jeudi	Thursday
vendredi	Friday
samedi	Saturday
dimanche	Sunday
Quand?	When?
lundi	on Monday
le lundi	on Mondays
tous les lundis	every Monday
mardi dernier	last Tuesday
vendredi prochain	next Friday
samedi en huit	a week on Saturday
samedi en quinze	two weeks on Saturday

i Note that days of the week are <u>NOT</u> written with a capital letter in French.

LES MOIS

janvier	January
février	February
mars	March
avril	April
mai	May
juin	June
juillet	July
août	August
septembre	September
octobre	October
novembre	November
décembre	December

MONTHS OF THE YEAR

Quand?

en février	in February
le 1er décembre	on December 1st
le premier décembre	on December first
en 1998	in 1998
en mille neuf cent quatre-vingt-dix-huit	in nineteen ninety-eight

When?

Quel jour sommes-nous?
Nous sommes le...

What day is it?
It's...

lundi 26 février *or* lundi vingt-six février	Monday 26 February *or* Monday twenty-sixth of February
dimanche 1er octobre *or* dimanche premier octobre	Sunday 1st October *or* Sunday the first of October

[i] Note that months of the year are NOT written with a capital letter in French.

VOCABULAIRE	USEFUL VOCABULARY
Quand?	**When?**
aujourd'hui	today
ce matin	this morning
cet après-midi	this afternoon
ce soir	this evening
Souvent?	**How often?**
tous les jours	every day
tous les deux jours	every other day
une fois par semaine	once a week
deux fois par semaine	twice a week
une fois par mois	once a month
Ça s'est passé quand?	**When did it happen?**
le matin	in the morning
le soir	in the evening
hier	yesterday
hier soir	yesterday evening
avant-hier	the day before yesterday
il y a une semaine	a week ago
il y a quinze jours	two weeks ago
l'an dernier *or* l'année dernière	last year
Ça va se passer quand?	**When is it going to happen?**
demain	tomorrow
demain matin	tomorrow morning
après-demain	the day after tomorrow
dans deux jours	in two days
dans une semaine	in a week
dans quinze jours	in two weeks
le mois prochain	next month
l'an prochain *or* l'année prochaine	next year

Some common difficulties

General problems

➤ You can't always translate French into English and English into French word for word. While occasionally it is possible to do this, often it is not. For example:

- English <u>phrasal verbs</u> (verbs followed by a preposition or adverb), for example, *to run away*, *to fall down*, are often translated by <u>ONE</u> word in French.

continuer	to go on
tomber	to fall down
rendre	to give back

⇨ *For more information on **Verbs**, see pages 69–137.*

- Sentences which contain a verb and preposition in English, might <u>NOT</u> contain a preposition in French.

payer quelque chose	to pay <u>for</u> something
regarder quelqu'un/quelque chose	to look <u>at</u> somebody/something
écouter quelqu'un/quelque chose	to listen <u>to</u> somebody/something

- Similarly, sentences which contain a verb and preposition in French, might <u>NOT</u> contain a preposition in English.

obéir <u>à</u> quelqu'un/quelque chose	to obey somebody/something
changer <u>de</u> quelque chose	to change something
manquer <u>de</u> quelque chose	to lack something

- The same French preposition may be translated into English in different ways.

parler <u>de</u> quelque chose	to talk <u>about</u> something
sûr <u>de</u> quelque chose	sure <u>of</u> something
voler quelque chose <u>à</u> quelqu'un	to steal something <u>from</u> someone
croire <u>à</u> quelque chose	to believe <u>in</u> something

⇨ *For more information on **Prepositions**, see page 162.*

• A word which is singular in English may not be in French.

les bagages	luggage
ses cheveux	his/her hair

• Similarly, a word which is singular in French may not be in English.

un short	shorts
mon pantalon	my trousers

➪ *For more information on **Nouns**, see page 1.*

• In English, you can use 's to show who or what something belongs to; in French, you have to use **de**.

la voiture de mon frère	my brother's car
la chambre des enfants	the children's bedroom

➪ *For more information on the preposition **de**, see page 166.*

Specific problems

1 -ing

➤ The -*ing* ending in English is translated in a number of different ways in French:

• *to be ...-ing* is translated by a verb consisting of one word.

Il part demain.	He's leaving tomorrow.
Je lisais un roman.	I was reading a book.

➪ *For more information on **Verbs**, see pages 69–137.*

ℹ Note that when you are talking about somebody's or something's physical position, you use a past participle.

Elle est assise là-bas.	She's sitting over there.
Il était couché par terre.	He was lying on the ground.

➪ *For more information on the **Past participle**, see page 111.*

➤ -*ing* can also be translated by:

• an infinitive

J'aime aller au cinéma.	I like going to the cinema.
Arrêtez de vous disputer!	Stop arguing!
Avant de partir...	Before leaving...

➪ *For more information on **Infinitives**, see page 133.*

For further explanation of grammatical terms, please see pages viii–xii.

- a present participle

| **Étant** plus timide que moi, elle... | Being shyer than me, she... |

➡ *For more information on the **Present participle**, see page 125.*

- a noun

| **Le ski** me maintient en forme. | Skiing keeps me fit. |

➡ *For more information on **Nouns**, see page 1.*

2 to be

➤ The verb *to be* is generally translated by **être**.

| Il **est** tard. | It's late. |
| Ce n'**est** pas possible! | It's not possible! |

➤ When you are talking about the physical position of something, **se trouver** may be used.

| Où **se trouve** la gare? | Where's the station? |

➤ In certain set phrases which describe how you are feeling or a state you are in, the verb **avoir** is used.

avoir chaud	to be warm
avoir froid	to be cold
avoir faim	to be hungry
avoir soif	to be thirsty
avoir peur	to be afraid
avoir tort	to be wrong
avoir raison	to be right

➤ When you are describing what the weather is like, use the verb **faire**.

Quel temps **fait**-il?	What's the weather like?
Il **fait** beau.	It's lovely.
Il **fait** mauvais.	It's miserable.
Il **fait** du vent.	It's windy.

➤ When you are talking about someone's age, use the verb **avoir**.

| Quel âge **as**-tu? | How old are you? |
| J'**ai** quinze ans. | I'm fifteen. |

➤ When talking about your health, use the verb **aller**.

| Comment **allez**-vous? | How are you? |
| Je **vais** très bien. | I'm very well. |

3 it is, it's

➤ *it is* and *it's* are usually translated by **il est** or **elle est** when referring to a noun.

'Où est mon parapluie?' – 'Il est là, dans le coin.'	'Where's my umbrella?' – 'It's there, in the corner.'
Descends la valise si elle n'est pas trop lourde.	Bring the case down if it isn't too heavy.

➤ When you are talking about the time, use **il est**.

'Quelle heure est-il?' – 'Il est sept heures et demie.'	'What time is it?' – 'It's half past seven.'

➤ When you are describing what the weather is like, use the verb **faire**.

Il fait beau.	It's lovely.
Il fait mauvais.	It's miserable.
Il fait du vent.	It's windy.

➤ If you want to say, for example, *it is difficult to do something* or *it is easy to do something*, use **il est**.

Il est difficile de répondre à cette question.	It is difficult to answer this question.

➤ In ALL other phrases and constructions, use **c'est**.

C'est moi qui ne l'aime pas.	It's me who doesn't like him.
C'est Charles qui l'a dit.	It's Charles who said so.
C'est ici que je les ai achetés.	It's here that I bought them.
C'est parce que la poste est fermée que...	It's because the post office is closed that...

4 there is, there are

➤ Both *there is* and *there are* are translated by **il y a**.

Il y a quelqu'un à la porte.	There is someone at the door.
Il y a cinq livres sur la table.	There are five books on the table.

5 can, to be able

➤ If you want to talk about someone's physical ability to do something, use **pouvoir**.

Pouvez-vous faire dix kilomètres à pied?	Can you walk ten kilometres?

For further explanation of grammatical terms, please see pages viii–xii.

➤ If you want to say that *you know how to do something*, use **savoir**.

    Elle ne <u>sait</u> pas nager.   She <u>can't</u> swim.

➤ When *can* is used with verbs to do with what you can see or hear, you do <u>NOT</u> use **pouvoir** in French.

    Je ne vois rien.   I <u>can't see</u> anything.
    Il les entendait.   He <u>could hear</u> them.

6 | <u>to</u>

➤ The preposition *to* is generally translated by **à**.

    Donne le livre <u>à</u> Patrick.   Give the book <u>to</u> Patrick.

⇨ *For more information on the preposition à, see page 163.*

➤ When you are talking about the time, use **moins**.

    dix heures <u>moins</u> cinq   five <u>to</u> ten
    à sept heures <u>moins</u> le quart   at a quarter <u>to</u> seven

➤ If you want to say *(in order) to*, use **pour**.

    Je l'ai fait <u>pour</u> vous aider.   I did it <u>to</u> help you.
    Il va en ville <u>pour</u> acheter un cadeau.   He's going into town <u>to</u> buy a present.

The Alphabet

➤ The French alphabet is pronounced differently from the way it is pronounced in English. Use the list below to help you sound out the letters.

A, a	[ɑ]	(ah)	like 'a' in 'la'
B, b	[be]	(bay)	
C, c	[se]	(say)	
D, d	[de]	(day)	
E, e	[ə]	(uh)	like 'e' in 'le'
F, f	[ɛf]	(eff)	
G, g	[ʒe]	(jay)	
H, h	[aʃ]	(ash)	
I, i	[i]	(ee)	
J, j	[ʒi]	(jee)	
K, k	[ka]	(ka)	
L, l	[ɛl]	(ell)	
M, m	[ɛm]	(emm)	
N, n	[ɛn]	(enn)	
O, o	[o]	(oh)	
P, p	[pe]	(pay)	
Q, q	[ky]	(ku)	like 'u' in 'une'
R, r	[ɛr]	(air)	
S, s	[ɛs]	(ess)	
T, t	[te]	(tay)	
U, u	[y]	(u)	like 'u' in 'une'
V, v	[ve]	(vay)	
W, w	[dubləve]	(doobla-vay)	
X, x	[iks]	(eex)	
Y, y	[igrɛk]	(ee-grek)	
Z, z	[zɛd]	(zed)	

For further explanation of grammatical terms, please see pages viii–xii.

Main Index

VERB TABLES

Introduction

The **Verb Tables** in the following section contain 93 tables of French verbs (some regular and some irregular) in alphabetical order. Each table shows you the following forms: **Present**, **Perfect**, **Future**, **Subjunctive**, **Imperfect**, **Conditional**, **Imperative** and the **Present** and **Past Participles**. For more information on these tenses, how they are formed, when they are used and so on, you should look at the section on **Verbs** in the main text on pages 69–137.

In order to help you use the verbs shown in the **Verb Tables** correctly, there are also a number of example phrases at the bottom of each page to show the verb as it is used in context.

In French there are both **regular** verbs (their forms follow the normal rules) and **irregular** verbs (their forms do not follow the normal rules). The regular verbs in these tables are:

donner (regular **-er** verb, Verb Table 29)
finir (regular **-ir** verb, Verb Table 39)
attendre (regular **-re** verb, Verb Table 8)

The irregular verbs are shown in full.

The **Verb Index** at the end of this section contains over 2000 verbs, each of which is cross-referred to one of the verbs given in the Verb Tables. The table shows the patterns that the verb listed in the index follows.

acheter (to buy)

PRESENT
j'	achète
tu	achètes
il/elle/on	achète
nous	achetons
vous	achetez
ils/elles	achètent

PRESENT SUBJUNCTIVE
j'	achète
tu	achètes
il/elle/on	achète
nous	achetions
vous	achetiez
ils/elles	achètent

PERFECT
j'	ai acheté
tu	as acheté
il/elle/on	a acheté
nous	avons acheté
vous	avez acheté
ils/elles	ont acheté

IMPERFECT
j'	achetais
tu	achetais
il/elle/on	achetait
nous	achetions
vous	achetiez
ils/elles	achetaient

FUTURE
j'	achèterai
tu	achèteras
il/elle/on	achètera
nous	achèterons
vous	achèterez
ils/elles	achèteront

CONDITIONAL
j'	achèterais
tu	achèterais
il/elle/on	achèterait
nous	achèterions
vous	achèteriez
ils/elles	achèteraient

IMPERATIVE
achète / achetons / achetez

PAST PARTICIPLE
acheté

PRESENT PARTICIPLE
achetant

EXAMPLE PHRASES

J'**ai acheté** des gâteaux à la pâtisserie. *I bought some cakes at the cake shop.*

Qu'est-ce que tu lui **as acheté** pour son anniversaire? *What did you buy him for his birthday?*

Je n'**achète** jamais de chips. *I never buy crisps.*

je/j' = I **tu** = you **il** = he/it **elle** = she/it **on** = we/one **nous** = we **vous** = you **ils/elles** = they

acquérir (to acquire)

PRESENT
j'	acquiers
tu	acquiers
il/elle/on	acquiert
nous	acquérons
vous	acquérez
ils/elles	acquièrent

PRESENT SUBJUNCTIVE
j'	acquière
tu	acquières
il/elle/on	acquière
nous	acquérions
vous	acquériez
ils/elles	acquièrent

PERFECT
j'	ai acquis
tu	as acquis
il/elle/on	a acquis
nous	avons acquis
vous	avez acquis
ils/elles	ont acquis

IMPERFECT
j'	acquérais
tu	acquérais
il/elle/on	acquérait
nous	acquérions
vous	acquériez
ils/elles	acquéraient

FUTURE
j'	acquerrai
tu	acquerras
il/elle/on	acquerra
nous	acquerrons
vous	acquerrez
ils/elles	acquerront

CONDITIONAL
j'	acquerrais
tu	acquerrais
il/elle/on	acquerrait
nous	acquerrions
vous	acquerriez
ils/elles	acquerraient

IMPERATIVE
acquiers / acquérons / acquérez

PAST PARTICIPLE
acquis

PRESENT PARTICIPLE
acquérant

EXAMPLE PHRASES

Elle **a acquis** la nationalité française en 2013. *She acquired French nationality in 2013.*

je/j' = I **tu** = you **il** = he/it **elle** = she/it **on** = we/one **nous** = we **vous** = you **ils/elles** = they

aller (to go)

PRESENT
je	**vais**
tu	**vas**
il/elle/on	**va**
nous	**allons**
vous	**allez**
ils/elles	**vont**

PRESENT SUBJUNCTIVE
j'	**aille**
tu	**ailles**
il/elle/on	**aille**
nous	**allions**
vous	**alliez**
ils/elles	**aillent**

PERFECT
je	**suis allé(e)**
tu	**es allé(e)**
il/elle/on	**est allé(e)**
nous	**sommes allé(e)s**
vous	**êtes allé(e)(s)**
ils/elles	**sont allé(e)s**

IMPERFECT
j'	**allais**
tu	**allais**
il/elle/on	**allait**
nous	**allions**
vous	**alliez**
ils/elles	**allaient**

FUTURE
j'	**irai**
tu	**iras**
il/elle/on	**ira**
nous	**irons**
vous	**irez**
ils/elles	**iront**

CONDITIONAL
j'	**irais**
tu	**irais**
il/elle/on	**irait**
nous	**irions**
vous	**iriez**
ils/elles	**iraient**

IMPERATIVE
va / allons / allez

PAST PARTICIPLE
allé

PRESENT PARTICIPLE
allant

EXAMPLE PHRASES

Vous **allez** au cinéma? *Are you going to the cinema?*

Je **suis allé** à Londres. *I went to London.*

Est-ce que tu **es** déjà **allé** en Allemagne? *Have you ever been to Germany?*

je/j' = I **tu** = you **il** = he/it **elle** = she/it **on** = we/one **nous** = we **vous** = you **ils/elles** = they

appeler (to call)

PRESENT

j'	appelle
tu	appelles
il/elle/on	appelle
nous	appelons
vous	appelez
ils/elles	appellent

PRESENT SUBJUNCTIVE

j'	appelle
tu	appelles
il/elle/on	appelle
nous	appelions
vous	appeliez
ils/elles	appellent

PERFECT

j'	ai appelé
tu	as appelé
il/elle/on	a appelé
nous	avons appelé
vous	avez appelé
ils/elles	ont appelé

IMPERFECT

j'	appelais
tu	appelais
il/elle/on	appelait
nous	appelions
vous	appeliez
ils/elles	appelaient

FUTURE

j'	appellerai
tu	appelleras
il/elle/on	appellera
nous	appellerons
vous	appellerez
ils/elles	appelleront

CONDITIONAL

j'	appellerais
tu	appellerais
il/elle/on	appellerait
nous	appellerions
vous	appelleriez
ils/elles	appelleraient

IMPERATIVE
appelle / appelons / appelez

PAST PARTICIPLE
appelé

PRESENT PARTICIPLE
appelant

EXAMPLE PHRASES

Elle **a appelé** le médecin. *She phoned the doctor.*

J'**ai appelé** Richard à Londres. *I phoned Richard in London.*

Comment tu **t'appelles**? *What's your name?*

⇨ See pages 88–91 for information on how to form the reflexive verb **s'appeler**.

je/j' = I **tu** = you **il** = he/it **elle** = she/it **on** = we/one **nous** = we **vous** = you **ils/elles** = they

arriver (to arrive; to happen)

PRESENT

j'	arrive
tu	arrives
il/elle/on	arrive
nous	arrivons
vous	arrivez
ils/elles	arrivent

PRESENT SUBJUNCTIVE

j'	arrive
tu	arrives
il/elle/on	arrive
nous	arrivions
vous	arriviez
ils/elles	arrivent

PERFECT

je	suis arrivé(e)
tu	es arrivé(e)
il/elle/on	est arrivé(e)
nous	sommes arrivé(e)s
vous	êtes arrivé(e)(s)
ils/elles	sont arrivé(e)s

IMPERFECT

j'	arrivais
tu	arrivais
il/elle/on	arrivait
nous	arrivions
vous	arriviez
ils/elles	arrivaient

FUTURE

j'	arriverai
tu	arriveras
il/elle/on	arrivera
nous	arriverons
vous	arriverez
ils/elles	arriveront

CONDITIONAL

j'	arriverais
tu	arriverais
il/elle/on	arriverait
nous	arriverions
vous	arriveriez
ils/elles	arriveraient

IMPERATIVE
arrive / arrivons / arrivez

PAST PARTICIPLE
arrivé

PRESENT PARTICIPLE
arrivant

EXAMPLE PHRASES

J'**arrive** à l'école à huit heures. *I arrive at school at 8 o'clock.*
Le prof n'**est** pas encore **arrivé**. *The teacher hasn't arrived yet.*
Qu'est-ce qui **est arrivé** à Aurélie? *What happened to Aurélie?*

je/j' = I **tu** = you **il** = he/it **elle** = she/it **on** = we/one **nous** = we **vous** = you **ils/elles** = they

s'asseoir (to sit down)

PRESENT
je	m'assieds/m'assois
tu	t'assieds/t'assois
il/elle/on	s'assied/s'assoit
nous	nous asseyons/nous assoyons
vous	vous asseyez/vous assoyez
ils/elles	s'asseyent/s'assoient

PRESENT SUBJUNCTIVE
je	m'asseye
tu	t'asseyes
il/elle/on	s'asseye
nous	nous asseyions
vous	vous asseyiez
ils/elles	s'asseyent

PERFECT
je	me suis assis(e)
tu	t'es assis(e)
il/elle/on	s'est assis(e)
nous	nous sommes assis(es)
vous	vous êtes assis(e) (es)
ils/elles	se sont assis(es)

IMPERFECT
je	m'asseyais
tu	t'asseyais
il/elle/on	s'asseyait
nous	nous asseyions
vous	vous asseyiez
ils/elles	s'asseyaient

FUTURE
je	m'assiérai
tu	t'assiéras
il/elle/on	s'assiéra
nous	nous assiérons
vous	vous assiérez
ils/elles	s'assiéront

CONDITIONAL
je	m'assiérais
tu	t'assiérais
il/elle/on	s'assiérait
nous	nous assiérions
vous	vous assiériez
ils/elles	s'assiéraient

IMPERATIVE
assieds-toi / asseyons-nous / asseyez-vous

PAST PARTICIPLE
assis

PRESENT PARTICIPLE
s'asseyant

EXAMPLE PHRASES
Assieds-toi, Nicole. *Sit down Nicole.*

Asseyez-vous, les enfants. *Sit down children.*

Je peux **m'asseoir**? *May I sit down?*

Je **me suis assise** sur un chewing-gum! *I've sat on some chewing gum!*

je/j' = I **tu** = you **il** = he/it **elle** = she/it **on** = we/one **nous** = we **vous** = you **ils/elles** = they

attendre (to wait)

PRESENT
j'	attends
tu	attends
il/elle/on	attend
nous	attendons
vous	attendez
ils/elles	attendent

PRESENT SUBJUNCTIVE
j'	attende
tu	attendes
il/elle/on	attende
nous	attendions
vous	attendiez
ils/elles	attendent

PERFECT
j'	ai attendu
tu	as attendu
il/elle/on	a attendu
nous	avons attendu
vous	avez attendu
ils/elles	ont attendu

IMPERFECT
j'	attendais
tu	attendais
il/elle/on	attendait
nous	attendions
vous	attendiez
ils/elles	attendaient

FUTURE
j'	attendrai
tu	attendras
il/elle/on	attendra
nous	attendrons
vous	attendrez
ils/elles	attendront

CONDITIONAL
j'	attendrais
tu	attendrais
il/elle/on	attendrait
nous	attendrions
vous	attendriez
ils/elles	attendraient

IMPERATIVE
attends / attendons / attendez

PAST PARTICIPLE
attendu

PRESENT PARTICIPLE
attendant

EXAMPLE PHRASES

Attends-moi! *Wait for me!*
Tu **attends** depuis longtemps? *Have you been waiting long?*
Je l'**ai attendu** à la poste. *I waited for him at the post office.*
Je **m'attends** à ce qu'il soit en retard. *I expect he'll be late.*

⇨ See pages 88–91 for information on how to form the reflexive verb **s'attendre**.

je/j' = I **tu** = you **il** = he/it **elle** = she/it **on** = we/one **nous** = we **vous** = you **ils/elles** = they

avoir (to have)

PRESENT

j'	**ai**
tu	**as**
il/elle/on	**a**
nous	**avons**
vous	**avez**
ils/elles	**ont**

PRESENT SUBJUNCTIVE

j'	**aie**
tu	**aies**
il/elle/on	**ait**
nous	**ayons**
vous	**ayez**
ils/elles	**aient**

PERFECT

j'	**ai eu**
tu	**as eu**
il/elle/on	**a eu**
nous	**avons eu**
vous	**avez eu**
ils/elles	**ont eu**

IMPERFECT

j'	**avais**
tu	**avais**
il/elle/on	**avait**
nous	**avions**
vous	**aviez**
ils/elles	**avaient**

FUTURE

j'	**aurai**
tu	**auras**
il/elle/on	**aura**
nous	**aurons**
vous	**aurez**
ils/elles	**auront**

CONDITIONAL

j'	**aurais**
tu	**aurais**
il/elle/on	**aurait**
nous	**aurions**
vous	**auriez**
ils/elles	**auraient**

IMPERATIVE
aie / ayons / ayez

PAST PARTICIPLE
eu

PRESENT PARTICIPLE
ayant

EXAMPLE PHRASES

Il **a** les yeux bleus. *He's got blue eyes.*

Quel âge **as**-tu? *How old are you?*

Il **a eu** un accident. *He's had an accident.*

J'**avais** faim. *I was hungry.*

Il y **a** beaucoup de monde. *There are lots of people.*

je/j' = I **tu** = you **il** = he/it **elle** = she/it **on** = we/one **nous** = we **vous** = you **ils/elles** = they

battre (to beat)

PRESENT
je	**bats**
tu	**bats**
il/elle/on	**bat**
nous	**battons**
vous	**battez**
ils/elles	**battent**

PRESENT SUBJUNCTIVE
je	**batte**
tu	**battes**
il/elle/on	**batte**
nous	**battions**
vous	**battiez**
ils/elles	**battent**

PERFECT
j'	**ai battu**
tu	**as battu**
il/elle/on	**a battu**
nous	**avons battu**
vous	**avez battu**
ils/elles	**ont battu**

IMPERFECT
je	**battais**
tu	**battais**
il/elle/on	**battait**
nous	**battions**
vous	**battiez**
ils/elles	**battaient**

FUTURE
je	**battrai**
tu	**battras**
il/elle/on	**battra**
nous	**battrons**
vous	**battrez**
ils/elles	**battront**

CONDITIONAL
je	**battrais**
tu	**battrais**
il/elle/on	**battrait**
nous	**battrions**
vous	**battriez**
ils/elles	**battraient**

IMPERATIVE
bats / battons / battez

PAST PARTICIPLE
battu

PRESENT PARTICIPLE
battant

EXAMPLE PHRASES

On les **a battus** deux à un. *We beat them 2-1.*

J'ai le cœur qui **bat**! *My heart's beating (fast)!*

Arrêtez de **vous battre**! *Stop fighting!*

➡ See pages 88–91 for information on how to form the reflexive verb **se battre**.

je/j' = I **tu** = you **il** = he/it **elle** = she/it **on** = we/one **nous** = we **vous** = you **ils/elles** = they

boire (to drink)

PRESENT

je	**bois**
tu	**bois**
il/elle/on	**boit**
nous	**buvons**
vous	**buvez**
ils/elles	**boivent**

PRESENT SUBJUNCTIVE

je	**boive**
tu	**boives**
il/elle/on	**boive**
nous	**buvions**
vous	**buviez**
ils/elles	**boivent**

PERFECT

j'	**ai bu**
tu	**as bu**
il/elle/on	**a bu**
nous	**avons bu**
vous	**avez bu**
ils/elles	**ont bu**

IMPERFECT

je	**buvais**
tu	**buvais**
il/elle/on	**buvait**
nous	**buvions**
vous	**buviez**
ils/elles	**buvaient**

FUTURE

je	**boirai**
tu	**boiras**
il/elle/on	**boira**
nous	**boirons**
vous	**boirez**
ils/elles	**boiront**

CONDITIONAL

je	**boirais**
tu	**boirais**
il/elle/on	**boirait**
nous	**boirions**
vous	**boiriez**
ils/elles	**boiraient**

IMPERATIVE
bois / buvons / buvez

PAST PARTICIPLE
bu

PRESENT PARTICIPLE
buvant

EXAMPLE PHRASES

Qu'est-ce que tu veux **boire**? *What would you like to drink?*

Il ne **boit** jamais d'alcool. *He never drinks alcohol.*

J'**ai bu** un litre d'eau. *I drank a litre of water.*

---

je/j' = I **tu** = you **il** = he/it **elle** = she/it **on** = we/one **nous** = we **vous** = you **ils/elles** = they

bouillir (to boil)

PRESENT

je	**bous**
tu	**bous**
il/elle/on	**bout**
nous	**bouillons**
vous	**bouillez**
ils/elles	**bouillent**

PRESENT SUBJUNCTIVE

je	**bouille**
tu	**bouilles**
il/elle/on	**bouille**
nous	**bouillions**
vous	**bouilliez**
ils/elles	**bouillent**

PERFECT

j'	**ai bouilli**
tu	**as bouilli**
il/elle/on	**a bouilli**
nous	**avons bouilli**
vous	**avez bouilli**
ils/elles	**ont bouilli**

IMPERFECT

je	**bouillais**
tu	**bouillais**
il/elle/on	**bouillait**
nous	**bouillions**
vous	**bouilliez**
ils/elles	**bouillaient**

FUTURE

je	**bouillirai**
tu	**bouilliras**
il/elle/on	**bouillira**
nous	**bouillirons**
vous	**bouillirez**
ils/elles	**bouilliront**

CONDITIONAL

je	**bouillirais**
tu	**bouillirais**
il/elle/on	**bouillirait**
nous	**bouillirions**
vous	**bouilliriez**
ils/elles	**bouilliraient**

IMPERATIVE
bous / bouillons / bouillez

PAST PARTICIPLE
bouilli

PRESENT PARTICIPLE
bouillant

EXAMPLE PHRASES

L'eau **bout**. *The water's boiling.*

Tu peux mettre de l'eau à **bouillir**? *Can you boil some water?*

je/j' = I **tu** = you **il** = he/it **elle** = she/it **on** = we/one **nous** = we **vous** = you **ils/elles** = they

commencer (to begin)

PRESENT

je	commence
tu	commences
il/elle/on	commence
nous	commençons
vous	commencez
ils/elles	commencent

PRESENT SUBJUNCTIVE

je	commence
tu	commences
il/elle/on	commence
nous	commencions
vous	commenciez
ils/elles	commencent

PERFECT

j'	ai commencé
tu	as commencé
il/elle/on	a commencé
nous	avons commencé
vous	avez commencé
ils/elles	ont commencé

IMPERFECT

je	commençais
tu	commençais
il/elle/on	commençait
nous	commencions
vous	commenciez
ils/elles	commençaient

FUTURE

je	commencerai
tu	commenceras
il/elle/on	commencera
nous	commencerons
vous	commencerez
ils/elles	commenceront

CONDITIONAL

je	commencerais
tu	commencerais
il/elle/on	commencerait
nous	commencerions
vous	commenceriez
ils/elles	commenceraient

IMPERATIVE
commence / commençons / commencez

PAST PARTICIPLE
commencé

PRESENT PARTICIPLE
commençant

EXAMPLE PHRASES

Il **a commencé** à pleuvoir. *It started to rain.*

Les cours **commencent** à neuf heures. *Lessons start at 9 o'clock.*

Tu **as** déjà **commencé** à réviser pour les examens? *Have you started revising for the exams?*

je/j' = I **tu** = you **il** = he/it **elle** = she/it **on** = we/one **nous** = we **vous** = you **ils/elles** = they

conclure (to conclude)

PRESENT

je	conclus
tu	conclus
il/elle/on	conclut
nous	concluons
vous	concluez
ils/elles	concluent

PRESENT SUBJUNCTIVE

je	conclue
tu	conclues
il/elle/on	conclue
nous	concluions
vous	concluiez
ils/elles	concluent

PERFECT

j'	ai conclu
tu	as conclu
il/elle/on	a conclu
nous	avons conclu
vous	avez conclu
ils/elles	ont conclu

IMPERFECT

je	concluais
tu	concluais
il/elle/on	concluait
nous	concluions
vous	concluiez
ils/elles	concluaient

FUTURE

je	conclurai
tu	concluras
il/elle/on	conclura
nous	conclurons
vous	conclurez
ils/elles	concluront

CONDITIONAL

je	conclurais
tu	conclurais
il/elle/on	conclurait
nous	conclurions
vous	concluriez
ils/elles	concluraient

IMPERATIVE
conclus / concluons / concluez

PAST PARTICIPLE
conclu

PRESENT PARTICIPLE
concluant

EXAMPLE PHRASES

Ils **ont conclu** un marché. *They concluded a deal.*

J'en **ai conclu** qu'il était parti. *I concluded that he had gone.*

Je **conclurai** par ces mots… *I will conclude with these words…*

Verb Tables **15**

connaître (to know)

PRESENT

je	connais
tu	connais
il/elle/on	connaît
nous	connaissons
vous	connaissez
ils/elles	connaissent

PRESENT SUBJUNCTIVE

je	connaisse
tu	connaisses
il/elle/on	connaisse
nous	connaissions
vous	connaissiez
ils/elles	connaissent

PERFECT

j'	ai connu
tu	as connu
il/elle/on	a connu
nous	avons connu
vous	avez connu
ils/elles	ont connu

IMPERFECT

je	connaissais
tu	connaissais
il/elle/on	connaissait
nous	connaissions
vous	connaissiez
ils/elles	connaissaient

FUTURE

je	connaîtrai
tu	connaîtras
il/elle/on	connaîtra
nous	connaîtrons
vous	connaîtrez
ils/elles	connaîtront

CONDITIONAL

je	connaîtrais
tu	connaîtrais
il/elle/on	connaîtrait
nous	connaîtrions
vous	connaîtriez
ils/elles	connaîtraient

IMPERATIVE
connais / connaissons / connaissez

PAST PARTICIPLE
connu

PRESENT PARTICIPLE
connaissant

EXAMPLE PHRASES

Je ne **connais** pas du tout cette région. *I don't know the area at all.*

Vous **connaissez** M. Amiot? *Do you know Mr Amiot?*

Il n'**a** pas **connu** son grand-père. *He never knew his granddad.*

Ils **se sont connus** à Rouen. *They first met in Rouen.*

⇨ See pages 88–91 for information on how to form the reflexive verb **se connaître**.

je/j' = I **tu** = you **il** = he/it **elle** = she/it **on** = we/one **nous** = we **vous** = you **ils/elles** = they

coudre (to sew)

PRESENT

je	**couds**
tu	**couds**
il/elle/on	**coud**
nous	**cousons**
vous	**cousez**
ils/elles	**cousent**

PRESENT SUBJUNCTIVE

je	**couse**
tu	**couses**
il/elle/on	**couse**
nous	**cousions**
vous	**cousiez**
ils/elles	**cousent**

PERFECT

j'	**ai cousu**
tu	**as cousu**
il/elle/on	**a cousu**
nous	**avons cousu**
vous	**avez cousu**
ils/elles	**ont cousu**

IMPERFECT

je	**cousais**
tu	**cousais**
il/elle/on	**cousait**
nous	**cousions**
vous	**cousiez**
ils/elles	**cousaient**

FUTURE

je	**coudrai**
tu	**coudras**
il/elle/on	**coudra**
nous	**coudrons**
vous	**coudrez**
ils/elles	**coudront**

CONDITIONAL

je	**coudrais**
tu	**coudrais**
il/elle/on	**coudrait**
nous	**coudrions**
vous	**coudriez**
ils/elles	**coudraient**

IMPERATIVE
couds / cousons / cousez

PAST PARTICIPLE
cousu

PRESENT PARTICIPLE
cousant

EXAMPLE PHRASES

Tu sais **coudre**? *Can you sew?*

Elle **a cousu** elle-même son costume. *She made her costume herself.*

---

je/j' = I **tu** = you **il** = he/it **elle** = she/it **on** = we/one **nous** = we **vous** = you **ils/elles** = they

courir (to run)

PRESENT
je	**cours**
tu	**cours**
il/elle/on	**court**
nous	**courons**
vous	**courez**
ils/elles	**courent**

PRESENT SUBJUNCTIVE
je	**coure**
tu	**coures**
il/elle/on	**coure**
nous	**courions**
vous	**couriez**
ils/elles	**courent**

PERFECT
j'	**ai couru**
tu	**as couru**
il/elle/on	**a couru**
nous	**avons couru**
vous	**avez couru**
ils/elles	**ont couru**

IMPERFECT
je	**courais**
tu	**courais**
il/elle/on	**courait**
nous	**courions**
vous	**couriez**
ils/elles	**couraient**

FUTURE
je	**courrai**
tu	**courras**
il/elle/on	**courra**
nous	**courrons**
vous	**courrez**
ils/elles	**courront**

CONDITIONAL
je	**courrais**
tu	**courrais**
il/elle/on	**courrait**
nous	**courrions**
vous	**courriez**
ils/elles	**courraient**

IMPERATIVE
cours / courons / courez

PAST PARTICIPLE
couru

PRESENT PARTICIPLE
courant

EXAMPLE PHRASES

Je ne **cours** pas très vite. *I can't run very fast.*

Elle est sortie en **courant**. *She ran out.*

Ne **courez** pas dans le couloir. *Don't run in the corridor.*

J'**ai couru** jusqu'à l'école. *I ran all the way to school.*

je/j' = I **tu** = you **il** = he/it **elle** = she/it **on** = we/one **nous** = we **vous** = you **ils/elles** = they

craindre (to fear)

PRESENT

je	crains
tu	crains
il/elle/on	craint
nous	craignons
vous	craignez
ils/elles	craignent

PRESENT SUBJUNCTIVE

je	craigne
tu	craignes
il/elle/on	craigne
nous	craignions
vous	craigniez
ils/elles	craignent

PERFECT

j'	ai craint
tu	as craint
il/elle/on	a craint
nous	avons craint
vous	avez craint
ils/elles	ont craint

IMPERFECT

je	craignais
tu	craignais
il/elle/on	craignait
nous	craignions
vous	craigniez
ils/elles	craignaient

FUTURE

je	craindrai
tu	craindras
il/elle/on	craindra
nous	craindrons
vous	craindrez
ils/elles	craindront

CONDITIONAL

je	craindrais
tu	craindrais
il/elle/on	craindrait
nous	craindrions
vous	craindriez
ils/elles	craindraient

IMPERATIVE
crains / craignons / craignez

PAST PARTICIPLE
craint

PRESENT PARTICIPLE
craignant

EXAMPLE PHRASES

Tu n'as rien à **craindre**. *You've got nothing to fear.*
Je **crains** le pire. *I fear the worst.*

je/j' = I **tu** = you **il** = he/it **elle** = she/it **on** = we/one **nous** = we **vous** = you **ils/elles** = they

créer (to create)

PRESENT
je	**crée**
tu	**crées**
il/elle/on	**crée**
nous	**créons**
vous	**créez**
ils/elles	**créent**

PRESENT SUBJUNCTIVE
je	**crée**
tu	**crées**
il/elle/on	**crée**
nous	**créions**
vous	**créiez**
ils/elles	**créent**

PERFECT
j'	**ai créé**
tu	**as créé**
il/elle/on	**a créé**
nous	**avons créé**
vous	**avez créé**
ils/elles	**ont créé**

IMPERFECT
je	**créais**
tu	**créais**
il/elle/on	**créait**
nous	**créions**
vous	**créiez**
ils/elles	**créaient**

FUTURE
je	**créerai**
tu	**créeras**
il/elle/on	**créera**
nous	**créerons**
vous	**créerez**
ils/elles	**créeront**

CONDITIONAL
je	**créerais**
tu	**créerais**
il/elle/on	**créerait**
nous	**créerions**
vous	**créeriez**
ils/elles	**créeraient**

IMPERATIVE
crée / créons / créez

PAST PARTICIPLE
créé

PRESENT PARTICIPLE
créant

EXAMPLE PHRASES

Il **a créé** une nouvelle invention. *He's created a new invention.*

Ce virus **crée** des difficultés dans le monde entier. *This virus is creating difficulties all over the world.*

Le gouvernement **créera** deux mille emplois supplémentaires. *The government will create an extra two thousand jobs.*

je/j' = I **tu** = you **il** = he/it **elle** = she/it **on** = we/one **nous** = we **vous** = you **ils/elles** = they

crier (to shout)

PRESENT

je	crie
tu	cries
il/elle/on	crie
nous	crions
vous	criez
ils/elles	crient

PRESENT SUBJUNCTIVE

je	crie
tu	cries
il/elle/on	crie
nous	criions
vous	criiez
ils/elles	crient

PERFECT

j'	ai crié
tu	as crié
il/elle/on	a crié
nous	avons crié
vous	avez crié
ils/elles	ont crié

IMPERFECT

je	criais
tu	criais
il/elle/on	criait
nous	criions
vous	criiez
ils/elles	criaient

FUTURE

je	crierai
tu	crieras
il/elle/on	criera
nous	crierons
vous	crierez
ils/elles	crieront

CONDITIONAL

je	crierais
tu	crierais
il/elle/on	crierait
nous	crierions
vous	crieriez
ils/elles	crieraient

IMPERATIVE
crie / crions / criez

PAST PARTICIPLE
crié

PRESENT PARTICIPLE
criant

EXAMPLE PHRASES

Ne **crie** pas comme ça! *Don't shout!*

Elle **a crié** au secours. *She cried for help.*

"Attention!", **a**-t-il **crié**. *"Watch out!" he shouted.*

---

je/j' = I **tu** = you **il** = he/it **elle** = she/it **on** = we/one **nous** = we **vous** = you **ils/elles** = they

croire (to believe)

PRESENT

je	**crois**
tu	**crois**
il/elle/on	**croit**
nous	**croyons**
vous	**croyez**
ils/elles	**croient**

PRESENT SUBJUNCTIVE

je	**croie**
tu	**croies**
il/elle/on	**croie**
nous	**croyions**
vous	**croyiez**
ils/elles	**croient**

PERFECT

j'	**ai cru**
tu	**as cru**
il/elle/on	**a cru**
nous	**avons cru**
vous	**avez cru**
ils/elles	**ont cru**

IMPERFECT

je	**croyais**
tu	**croyais**
il/elle/on	**croyait**
nous	**croyions**
vous	**croyiez**
ils/elles	**croyaient**

FUTURE

je	**croirai**
tu	**croiras**
il/elle/on	**croira**
nous	**croirons**
vous	**croirez**
ils/elles	**croiront**

CONDITIONAL

je	**croirais**
tu	**croirais**
il/elle/on	**croirait**
nous	**croirions**
vous	**croiriez**
ils/elles	**croiraient**

IMPERATIVE
crois / croyons / croyez

PAST PARTICIPLE
cru

PRESENT PARTICIPLE
croyant

EXAMPLE PHRASES

Je ne te **crois** pas. *I don't believe you.*

J'**ai cru** que tu n'allais pas venir. *I thought you weren't going to come.*

Elle **croyait** encore au père Noël. *She still believed in Santa.*

---

je/j' = I tu = you il = he/it elle = she/it on = we/one nous = we vous = you ils/elles = they

croître (to grow)

PRESENT

je	**croîs**
tu	**croîs**
il/elle/on	**croît**
nous	**croissons**
vous	**croissez**
ils/elles	**croissent**

PRESENT SUBJUNCTIVE

je	**croisse**
tu	**croisses**
il/elle/on	**croisse**
nous	**croissions**
vous	**croissiez**
ils/elles	**croissent**

PERFECT

j'	**ai crû**
tu	**as crû**
il/elle/on	**a crû**
nous	**avons crû**
vous	**avez crû**
ils/elles	**ont crû**

IMPERFECT

je	**croissais**
tu	**croissais**
il/elle/on	**croissait**
nous	**croissions**
vous	**croissiez**
ils/elles	**croissaient**

FUTURE

je	**croîtrai**
tu	**croîtras**
il/elle/on	**croîtra**
nous	**croîtrons**
vous	**croîtrez**
ils/elles	**croîtront**

CONDITIONAL

je	**croîtrais**
tu	**croîtrais**
il/elle/on	**croîtrait**
nous	**croîtrions**
vous	**croîtriez**
ils/elles	**croîtraient**

IMPERATIVE
croîs / croissons / croissez

PAST PARTICIPLE
crû (*NB: crue, crus, crues*)

PRESENT PARTICIPLE
croissant

EXAMPLE PHRASES

Les ventes **croissent** de 6% par an. *Sales are growing by 6% per year.*

C'est une plante qui **croît** dans les pays chauds. *This plant grows in hot countries.*

cueillir (to pick)

PRESENT

je	cueille
tu	cueilles
il/elle/on	cueille
nous	cueillons
vous	cueillez
ils/elles	cueillent

PRESENT SUBJUNCTIVE

je	cueille
tu	cueilles
il/elle/on	cueille
nous	cueillions
vous	cueilliez
ils/elles	cueillent

PERFECT

j'	ai cueilli
tu	as cueilli
il/elle/on	a cueilli
nous	avons cueilli
vous	avez cueilli
ils/elles	ont cueilli

IMPERFECT

je	cueillais
tu	cueillais
il/elle/on	cueillait
nous	cueillions
vous	cueilliez
ils/elles	cueillaient

FUTURE

je	cueillerai
tu	cueilleras
il/elle/on	cueillera
nous	cueillerons
vous	cueillerez
ils/elles	cueilleront

CONDITIONAL

je	cueillerais
tu	cueillerais
il/elle/on	cueillerait
nous	cueillerions
vous	cueilleriez
ils/elles	cueilleraient

IMPERATIVE
cueille / cueillons / cueillez

PAST PARTICIPLE
cueilli

PRESENT PARTICIPLE
cueillant

EXAMPLE PHRASES

J'**ai cueilli** quelques fraises dans le jardin. *I've picked a few strawberries in the garden.*
Il est interdit de **cueillir** des fleurs sauvages dans la montagne. *It's forbidden to pick wild flowers in the mountains.*

je/j' = I **tu** = you **il** = he/it **elle** = she/it **on** = we/one **nous** = we **vous** = you **ils/elles** = they

cuire (to cook)

PRESENT

je	cuis
tu	cuis
il/elle/on	cuit
nous	cuisons
vous	cuisez
ils/elles	cuisent

PRESENT SUBJUNCTIVE

je	cuise
tu	cuises
il/elle/on	cuise
nous	cuisions
vous	cuisiez
ils/elles	cuisent

PERFECT

j'	ai cuit
tu	as cuit
il/elle/on	a cuit
nous	avons cuit
vous	avez cuit
ils/elles	ont cuit

IMPERFECT

je	cuisais
tu	cuisais
il/elle/on	cuisait
nous	cuisions
vous	cuisiez
ils/elles	cuisaient

FUTURE

je	cuirai
tu	cuiras
il/elle/on	cuira
nous	cuirons
vous	cuirez
ils/elles	cuiront

CONDITIONAL

je	cuirais
tu	cuirais
il/elle/on	cuirait
nous	cuirions
vous	cuiriez
ils/elles	cuiraient

IMPERATIVE
cuis / cuisons / cuisez

PAST PARTICIPLE
cuit

PRESENT PARTICIPLE
cuisant

EXAMPLE PHRASES

Je les **ai cuits** au beurre. *I cooked them in butter.*

En général, je **cuis** les légumes à la vapeur. *I usually steam vegetables.*

Ce gâteau prend environ une heure à **cuire**. *This cake takes about an hour to bake.*

---

je/j' = I **tu** = you **il** = he/it **elle** = she/it **on** = we/one **nous** = we **vous** = you **ils/elles** = they

descendre (to go down; to take down)

PRESENT
je	descends
tu	descends
il/elle/on	descend
nous	descendons
vous	descendez
ils/elles	descendent

PRESENT SUBJUNCTIVE
je	descende
tu	descendes
il/elle/on	descende
nous	descendions
vous	descendiez
ils/elles	descendent

PERFECT
je	suis descendu(e)
tu	es descendu(e)
il/elle/on	est descendu(e)
nous	sommes descendu(e)s
vous	êtes descendu(e)(s)
ils/elles	sont descendu(e)s

IMPERFECT
je	descendais
tu	descendais
il/elle/on	descendait
nous	descendions
vous	descendiez
ils/elles	descendaient

FUTURE
je	descendrai
tu	descendras
il/elle/on	descendra
nous	descendrons
vous	descendrez
ils/elles	descendront

CONDITIONAL
je	descendrais
tu	descendrais
il/elle/on	descendrait
nous	descendrions
vous	descendriez
ils/elles	descendraient

IMPERATIVE
descends / descendons / descendez

PAST PARTICIPLE
descendu

PRESENT PARTICIPLE
descendant

EXAMPLE PHRASES

Descendez la rue jusqu'au rond-point. *Go down the street to the roundabout.*

Reste en bas: je **descends**! *Stay downstairs – I'm coming down!*

Nous **sommes descendus** à la station Trocadéro. *We got off at the Trocadéro station.*

Vous pouvez **descendre** ma valise, s'il vous plaît? *Can you get my suitcase down, please?*

i Note that **descendre** takes **avoir** in the perfect tense when it is used with a direct object; see page 114.

je/j' = I **tu** = you **il** = he/it **elle** = she/it **on** = we/one **nous** = we **vous** = you **ils/elles** = they

devenir (to become)

PRESENT		PRESENT SUBJUNCTIVE	
je	deviens	je	devienne
tu	deviens	tu	deviennes
il/elle/on	devient	il/elle/on	devienne
nous	devenons	nous	devenions
vous	devenez	vous	deveniez
ils/elles	deviennent	ils/elles	deviennent

PERFECT		IMPERFECT	
je	suis devenu(e)	je	devenais
tu	es devenu(e)	tu	devenais
il/elle/on	est devenu(e)	il/elle/on	devenait
nous	sommes devenu(e)s	nous	devenions
vous	êtes devenu(e)(s)	vous	deveniez
ils/elles	sont devenu(e)s	ils/elles	devenaient

FUTURE		CONDITIONAL	
je	deviendrai	je	deviendrais
tu	deviendras	tu	deviendrais
il/elle/on	deviendra	il/elle/on	deviendrait
nous	deviendrons	nous	deviendrions
vous	deviendrez	vous	deviendriez
ils/elles	deviendront	ils/elles	deviendraient

IMPERATIVE
deviens / devenons / devenez

PAST PARTICIPLE
devenu

PRESENT PARTICIPLE
devenant

EXAMPLE PHRASES

Il **est devenu** médecin. *He became a doctor.*

Cet ordinateur **devient** de plus en plus lent. *This computer is becoming slower and slower.*

Qu'est-ce qu'elle **est devenue**? *What has become of her?*

---

je/j' = I **tu** = you **il** = he/it **elle** = she/it **on** = we/one **nous** = we **vous** = you **ils/elles** = they

devoir (to have to; to owe)

PRESENT
je	**dois**
tu	**dois**
il/elle/on	**doit**
nous	**devons**
vous	**devez**
ils/elles	**doivent**

PRESENT SUBJUNCTIVE
je	**doive**
tu	**doives**
il/elle/on	**doive**
nous	**devions**
vous	**deviez**
ils/elles	**doivent**

PERFECT
j'	**ai dû**
tu	**as dû**
il/elle/on	**a dû**
nous	**avons dû**
vous	**avez dû**
ils/elles	**ont dû**

IMPERFECT
je	**devais**
tu	**devais**
il/elle/on	**devait**
nous	**devions**
vous	**deviez**
ils/elles	**devaient**

FUTURE
je	**devrai**
tu	**devras**
il/elle/on	**devra**
nous	**devrons**
vous	**devrez**
ils/elles	**devront**

CONDITIONAL
je	**devrais**
tu	**devrais**
il/elle/on	**devrait**
nous	**devrions**
vous	**devriez**
ils/elles	**devraient**

IMPERATIVE
dois / devons / devez

PAST PARTICIPLE
dû (*NB*: due, dus, dues)

PRESENT PARTICIPLE
devant

EXAMPLE PHRASES
Je **dois** aller faire les courses ce matin. *I have to do the shopping this morning.*
À quelle heure est-ce que tu **dois** partir? *What time do you have to leave?*
Il **a dû** faire ses devoirs hier soir. *He had to do his homework last night.*
Il **devait** prendre le train pour aller travailler. *He had to go to work by train.*

je/j' = I **tu** = you **il** = he/it **elle** = she/it **on** = we/one **nous** = we **vous** = you **ils/elles** = they

dire (to say)

PRESENT
je	dis
tu	dis
il/elle/on	dit
nous	disons
vous	dites
ils/elles	disent

PRESENT SUBJUNCTIVE
je	dise
tu	dises
il/elle/on	dise
nous	disions
vous	disiez
ils/elles	disent

PERFECT
j'	ai dit
tu	as dit
il/elle/on	a dit
nous	avons dit
vous	avez dit
ils/elles	ont dit

IMPERFECT
je	disais
tu	disais
il/elle/on	disait
nous	disions
vous	disiez
ils/elles	disaient

FUTURE
je	dirai
tu	diras
il/elle/on	dira
nous	dirons
vous	direz
ils/elles	diront

CONDITIONAL
je	dirais
tu	dirais
il/elle/on	dirait
nous	dirions
vous	diriez
ils/elles	diraient

IMPERATIVE
dis / disons / dites

PAST PARTICIPLE
dit

PRESENT PARTICIPLE
disant

EXAMPLE PHRASES

Qu'est-ce qu'elle **dit**? *What is she saying?*

"Bonjour!", **a**-t-il **dit**. *"Hello!" he said.*

Ils m'**ont dit** que le film était nul. *They told me that the film was rubbish.*

Comment ça **se dit** en anglais? *How do you say that in English?*

⇨ See pages 88–91 for information on how to form the reflexive verb **se dire**.

je/j' = I   **tu** = you   **il** = he/it   **elle** = she/it   **on** = we/one   **nous** = we   **vous** = you   **ils/elles** = they

donner (to give)

PRESENT		PRESENT SUBJUNCTIVE	
je	**donne**	je	**donne**
tu	**donnes**	tu	**donnes**
il/elle/on	**donne**	il/elle/on	**donne**
nous	**donnons**	nous	**donnions**
vous	**donnez**	vous	**donniez**
ils/elles	**donnent**	ils/elles	**donnent**

PERFECT		IMPERFECT	
j'	**ai donné**	je	**donnais**
tu	**as donné**	tu	**donnais**
il/elle/on	**a donné**	il/elle/on	**donnait**
nous	**avons donné**	nous	**donnions**
vous	**avez donné**	vous	**donniez**
ils/elles	**ont donné**	ils/elles	**donnaient**

FUTURE		CONDITIONAL	
je	**donnerai**	je	**donnerais**
tu	**donneras**	tu	**donnerais**
il/elle/on	**donnera**	il/elle/on	**donnerait**
nous	**donnerons**	nous	**donnerions**
vous	**donnerez**	vous	**donneriez**
ils/elles	**donneront**	ils/elles	**donneraient**

IMPERATIVE	PAST PARTICIPLE
donne / donnons / donnez	donné

PRESENT PARTICIPLE
donnant

EXAMPLE PHRASES

Donne-moi la main. *Give me your hand.*

Est-ce que je t'**ai donné** mon adresse? *Did I give you my address?*

L'appartement **donne** sur la place. *The flat overlooks the square.*

je/j' = I **tu** = you **il** = he/it **elle** = she/it **on** = we/one **nous** = we **vous** = you **ils/elles** = they

dormir (to sleep)

PRESENT
je	dors
tu	dors
il/elle/on	dort
nous	dormons
vous	dormez
ils/elles	dorment

PRESENT SUBJUNCTIVE
je	dorme
tu	dormes
il/elle/on	dorme
nous	dormions
vous	dormiez
ils/elles	dorment

PERFECT
j'	ai dormi
tu	as dormi
il/elle/on	a dormi
nous	avons dormi
vous	avez dormi
ils/elles	ont dormi

IMPERFECT
je	dormais
tu	dormais
il/elle/on	dormait
nous	dormions
vous	dormiez
ils/elles	dormaient

FUTURE
je	dormirai
tu	dormiras
il/elle/on	dormira
nous	dormirons
vous	dormirez
ils/elles	dormiront

CONDITIONAL
je	dormirais
tu	dormirais
il/elle/on	dormirait
nous	dormirions
vous	dormiriez
ils/elles	dormiraient

IMPERATIVE
dors / dormons / dormez

PAST PARTICIPLE
dormi

PRESENT PARTICIPLE
dormant

EXAMPLE PHRASES
Tu **as** bien **dormi**? *Did you sleep well?*
Nous **dormons** dans la même chambre. *We sleep in the same bedroom.*
À 9 heures, il **dormait** déjà. *He was already asleep by nine.*

écrire (to write)

PRESENT

j'	écris
tu	écris
il/elle/on	écrit
nous	écrivons
vous	écrivez
ils/elles	écrivent

PRESENT SUBJUNCTIVE

j'	écrive
tu	écrives
il/elle/on	écrive
nous	écrivions
vous	écriviez
ils/elles	écrivent

PERFECT

j'	ai écrit
tu	as écrit
il/elle/on	a écrit
nous	avons écrit
vous	avez écrit
ils/elles	ont écrit

IMPERFECT

j'	écrivais
tu	écrivais
il/elle/on	écrivait
nous	écrivions
vous	écriviez
ils/elles	écrivaient

FUTURE

j'	écrirai
tu	écriras
il/elle/on	écrira
nous	écrirons
vous	écrirez
ils/elles	écriront

CONDITIONAL

j'	écrirais
tu	écrirais
il/elle/on	écrirait
nous	écririons
vous	écririez
ils/elles	écriraient

IMPERATIVE
écris / écrivons / écrivez

PAST PARTICIPLE
écrit

PRESENT PARTICIPLE
écrivant

EXAMPLE PHRASES

Les prof **a écrit** sur le tableau blanc. *The teacher wrote on the whiteboard.*

Elle **écrit** des romans. *She writes novels.*

Comment ça **s'écrit**, "brouillard"? *How do you spell "brouillard"?*

⇨ See pages 88–91 for information on how to form the reflexive verb **s'écrire**.

je/j' = I **tu** = you **il** = he/it **elle** = she/it **on** = we/one **nous** = we **vous** = you **ils/elles** = they

émouvoir (to move)

PRESENT

j'	émeus
tu	émeus
il/elle/on	émeut
nous	émouvons
vous	émouvez
ils/elles	émeuvent

PRESENT SUBJUNCTIVE

j'	émeuve
tu	émeuves
il/elle/on	émeuve
nous	émouvions
vous	émouviez
ils/elles	émeuvent

PERFECT

j'	ai ému
tu	as ému
il/elle/on	a ému
nous	avons ému
vous	avez ému
ils/elles	ont ému

IMPERFECT

j'	émouvais
tu	émouvais
il/elle/on	émouvait
nous	émouvions
vous	émouviez
ils/elles	émouvaient

FUTURE

j'	émouvrai
tu	émouvras
il/elle/on	émouvra
nous	émouvrons
vous	émouvrez
ils/elles	émouvront

CONDITIONAL

j'	émouvrais
tu	émouvrais
il/elle/on	émouvrait
nous	émouvrions
vous	émouvriez
ils/elles	émouvraient

IMPERATIVE
émeus / émouvons / émouvez

PAST PARTICIPLE
ému

PRESENT PARTICIPLE
émouvant

EXAMPLE PHRASES

Ce film nous **a émus**. *This film moved us.*

Cette histoire m'**émeut** toujours beaucoup. *This story always moves me deeply.*

entrer (to enter)

PRESENT

j'	entre
tu	entres
il/elle/on	entre
nous	entrons
vous	entrez
ils/elles	entrent

PRESENT SUBJUNCTIVE

j'	entre
tu	entres
il/elle/on	entre
nous	entrions
vous	entriez
ils/elles	entrent

PERFECT

je	suis entré(e)
tu	es entré(e)
il/elle/on	est entré(e)
nous	sommes entré(e)s
vous	êtes entré(e)(s)
ils/elles	sont entré(e)s

IMPERFECT

j'	entrais
tu	entrais
il/elle/on	entrait
nous	entrions
vous	entriez
ils/elles	entraient

FUTURE

j'	entrerai
tu	entreras
il/elle/on	entrera
nous	entrerons
vous	entrerez
ils/elles	entreront

CONDITIONAL

j'	entrerais
tu	entrerais
il/elle/on	entrerait
nous	entrerions
vous	entreriez
ils/elles	entreraient

IMPERATIVE
entre / entrons / entrez

PAST PARTICIPLE
entré

PRESENT PARTICIPLE
entrant

EXAMPLE PHRASES

Je peux **entrer**? *Can I come in?*

Essuie-toi les pieds en **entrant**. *Wipe your feet as you come in.*

Ils **sont** tous **entrés** dans la maison. *They all went into the house.*

je/j' = I **tu** = you **il** = he/it **elle** = she/it **on** = we/one **nous** = we **vous** = you **ils/elles** = they

envoyer (to send)

PRESENT

j'	envoie
tu	envoies
il/elle/on	envoie
nous	envoyons
vous	envoyez
ils/elles	envoient

PRESENT SUBJUNCTIVE

j'	envoie
tu	envoies
il/elle/on	envoie
nous	envoyions
vous	envoyiez
ils/elles	envoient

PERFECT

j'	ai envoyé
tu	as envoyé
il/elle/on	a envoyé
nous	avons envoyé
vous	avez envoyé
ils/elles	ont envoyé

IMPERFECT

j'	envoyais
tu	envoyais
il/elle/on	envoyait
nous	envoyions
vous	envoyiez
ils/elles	envoyaient

FUTURE

j'	enverrai
tu	enverras
il/elle/on	enverra
nous	enverrons
vous	enverrez
ils/elles	enverront

CONDITIONAL

j'	enverrais
tu	enverrais
il/elle/on	enverrait
nous	enverrions
vous	enverriez
ils/elles	enverraient

IMPERATIVE
envoie / envoyons / envoyez

PAST PARTICIPLE
envoyé

PRESENT PARTICIPLE
envoyant

EXAMPLE PHRASES

J'**ai envoyé** une carte postale à ma tante. *I sent my aunt a postcard.*
Envoie-moi un e-mail. *Send me an email.*
Je t'**enverrai** ton cadeau par la poste. *I'll send you your present by post.*

je/j' = I **tu** = you **il** = he/it **elle** = she/it **on** = we/one **nous** = we **vous** = you **ils/elles** = they

espérer (to hope)

PRESENT

j'	espère
tu	espères
il/elle/on	espère
nous	espérons
vous	espérez
ils/elles	espèrent

PRESENT SUBJUNCTIVE

j'	espère
tu	espères
il/elle/on	espère
nous	espérions
vous	espériez
ils/elles	espèrent

PERFECT

j'	ai espéré
tu	as espéré
il/elle/on	a espéré
nous	avons espéré
vous	avez espéré
ils/elles	ont espéré

IMPERFECT

j'	espérais
tu	espérais
il/elle/on	espérait
nous	espérions
vous	espériez
ils/elles	espéraient

FUTURE

j'	espérerai
tu	espéreras
il/elle/on	espérera
nous	espérerons
vous	espérerez
ils/elles	espéreront

CONDITIONAL

j'	espérerais
tu	espérerais
il/elle/on	espérerait
nous	espérerions
vous	espéreriez
ils/elles	espéreraient

IMPERATIVE
espère / espérons / espérez

PAST PARTICIPLE
espéré

PRESENT PARTICIPLE
espérant

EXAMPLE PHRASES

J'**espère** que tu vas bien. *I hope you're well.*

Il **espérait** pouvoir venir. *He was hoping he'd be able to come.*

Tu penses réussir tes examens? – J'**espère** bien! *Do you think you'll pass your exams? – I hope so!*

je/j' = I **tu** = you **il** = he/it **elle** = she/it **on** = we/one **nous** = we **vous** = you **ils/elles** = they

être (to be)

PRESENT

je	**suis**
tu	**es**
il/elle/on	**est**
nous	**sommes**
vous	**êtes**
ils/elles	**sont**

PRESENT SUBJUNCTIVE

je	**sois**
tu	**sois**
il/elle/on	**soit**
nous	**soyons**
vous	**soyez**
ils/elles	**soient**

PERFECT

j'	**ai été**
tu	**as été**
il/elle/on	**a été**
nous	**avons été**
vous	**avez été**
ils/elles	**ont été**

IMPERFECT

j'	**étais**
tu	**étais**
il/elle/on	**était**
nous	**étions**
vous	**étiez**
ils/elles	**étaient**

FUTURE

je	**serai**
tu	**seras**
il/elle/on	**sera**
nous	**serons**
vous	**serez**
ils/elles	**seront**

CONDITIONAL

je	**serais**
tu	**serais**
il/elle/on	**serait**
nous	**serions**
vous	**seriez**
ils/elles	**seraient**

IMPERATIVE
sois / soyons / soyez

PAST PARTICIPLE
été

PRESENT PARTICIPLE
étant

EXAMPLE PHRASES

Mon père **est** professeur. *My father's a teacher.*

Quelle heure **est**-il? – Il **est** dix heures. *What time is it? – It's 10 o'clock.*

Ils ne **sont** pas encore arrivés. *They haven't arrived yet.*

je/j' = I **tu** = you **il** = he/it **elle** = she/it **on** = we/one **nous** = we **vous** = you **ils/elles** = they

faire (to do; to make)

PRESENT
je	fais
tu	fais
il/elle/on	fait
nous	faisons
vous	faites
ils/elles	font

PRESENT SUBJUNCTIVE
je	fasse
tu	fasses
il/elle/on	fasse
nous	fassions
vous	fassiez
ils/elles	fassent

PERFECT
j'	ai fait
tu	as fait
il/elle/on	a fait
nous	avons fait
vous	avez fait
ils/elles	ont fait

IMPERFECT
je	faisais
tu	faisais
il/elle/on	faisait
nous	faisions
vous	faisiez
ils/elles	faisaient

FUTURE
je	ferai
tu	feras
il/elle/on	fera
nous	ferons
vous	ferez
ils/elles	feront

CONDITIONAL
je	ferais
tu	ferais
il/elle/on	ferait
nous	ferions
vous	feriez
ils/elles	feraient

IMPERATIVE
fais / faisons / faites

PAST PARTICIPLE
fait

PRESENT PARTICIPLE
faisant

EXAMPLE PHRASES

Qu'est-ce que tu **fais**? *What are you doing?*
Qu'est-ce qu'il **a fait**? *What has he done?* or *What did he do?*
J'**ai fait** un gâteau. *I've made a cake* or *I made a cake.*
Il **s'est fait** couper les cheveux. *He's had his hair cut.*

⇨ See pages 88–91 for information on how to form the reflexive verb **se faire**.

je/j' = I **tu** = you **il** = he/it **elle** = she/it **on** = we/one **nous** = we **vous** = you **ils/elles** = they

falloir (to be necessary)

PRESENT
    il **faut**

PRESENT SUBJUNCTIVE
    il **faille**

PERFECT
    il **a fallu**

IMPERFECT
    il **fallait**

FUTURE
    il **faudra**

CONDITIONAL
    il **faudrait**

IMPERATIVE
not used

PAST PARTICIPLE
    fallu

PRESENT PARTICIPLE
not used

EXAMPLE PHRASES

Il **faut** se dépêcher! *We have to hurry up!*

Il me **fallait** de l'argent. *I needed money.*

Il **faudra** que tu sois là à 8 heures. *You'll have to be there at 8.*

---

je/j' = I   **tu** = you   **il** = he/it   **elle** = she/it   **on** = we/one   **nous** = we   **vous** = you   **ils/elles** = they

finir (to finish)

PRESENT
je	finis
tu	finis
il/elle/on	finit
nous	finissons
vous	finissez
ils/elles	finissent

PRESENT SUBJUNCTIVE
je	finisse
tu	finisses
il/elle/on	finisse
nous	finissions
vous	finissiez
ils/elles	finissent

PERFECT
j'	ai fini
tu	as fini
il/elle/on	a fini
nous	avons fini
vous	avez fini
ils/elles	ont fini

IMPERFECT
je	finissais
tu	finissais
il/elle/on	finissait
nous	finissions
vous	finissiez
ils/elles	finissaient

FUTURE
je	finirai
tu	finiras
il/elle/on	finira
nous	finirons
vous	finirez
ils/elles	finiront

CONDITIONAL
je	finirais
tu	finirais
il/elle/on	finirait
nous	finirions
vous	finiriez
ils/elles	finiraient

IMPERATIVE
finis / finissons / finissez

PAST PARTICIPLE
fini

PRESENT PARTICIPLE
finissant

EXAMPLE PHRASES

Finis ta soupe! *Finish your soup!*

J'ai **fini**! *I've finished!*

Je **finirai** mes devoirs demain. *I'll finish my homework tomorrow.*

je/j' = I **tu** = you **il** = he/it **elle** = she/it **on** = we/one **nous** = we **vous** = you **ils/elles** = they

fuir (to flee; to leak)

PRESENT

je	**fuis**
tu	**fuis**
il/elle/on	**fuit**
nous	**fuyons**
vous	**fuyez**
ils/elles	**fuient**

PRESENT SUBJUNCTIVE

je	**fuie**
tu	**fuies**
il/elle/on	**fuie**
nous	**fuyions**
vous	**fuyiez**
ils/elles	**fuient**

PERFECT

j'	**ai fui**
tu	**as fui**
il/elle/on	**a fui**
nous	**avons fui**
vous	**avez fui**
ils/elles	**ont fui**

IMPERFECT

je	**fuyais**
tu	**fuyais**
il/elle/on	**fuyait**
nous	**fuyions**
vous	**fuyiez**
ils/elles	**fuyaient**

FUTURE

je	**fuirai**
tu	**fuiras**
il/elle/on	**fuira**
nous	**fuirons**
vous	**fuirez**
ils/elles	**fuiront**

CONDITIONAL

je	**fuirais**
tu	**fuirais**
il/elle/on	**fuirait**
nous	**fuirions**
vous	**fuiriez**
ils/elles	**fuiraient**

IMPERATIVE
fuis / fuyons / fuyez

PAST PARTICIPLE
fui

PRESENT PARTICIPLE
fuyant

EXAMPLE PHRASES

Ils **ont fui** leur pays. *They fled their country.*
J'ai un stylo qui **fuit**. *My pen leaks.*

haïr (to hate)

PRESENT

je	hais
tu	hais
il/elle/on	hait
nous	haïssons
vous	haïssez
ils/elles	haïssent

PRESENT SUBJUNCTIVE

je	haïsse
tu	haïsses
il/elle/on	haïsse
nous	haïssions
vous	haïssiez
ils/elles	haïssent

PERFECT

j'	ai haï
tu	as haï
il/elle/on	a haï
nous	avons haï
vous	avez haï
ils/elles	ont haï

IMPERFECT

je	haïssais
tu	haïssais
il/elle/on	haïssait
nous	haïssions
vous	haïssiez
ils/elles	haïssaient

FUTURE

je	haïrai
tu	haïras
il/elle/on	haïra
nous	haïrons
vous	haïrez
ils/elles	haïront

CONDITIONAL

je	haïrais
tu	haïrais
il/elle/on	haïrait
nous	haïrions
vous	haïriez
ils/elles	haïraient

IMPERATIVE
hais / haïssons / haïssez

PAST PARTICIPLE
haï

PRESENT PARTICIPLE
haïssant

EXAMPLE PHRASES

Je te **hais**! *I hate you!*

Elle **haïssait** tout le monde. *She hated everyone.*

Ils **se haïssent**. *They hate each other.*

je/j' = I **tu** = you **il** = he/it **elle** = she/it **on** = we/one **nous** = we **vous** = you **ils/elles** = they

jeter (to throw)

PRESENT
je	jette
tu	jettes
il/elle/on	jette
nous	jetons
vous	jetez
ils/elles	jettent

PERFECT
j'	ai jeté
tu	as jeté
il/elle/on	a jeté
nous	avons jeté
vous	avez jeté
ils/elles	ont jeté

FUTURE
je	jetterai
tu	jetteras
il/elle/on	jettera
nous	jetterons
vous	jetterez
ils/elles	jetteront

IMPERATIVE
jette / jetons / jetez

PRESENT PARTICIPLE
jetant

PRESENT SUBJUNCTIVE
je	jette
tu	jettes
il/elle/on	jette
nous	jetions
vous	jetiez
ils/elles	jettent

IMPERFECT
je	jetais
tu	jetais
il/elle/on	jetait
nous	jetions
vous	jetiez
ils/elles	jetaient

CONDITIONAL
je	jetterais
tu	jetterais
il/elle/on	jetterait
nous	jetterions
vous	jetteriez
ils/elles	jetteraient

PAST PARTICIPLE
jeté

EXAMPLE PHRASES
Ne **jette** pas tes vêtements par terre. *Don't throw your clothes on the floor.*
Elle **a jeté** son chewing-gum par la fenêtre. *She threw her chewing gum out of the window.*
Ils ne **jettent** jamais rien. *They never throw anything away.*

joindre (to join; to contact)

PRESENT
je	**joins**
tu	**joins**
il/elle/on	**joint**
nous	**joignons**
vous	**joignez**
ils/elles	**joignent**

PRESENT SUBJUNCTIVE
je	**joigne**
tu	**joignes**
il/elle/on	**joigne**
nous	**joignions**
vous	**joigniez**
ils/elles	**joignent**

PERFECT
j'	**ai joint**
tu	**as joint**
il/elle/on	**a joint**
nous	**avons joint**
vous	**avez joint**
ils/elles	**ont joint**

IMPERFECT
je	**joignais**
tu	**joignais**
il/elle/on	**joignait**
nous	**joignions**
vous	**joigniez**
ils/elles	**joignaient**

FUTURE
je	**joindrai**
tu	**joindras**
il/elle/on	**joindra**
nous	**joindrons**
vous	**joindrez**
ils/elles	**joindront**

CONDITIONAL
je	**joindrais**
tu	**joindrais**
il/elle/on	**joindrait**
nous	**joindrions**
vous	**joindriez**
ils/elles	**joindraient**

IMPERATIVE
joins / joignons / joignez

PAST PARTICIPLE
joint

PRESENT PARTICIPLE
joignant

EXAMPLE PHRASES

J'espère que vous vous **joindrez** à nous dimanche. *I hope you'll join us on Sunday.*

Où est-ce qu'on peut te **joindre** ce week-end? *Where can we contact you this weekend?*

On **a joint** les deux tables. *We put the two tables together.*

je/j' = I **tu** = you **il** = he/it **elle** = she/it **on** = we/one **nous** = we **vous** = you **ils/elles** = they

lever (to lift)

PRESENT
je	**lève**
tu	**lèves**
il/elle/on	**lève**
nous	**levons**
vous	**levez**
ils/elles	**lèvent**

PRESENT SUBJUNCTIVE
je	**lève**
tu	**lèves**
il/elle/on	**lève**
nous	**levions**
vous	**leviez**
ils/elles	**lèvent**

PERFECT
j'	**ai levé**
tu	**as levé**
il/elle/on	**a levé**
nous	**avons levé**
vous	**avez levé**
ils/elles	**ont levé**

IMPERFECT
je	**levais**
tu	**levais**
il/elle/on	**levait**
nous	**levions**
vous	**leviez**
ils/elles	**levaient**

FUTURE
je	**lèverai**
tu	**lèveras**
il/elle/on	**lèvera**
nous	**lèverons**
vous	**lèverez**
ils/elles	**lèveront**

CONDITIONAL
je	**lèverais**
tu	**lèverais**
il/elle/on	**lèverait**
nous	**lèverions**
vous	**lèveriez**
ils/elles	**lèveraient**

IMPERATIVE
lève / levons / levez

PAST PARTICIPLE
levé

PRESENT PARTICIPLE
levant

EXAMPLE PHRASES

Lève la tête. *Lift your head up.*

Levez la main! *Put your hand up!*

Je **me lève** tous les jours à sept heures. *I get up at 7 every day.*

⇨ See pages 88–91 for information on how to form the reflexive verb **se lever**.

lire (to read)

PRESENT

je	**lis**
tu	**lis**
il/elle/on	**lit**
nous	**lisons**
vous	**lisez**
ils/elles	**lisent**

PRESENT SUBJUNCTIVE

je	**lise**
tu	**lises**
il/elle/on	**lise**
nous	**lisions**
vous	**lisiez**
ils/elles	**lisent**

PERFECT

j'	**ai lu**
tu	**as lu**
il/elle/on	**a lu**
nous	**avons lu**
vous	**avez lu**
ils/elles	**ont lu**

IMPERFECT

je	**lisais**
tu	**lisais**
il/elle/on	**lisait**
nous	**lisions**
vous	**lisiez**
ils/elles	**lisaient**

FUTURE

je	**lirai**
tu	**liras**
il/elle/on	**lira**
nous	**lirons**
vous	**lirez**
ils/elles	**liront**

CONDITIONAL

je	**lirais**
tu	**lirais**
il/elle/on	**lirait**
nous	**lirions**
vous	**liriez**
ils/elles	**liraient**

IMPERATIVE
lis / lisons / lisez

PAST PARTICIPLE
lu

PRESENT PARTICIPLE
lisant

EXAMPLE PHRASES

Vous **avez lu** "Madame Bovary"? *Have you read "Madame Bovary"?*
Je le **lirai** dans l'avion. *I'll read it on the plane.*
Elle lui **lisait** une histoire. *She was reading him a story.*

je/j' = I **tu** = you **il** = he/it **elle** = she/it **on** = we/one **nous** = we **vous** = you **ils/elles** = they

manger (to eat)

PRESENT

je	mange
tu	manges
il/elle/on	mange
nous	mangeons
vous	mangez
ils/elles	mangent

PRESENT SUBJUNCTIVE

je	mange
tu	manges
il/elle/on	mange
nous	mangions
vous	mangiez
ils/elles	mangent

PERFECT

j'	ai mangé
tu	as mangé
il/elle/on	a mangé
nous	avons mangé
vous	avez mangé
ils/elles	ont mangé

IMPERFECT

je	mangeais
tu	mangeais
il/elle/on	mangeait
nous	mangions
vous	mangiez
ils/elles	mangeaient

FUTURE

je	mangerai
tu	mangeras
il/elle/on	mangera
nous	mangerons
vous	mangerez
ils/elles	mangeront

CONDITIONAL

je	mangerais
tu	mangerais
il/elle/on	mangerait
nous	mangerions
vous	mangeriez
ils/elles	mangeraient

IMPERATIVE
mange / mangeons / mangez

PAST PARTICIPLE
mangé

PRESENT PARTICIPLE
mangeant

EXAMPLE PHRASES

Nous ne **mangeons** pas souvent ensemble. *We don't often eat together.*

Tu **as** assez **mangé**? *Have you had enough to eat?*

Je **mangerai** plus tard. *I'll eat later on.*

---

je/j' = I **tu** = you **il** = he/it **elle** = she/it **on** = we/one **nous** = we **vous** = you **ils/elles** = they

maudire (to curse)

PRESENT

je	maudis
tu	maudis
il/elle/on	maudit
nous	maudissons
vous	maudissez
ils/elles	maudissent

PRESENT SUBJUNCTIVE

je	maudisse
tu	maudisses
il/elle/on	maudisse
nous	maudissions
vous	maudissiez
ils/elles	maudissent

PERFECT

j'	ai maudit
tu	as maudit
il/elle/on	a maudit
nous	avons maudit
vous	avez maudit
ils/elles	ont maudit

IMPERFECT

je	maudissais
tu	maudissais
il/elle/on	maudissait
nous	maudissions
vous	maudissiez
ils/elles	maudissaient

FUTURE

je	maudirai
tu	maudiras
il/elle/on	maudira
nous	maudirons
vous	maudirez
ils/elles	maudiront

CONDITIONAL

je	maudirais
tu	maudirais
il/elle/on	maudirait
nous	maudirions
vous	maudiriez
ils/elles	maudiraient

IMPERATIVE
maudis / maudissons / maudissez

PAST PARTICIPLE
maudit

PRESENT PARTICIPLE
maudissant

EXAMPLE PHRASES

Ils **maudissent** leurs ennemis. *They curse their enemies.*
Ce **maudit** stylo ne marche pas! *This blasted pen doesn't work!*

mettre (to put)

PRESENT

je	mets
tu	mets
il/elle/on	met
nous	mettons
vous	mettez
ils/elles	mettent

PRESENT SUBJUNCTIVE

je	mette
tu	mettes
il/elle/on	mette
nous	mettions
vous	mettiez
ils/elles	mettent

PERFECT

j'	ai mis
tu	as mis
il/elle/on	a mis
nous	avons mis
vous	avez mis
ils/elles	ont mis

IMPERFECT

je	mettais
tu	mettais
il/elle/on	mettait
nous	mettions
vous	mettiez
ils/elles	mettaient

FUTURE

je	mettrai
tu	mettras
il/elle/on	mettra
nous	mettrons
vous	mettrez
ils/elles	mettront

CONDITIONAL

je	mettrais
tu	mettrais
il/elle/on	mettrait
nous	mettrions
vous	mettriez
ils/elles	mettraient

IMPERATIVE
mets / mettons / mettez

PAST PARTICIPLE
mis

PRESENT PARTICIPLE
mettant

EXAMPLE PHRASES

Mets ton manteau! *Put your coat on!*

Où est-ce que tu **as mis** les clés? *Where have you put the keys?*

J'**ai mis** le livre sur la table. *I put the book on the table.*

Elle **s'est mise** à pleurer. *She started crying.*

⇨ See pages 88–91 for information on how to form the reflexive verb **se mettre**.

je/j' = I **tu** = you **il** = he/it **elle** = she/it **on** = we/one **nous** = we **vous** = you **ils/elles** = they

monter (to go up)

PRESENT

je	monte
tu	montes
il/elle/on	monte
nous	montons
vous	montez
ils/elles	montent

PRESENT SUBJUNCTIVE

je	monte
tu	montes
il/elle/on	monte
nous	montions
vous	montiez
ils/elles	montent

PERFECT

je	suis monté(e)
tu	es monté(e)
il/elle/on	est monté(e)
nous	sommes monté(e)s
vous	êtes monté(e)(s)
ils/elles	sont monté(e)s

IMPERFECT

je	montais
tu	montais
il/elle/on	montait
nous	montions
vous	montiez
ils/elles	montaient

FUTURE

je	monterai
tu	monteras
il/elle/on	montera
nous	monterons
vous	monterez
ils/elles	monteront

CONDITIONAL

je	monterais
tu	monterais
il/elle/on	monterait
nous	monterions
vous	monteriez
ils/elles	monteraient

IMPERATIVE
monte / montons / montez

PAST PARTICIPLE
monté

PRESENT PARTICIPLE
montant

EXAMPLE PHRASES

Je **suis montée** tout en haut de la tour. *I went all the way up the tower.*

Monte dans la voiture, je t'emmène. *Get into the car, I'll take you there.*

Il s'est tordu la cheville en **montant** à une échelle. *He twisted his ankle going up a ladder.*

i Note that **monter** takes **avoir** in the perfect tense when it is used with a direct object; see page 114.

je/j' = I **tu** = you **il** = he/it **elle** = she/it **on** = we/one **nous** = we **vous** = you **ils/elles** = they

mordre (to bite)

PRESENT

je	mords
tu	mords
il/elle/on	mord
nous	mordons
vous	mordez
ils/elles	mordent

PRESENT SUBJUNCTIVE

je	morde
tu	mordes
il/elle/on	morde
nous	mordions
vous	mordiez
ils/elles	mordent

PERFECT

j'	ai mordu
tu	as mordu
il/elle/on	a mordu
nous	avons mordu
vous	avez mordu
ils/elles	ont mordu

IMPERFECT

je	mordais
tu	mordais
il/elle/on	mordait
nous	mordions
vous	mordiez
ils/elles	mordaient

FUTURE

je	mordrai
tu	mordras
il/elle/on	mordra
nous	mordrons
vous	mordrez
ils/elles	mordront

CONDITIONAL

je	mordrais
tu	mordrais
il/elle/on	mordrait
nous	mordrions
vous	mordriez
ils/elles	mordraient

IMPERATIVE
mords / mordons / mordez

PAST PARTICIPLE
mordu

PRESENT PARTICIPLE
mordant

EXAMPLE PHRASES

Le chien m'**a mordue**. *The dog bit me.*

Il ne va pas te **mordre**! *He won't bite!*

---

je/j' = I **tu** = you **il** = he/it **elle** = she/it **on** = we/one **nous** = we **vous** = you **ils/elles** = they

moudre (to grind)

PRESENT

je	mouds
tu	mouds
il/elle/on	moud
nous	moulons
vous	moulez
ils/elles	moulent

PRESENT SUBJUNCTIVE

je	moule
tu	moules
il/elle/on	moule
nous	moulions
vous	mouliez
ils/elles	moulent

PERFECT

j'	ai moulu
tu	as moulu
il/elle/on	a moulu
nous	avons moulu
vous	avez moulu
ils/elles	ont moulu

IMPERFECT

je	moulais
tu	moulais
il/elle/on	moulait
nous	moulions
vous	mouliez
ils/elles	moulaient

FUTURE

je	moudrai
tu	moudras
il/elle/on	moudra
nous	moudrons
vous	moudrez
ils/elles	moudront

CONDITIONAL

je	moudrais
tu	moudrais
il/elle/on	moudrait
nous	moudrions
vous	moudriez
ils/elles	moudraient

IMPERATIVE
mouds / moulons / moulez

PAST PARTICIPLE
moulu

PRESENT PARTICIPLE
moulant

EXAMPLE PHRASES

J'**ai moulu** du café pour demain matin. *I've ground some coffee for tomorrow morning.*

---

je/j' = I **tu** = you **il** = he/it **elle** = she/it **on** = we/one **nous** = we **vous** = you **ils/elles** = they

mourir (to die)

PRESENT
je	meurs
tu	meurs
il/elle/on	meurt
nous	mourons
vous	mourez
ils/elles	meurent

PRESENT SUBJUNCTIVE
je	meure
tu	meures
il/elle/on	meure
nous	mourions
vous	mouriez
ils/elles	meurent

PERFECT
je	suis mort(e)
tu	es mort(e)
il/elle/on	est mort(e)
nous	sommes mort(e)s
vous	êtes mort(e)(s)
ils/elles	sont mort(e)s

IMPERFECT
je	mourais
tu	mourais
il/elle/on	mourait
nous	mourions
vous	mouriez
ils/elles	mouraient

FUTURE
je	mourrai
tu	mourras
il/elle/on	mourra
nous	mourrons
vous	mourrez
ils/elles	mourront

CONDITIONAL
je	mourrais
tu	mourrais
il/elle/on	mourrait
nous	mourrions
vous	mourriez
ils/elles	mourraient

IMPERATIVE
meurs / mourons / mourez

PAST PARTICIPLE
mort

PRESENT PARTICIPLE
mourant

EXAMPLE PHRASES
Elle **est morte** en 1998. *She died in 1998.*
Ils **sont morts**. *They're dead.*
On **meurt** de froid ici! *We're freezing to death in here!*

je/j' = I **tu** = you **il** = he/it **elle** = she/it **on** = we/one **nous** = we **vous** = you **ils/elles** = they

naître (to be born)

PRESENT

je	nais
tu	nais
il/elle/on	naît
nous	naissons
vous	naissez
ils/elles	naissent

PRESENT SUBJUNCTIVE

je	naisse
tu	naisses
il/elle/on	naisse
nous	naissions
vous	naissiez
ils/elles	naissent

PERFECT

je	suis né(e)
tu	es né(e)
il/elle/on	est né(e)
nous	sommes né(e)s
vous	êtes né(e)(s)
ils/elles	sont né(e)s

IMPERFECT

je	naissais
tu	naissais
il/elle/on	naissait
nous	naissions
vous	naissiez
ils/elles	naissaient

FUTURE

je	naîtrai
tu	naîtras
il/elle/on	naîtra
nous	naîtrons
vous	naîtrez
ils/elles	naîtront

CONDITIONAL

je	naîtrais
tu	naîtrais
il/elle/on	naîtrait
nous	naîtrions
vous	naîtriez
ils/elles	naîtraient

IMPERATIVE
nais / naissons / naissez

PAST PARTICIPLE
né

PRESENT PARTICIPLE
naissant

EXAMPLE PHRASES

Je **suis née** le 12 février. *I was born on 12 February.*

Le bébé de Delphine **naîtra** en mars. *Delphine is going to have a baby in March.*

Quand est-ce que tu **es né**? *When were you born?*

je/j' = I **tu** = you **il** = he/it **elle** = she/it **on** = we/one **nous** = we **vous** = you **ils/elles** = they

nettoyer (to clean)

PRESENT

je	**nettoie**
tu	**nettoies**
il/elle/on	**nettoie**
nous	**nettoyons**
vous	**nettoyez**
ils/elles	**nettoient**

PRESENT SUBJUNCTIVE

je	**nettoie**
tu	**nettoies**
il/elle/on	**nettoie**
nous	**nettoyions**
vous	**nettoyiez**
ils/elles	**nettoient**

PERFECT

j'	**ai nettoyé**
tu	**as nettoyé**
il/elle/on	**a nettoyé**
nous	**avons nettoyé**
vous	**avez nettoyé**
ils/elles	**ont nettoyé**

IMPERFECT

je	**nettoyais**
tu	**nettoyais**
il/elle/on	**nettoyait**
nous	**nettoyions**
vous	**nettoyiez**
ils/elles	**nettoyaient**

FUTURE

je	**nettoierai**
tu	**nettoieras**
il/elle/on	**nettoiera**
nous	**nettoierons**
vous	**nettoierez**
ils/elles	**nettoieront**

CONDITIONAL

je	**nettoierais**
tu	**nettoierais**
il/elle/on	**nettoierait**
nous	**nettoierions**
vous	**nettoieriez**
ils/elles	**nettoieraient**

IMPERATIVE
nettoie / nettoyons / nettoyez

PAST PARTICIPLE
nettoyé

PRESENT PARTICIPLE
nettoyant

EXAMPLE PHRASES

Richard **a nettoyé** tout l'appartement. *Richard has cleaned the whole flat.*

Elle **nettoyait** le sol en écoutant la radio. *She was cleaning the floor while listening to the radio.*

Je ne **nettoie** pas souvent l'écran de mon ordi. *I don't clean my computer screen very often.*

offrir (to offer; to give)

PRESENT

j'	**offre**
tu	**offres**
il/elle/on	**offre**
nous	**offrons**
vous	**offrez**
ils/elles	**offrent**

PRESENT SUBJUNCTIVE

j'	**offre**
tu	**offres**
il/elle/on	**offre**
nous	**offrions**
vous	**offriez**
ils/elles	**offrent**

PERFECT

j'	**ai offert**
tu	**as offert**
il/elle/on	**a offert**
nous	**avons offert**
vous	**avez offert**
ils/elles	**ont offert**

IMPERFECT

j'	**offrais**
tu	**offrais**
il/elle/on	**offrait**
nous	**offrions**
vous	**offriez**
ils/elles	**offraient**

FUTURE

j'	**offrirai**
tu	**offriras**
il/elle/on	**offrira**
nous	**offrirons**
vous	**offrirez**
ils/elles	**offriront**

CONDITIONAL

j'	**offrirais**
tu	**offrirais**
il/elle/on	**offrirait**
nous	**offririons**
vous	**offririez**
ils/elles	**offriraient**

IMPERATIVE
offre / offrons / offrez

PAST PARTICIPLE
offert

PRESENT PARTICIPLE
offrant

EXAMPLE PHRASES

On lui **a offert** un poste de secrétaire. *They offered her a secreterial post.*

Offre-lui des fleurs. *Give her some flowers.*

Viens, je t'**offre** à boire. *Come on, I'll buy you a drink.*

Je **me suis offert** un nouveau stylo. *I treated myself to a new pen.*

⇨ See pages 88–91 for information on how to form the reflexive verb **s'offrir**.

je/j' = I **tu** = you **il** = he/it **elle** = she/it **on** = we/one **nous** = we **vous** = you **ils/elles** = they

ouvrir (to open)

PRESENT

j'	ouvre
tu	ouvres
il/elle/on	ouvre
nous	ouvrons
vous	ouvrez
ils/elles	ouvrent

PRESENT SUBJUNCTIVE

j'	ouvre
tu	ouvres
il/elle/on	ouvre
nous	ouvrions
vous	ouvriez
ils/elles	ouvrent

PERFECT

j'	ai ouvert
tu	as ouvert
il/elle/on	a ouvert
nous	avons ouvert
vous	avez ouvert
ils/elles	ont ouvert

IMPERFECT

j'	ouvrais
tu	ouvrais
il/elle/on	ouvrait
nous	ouvrions
vous	ouvriez
ils/elles	ouvraient

FUTURE

j'	ouvrirai
tu	ouvriras
il/elle/on	ouvrira
nous	ouvrirons
vous	ouvrirez
ils/elles	ouvriront

CONDITIONAL

j'	ouvrirais
tu	ouvrirais
il/elle/on	ouvrirait
nous	ouvririons
vous	ouvririez
ils/elles	ouvriraient

IMPERATIVE
ouvre / ouvrons / ouvrez

PAST PARTICIPLE
ouvert

PRESENT PARTICIPLE
ouvrant

EXAMPLE PHRASES

Elle **a ouvert** la porte. *She opened the door.*

Est-ce que tu pourrais **ouvrir** la fenêtre? *Could you open the window?*

Je me suis coupé en **ouvrant** une boîte de conserve. *I cut myself opening a tin.*

La porte **s'est ouverte**. *The door opened.*

⇨ See pages 88–91 for information on how to form the reflexive verb **s'ouvrir**.

je/j' = I **tu** = you **il** = he/it **elle** = she/it **on** = we/one **nous** = we **vous** = you **ils/elles** = they

paraître (to seem)

PRESENT

je	**parais**
tu	**parais**
il/elle/on	**paraît**
nous	**paraissons**
vous	**paraissez**
ils/elles	**paraissent**

PRESENT SUBJUNCTIVE

je	**paraisse**
tu	**paraisses**
il/elle/on	**paraisse**
nous	**paraissions**
vous	**paraissiez**
ils/elles	**paraissent**

PERFECT

j'	**ai paru**
tu	**as paru**
il/elle/on	**a paru**
nous	**avons paru**
vous	**avez paru**
ils/elles	**ont paru**

IMPERFECT

je	**paraissais**
tu	**paraissais**
il/elle/on	**paraissait**
nous	**paraissions**
vous	**paraissiez**
ils/elles	**paraissaient**

FUTURE

je	**paraîtrai**
tu	**paraîtras**
il/elle/on	**paraîtra**
nous	**paraîtrons**
vous	**paraîtrez**
ils/elles	**paraîtront**

CONDITIONAL

je	**paraîtrais**
tu	**paraîtrais**
il/elle/on	**paraîtrait**
nous	**paraîtrions**
vous	**paraîtriez**
ils/elles	**paraîtraient**

IMPERATIVE
parais / paraissons / paraissez

PAST PARTICIPLE
paru

PRESENT PARTICIPLE
paraissant

EXAMPLE PHRASES

Elle **paraissait** fatiguée. *She seemed tired.*

Gisèle **paraît** plus jeune que son âge. *Gisèle doesn't look her age.*

Il **paraît** qu'il fait chaud toute l'année là-bas. *Apparently it's hot all year round over there.*

je/j' = I **tu** = you **il** = he/it **elle** = she/it **on** = we/one **nous** = we **vous** = you **ils/elles** = they

partir (to go; to leave)

PRESENT

je	**pars**
tu	**pars**
il/elle/on	**part**
nous	**partons**
vous	**partez**
ils/elles	**partent**

PRESENT SUBJUNCTIVE

je	**parte**
tu	**partes**
il/elle/on	**parte**
nous	**partions**
vous	**partiez**
ils/elles	**partent**

PERFECT

je	**suis parti(e)**
tu	**es parti(e)**
il/elle/on	**est parti(e)**
nous	**sommes parti(e)s**
vous	**êtes parti(e)(s)**
ils/elles	**sont parti(e)s**

IMPERFECT

je	**partais**
tu	**partais**
il/elle/on	**partait**
nous	**partions**
vous	**partiez**
ils/elles	**partaient**

FUTURE

je	**partirai**
tu	**partiras**
il/elle/on	**partira**
nous	**partirons**
vous	**partirez**
ils/elles	**partiront**

CONDITIONAL

je	**partirais**
tu	**partirais**
il/elle/on	**partirait**
nous	**partirions**
vous	**partiriez**
ils/elles	**partiraient**

IMPERATIVE
pars / partons / partez

PAST PARTICIPLE
parti

PRESENT PARTICIPLE
partant

EXAMPLE PHRASES

On **part** en vacances le 15 août. *We're going on holiday on 15 August.*
Ne **partez** pas sans moi! *Don't leave without me!*
Elle **est partie** tôt ce matin. *She left early this morning.*

passer (to pass; to spend)

PRESENT

je	passe
tu	passes
il/elle/on	passe
nous	passons
vous	passez
ils/elles	passent

PRESENT SUBJUNCTIVE

je	passe
tu	passes
il/elle/on	passe
nous	passions
vous	passiez
ils/elles	passent

PERFECT

j'	ai passé
tu	as passé
il/elle/on	a passé
nous	avons passé
vous	avez passé
ils/elles	ont passé

IMPERFECT

je	passais
tu	passais
il/elle/on	passait
nous	passions
vous	passiez
ils/elles	passaient

FUTURE

je	passerai
tu	passeras
il/elle/on	passera
nous	passerons
vous	passerez
ils/elles	passeront

CONDITIONAL

je	passerais
tu	passerais
il/elle/on	passerait
nous	passerions
vous	passeriez
ils/elles	passeraient

IMPERATIVE
passe / passons / passez

PAST PARTICIPLE
passé

PRESENT PARTICIPLE
passant

EXAMPLE PHRASES

Les mois **ont passé**. *Months passed.*

Il **a passé** son examen en juin. *He took his exam in June.*

Je vais **passer** les vacances chez mes grands-parents. *I'm going to spend the holidays at my grandparents' house.*

Elle **est passée** me dire bonjour. *She came by to say hello.*

L'histoire **se passe** au Mexique. *The story takes place in Mexico.*

ℹ Note that **passer** can also take **être** in the perfect tense; see page 114.

⇨ See pages 88–91 for information on how to form the reflexive verb **se passer**.

payer (to pay)

PRESENT

je	**paye**
tu	**payes**
il/elle/on	**paye**
nous	**payons**
vous	**payez**
ils/elles	**payent**

PRESENT SUBJUNCTIVE

je	**paye**
tu	**payes**
il/elle/on	**paye**
nous	**payions**
vous	**payiez**
ils/elles	**payent**

PERFECT

j'	**ai payé**
tu	**as payé**
il/elle/on	**a payé**
nous	**avons payé**
vous	**avez payé**
ils/elles	**ont payé**

IMPERFECT

je	**payais**
tu	**payais**
il/elle/on	**payait**
nous	**payions**
vous	**payiez**
ils/elles	**payaient**

FUTURE

je	**payerai**
tu	**payeras**
il/elle/on	**payera**
nous	**payerons**
vous	**payerez**
ils/elles	**payeront**

CONDITIONAL

je	**payerais**
tu	**payerais**
il/elle/on	**payerait**
nous	**payerions**
vous	**payeriez**
ils/elles	**payeraient**

IMPERATIVE
paye / payons / payez

PAST PARTICIPLE
payé

PRESENT PARTICIPLE
payant

EXAMPLE PHRASES

Tu l'**as payé** combien? *How much did you pay for it?*

Ma patronne me **payera** demain. *My boss will pay me tomorrow.*

Les étudiants **payent** moitié prix. *Students pay half price.*

---

je/j' = I   **tu** = you   **il** = he/it   **elle** = she/it   **on** = we/one   **nous** = we   **vous** = you   **ils/elles** = they

peindre (to paint)

PRESENT
je	peins
tu	peins
il/elle/on	peint
nous	peignons
vous	peignez
ils/elles	peignent

PRESENT SUBJUNCTIVE
je	peigne
tu	peignes
il/elle/on	peigne
nous	peignions
vous	peigniez
ils/elles	peignent

PERFECT
j'	ai peint
tu	as peint
il/elle/on	a peint
nous	avons peint
vous	avez peint
ils/elles	ont peint

IMPERFECT
je	peignais
tu	peignais
il/elle/on	peignait
nous	peignions
vous	peigniez
ils/elles	peignaient

FUTURE
je	peindrai
tu	peindras
il/elle/on	peindra
nous	peindrons
vous	peindrez
ils/elles	peindront

CONDITIONAL
je	peindrais
tu	peindrais
il/elle/on	peindrait
nous	peindrions
vous	peindriez
ils/elles	peindraient

IMPERATIVE
peins / peignons / peignez

PAST PARTICIPLE
peint

PRESENT PARTICIPLE
peignant

EXAMPLE PHRASES

On **a peint** l'entrée en bleu clair. *We painted the hall light blue.*
Ce tableau **a été peint** en 1913. *This picture was painted in 1913.*

je/j' = I **tu** = you **il** = he/it **elle** = she/it **on** = we/one **nous** = we **vous** = you **ils/elles** = they

perdre (to lose)

PRESENT

je	perds
tu	perds
il/elle/on	perd
nous	perdons
vous	perdez
ils/elles	perdent

PRESENT SUBJUNCTIVE

je	perde
tu	perdes
il/elle/on	perde
nous	perdions
vous	perdiez
ils/elles	perdent

PERFECT

j'	ai perdu
tu	as perdu
il/elle/on	a perdu
nous	avons perdu
vous	avez perdu
ils/elles	ont perdu

IMPERFECT

je	perdais
tu	perdais
il/elle/on	perdait
nous	perdions
vous	perdiez
ils/elles	perdaient

FUTURE

je	perdrai
tu	perdras
il/elle/on	perdra
nous	perdrons
vous	perdrez
ils/elles	perdront

CONDITIONAL

je	perdrais
tu	perdrais
il/elle/on	perdrait
nous	perdrions
vous	perdriez
ils/elles	perdraient

IMPERATIVE
perds / perdons / perdez

PAST PARTICIPLE
perdu

PRESENT PARTICIPLE
perdant

EXAMPLE PHRASES

J'**ai perdu** mon porte-monnaie dans le métro. *I lost my purse on the underground.*

L'Italie **a perdu** un à zéro. *Italy lost one-nil.*

Si tu **te perds**, appelle-moi. *Call me if you get lost.*

⇨ See pages 88–91 for information on how to form the reflexive verb **se perdre**.

---

je/j' = I **tu** = you **il** = he/it **elle** = she/it **on** = we/one **nous** = we **vous** = you **ils/elles** = they

plaire (to please)

PRESENT

je	**plais**
tu	**plais**
il/elle/on	**plaît**
nous	**plaisons**
vous	**plaisez**
ils/elles	**plaisent**

PRESENT SUBJUNCTIVE

je	**plaise**
tu	**plaises**
il/elle/on	**plaise**
nous	**plaisions**
vous	**plaisiez**
ils/elles	**plaisent**

PERFECT

j'	**ai plu**
tu	**as plu**
il/elle/on	**a plu**
nous	**avons plu**
vous	**avez plu**
ils/elles	**ont plu**

IMPERFECT

je	**plaisais**
tu	**plaisais**
il/elle/on	**plaisait**
nous	**plaisions**
vous	**plaisiez**
ils/elles	**plaisaient**

FUTURE

je	**plairai**
tu	**plairas**
il/elle/on	**plaira**
nous	**plairons**
vous	**plairez**
ils/elles	**plairont**

CONDITIONAL

je	**plairais**
tu	**plairais**
il/elle/on	**plairait**
nous	**plairions**
vous	**plairiez**
ils/elles	**plairaient**

IMPERATIVE
plais / plaisons / plaisez

PAST PARTICIPLE
plu

PRESENT PARTICIPLE
plaisant

EXAMPLE PHRASES

Le menu ne me **plaît** pas. *I don't like the menu.*

Ça te **plairait** d'aller à la mer? *Would you like to go to the seaside?*

Ça t'**a plu**, le film? *Did you like the film?*

Passe-moi le sel, s'il te **plaît**. *Pass me the salt, please.*

L'addition, s'il vous **plaît**! *Can we have the bill, please?*

je/j' = I **tu** = you **il** = he/it **elle** = she/it **on** = we/one **nous** = we **vous** = you **ils/elles** = they

pleuvoir (to rain)

PRESENT
   il **pleut**

PRESENT SUBJUNCTIVE
   il **pleuve**

PERFECT
   il **a plu**

IMPERFECT
   il **pleuvait**

FUTURE
   il **pleuvra**

CONDITIONAL
   il **pleuvrait**

IMPERATIVE
not used

PAST PARTICIPLE
plu

PRESENT PARTICIPLE
pleuvant

EXAMPLE PHRASES

Il **a plu** toute la journée. *It rained all day long.*

Il **pleut** beaucoup à Glasgow. *It rains a lot in Glasgow.*

J'espère qu'il ne **pleuvra** pas demain. *I hope it won't rain tomorrow.*

---

je/j' = I **tu** = you **il** = he/it **elle** = she/it **on** = we/one **nous** = we **vous** = you **ils/elles** = they

pouvoir (to be able)

PRESENT

je	**peux**
tu	**peux**
il/elle/on	**peut**
nous	**pouvons**
vous	**pouvez**
ils/elles	**peuvent**

PRESENT SUBJUNCTIVE

je	**puisse**
tu	**puisses**
il/elle/on	**puisse**
nous	**puissions**
vous	**puissiez**
ils/elles	**puissent**

PERFECT

j'	**ai pu**
tu	**as pu**
il/elle/on	**a pu**
nous	**avons pu**
vous	**avez pu**
ils/elles	**ont pu**

IMPERFECT

je	**pouvais**
tu	**pouvais**
il/elle/on	**pouvait**
nous	**pouvions**
vous	**pouviez**
ils/elles	**pouvaient**

FUTURE

je	**pourrai**
tu	**pourras**
il/elle/on	**pourra**
nous	**pourrons**
vous	**pourrez**
ils/elles	**pourront**

CONDITIONAL

je	**pourrais**
tu	**pourrais**
il/elle/on	**pourrait**
nous	**pourrions**
vous	**pourriez**
ils/elles	**pourraient**

IMPERATIVE
not used

PAST PARTICIPLE
pu

PRESENT PARTICIPLE
pouvant

EXAMPLE PHRASES

Je **peux** t'aider, si tu veux. *I can help you if you like.*

J'ai fait tout ce que j'**ai pu**. *I did all I could.*

Je ne **pourrai** pas venir samedi. *I won't be able to come on Saturday.*

---

je/j' = I **tu** = you **il** = he/it **elle** = she/it **on** = we/one **nous** = we **vous** = you **ils/elles** = they

prendre (to take)

PRESENT

je	**prends**
tu	**prends**
il/elle/on	**prend**
nous	**prenons**
vous	**prenez**
ils/elles	**prennent**

PRESENT SUBJUNCTIVE

je	**prenne**
tu	**prennes**
il/elle/on	**prenne**
nous	**prenions**
vous	**preniez**
ils/elles	**prennent**

PERFECT

j'	**ai pris**
tu	**as pris**
il/elle/on	**a pris**
nous	**avons pris**
vous	**avez pris**
ils/elles	**ont pris**

IMPERFECT

je	**prenais**
tu	**prenais**
il/elle/on	**prenait**
nous	**prenions**
vous	**preniez**
ils/elles	**prenaient**

FUTURE

je	**prendrai**
tu	**prendras**
il/elle/on	**prendra**
nous	**prendrons**
vous	**prendrez**
ils/elles	**prendront**

CONDITIONAL

je	**prendrais**
tu	**prendrais**
il/elle/on	**prendrait**
nous	**prendrions**
vous	**prendriez**
ils/elles	**prendraient**

IMPERATIVE
prends / prenons / prenez

PAST PARTICIPLE
pris

PRESENT PARTICIPLE
prenant

EXAMPLE PHRASES

J'**ai pris** plein de photos. *I took lots of pictures.*

N'oublie pas de **prendre** ton passeport. *Don't forget to take your passport.*

Il **prendra** le train de 8h20. *He'll take the 8.20 train.*

Pour qui est-ce qu'il **se prend**? *Who does he think he is?*

⇨ See pages 88–91 for information on how to form the reflexive verb **se prendre**.

je/j' = I **tu** = you **il** = he/it **elle** = she/it **on** = we/one **nous** = we **vous** = you **ils/elles** = they

protéger (to protect)

PRESENT		PRESENT SUBJUNCTIVE	
je	**protège**	je	**protège**
tu	**protèges**	tu	**protèges**
il/elle/on	**protège**	il/elle/on	**protège**
nous	**protégeons**	nous	**protégions**
vous	**protégez**	vous	**protégiez**
ils/elles	**protègent**	ils/elles	**protègent**

PERFECT		IMPERFECT	
j'	**ai protégé**	je	**protégeais**
tu	**as protégé**	tu	**protégeais**
il/elle/on	**a protégé**	il/elle/on	**protégeait**
nous	**avons protégé**	nous	**protégions**
vous	**avez protégé**	vous	**protégiez**
ils/elles	**ont protégé**	ils/elles	**protégeaient**

FUTURE		CONDITIONAL	
je	**protégerai**	je	**protégerais**
tu	**protégeras**	tu	**protégerais**
il/elle/on	**protégera**	il/elle/on	**protégerait**
nous	**protégerons**	nous	**protégerions**
vous	**protégerez**	vous	**protégeriez**
ils/elles	**protégeront**	ils/elles	**protégeraient**

IMPERATIVE	PAST PARTICIPLE
protège / protégeons / protégez	**protégé**

PRESENT PARTICIPLE
protégeant

EXAMPLE PHRASES

Il **protège** sa petite sœur à l'école. *He protects his little sister at school.*

Protège ton livre de la pluie. *Protect your book from the rain.*

Le champ **est protégé** du vent par la colline. *The field is sheltered from the wind by the hill.*

---

je/j' = I **tu** = you **il** = he/it **elle** = she/it **on** = we/one **nous** = we **vous** = you **ils/elles** = they

recevoir (to receive)

PRESENT
je	**reçois**
tu	**reçois**
il/elle/on	**reçoit**
nous	**recevons**
vous	**recevez**
ils/elles	**reçoivent**

PRESENT SUBJUNCTIVE
je	**reçoive**
tu	**reçoives**
il/elle/on	**reçoive**
nous	**recevions**
vous	**receviez**
ils/elles	**reçoivent**

PERFECT
j'	**ai reçu**
tu	**as reçu**
il/elle/on	**a reçu**
nous	**avons reçu**
vous	**avez reçu**
ils/elles	**ont reçu**

IMPERFECT
je	**recevais**
tu	**recevais**
il/elle/on	**recevait**
nous	**recevions**
vous	**receviez**
ils/elles	**recevaient**

FUTURE
je	**recevrai**
tu	**recevras**
il/elle/on	**recevra**
nous	**recevrons**
vous	**recevrez**
ils/elles	**recevront**

CONDITIONAL
je	**recevrais**
tu	**recevrais**
il/elle/on	**recevrait**
nous	**recevrions**
vous	**recevriez**
ils/elles	**recevraient**

IMPERATIVE
reçois / recevons / recevez

PAST PARTICIPLE
reçu

PRESENT PARTICIPLE
recevant

EXAMPLE PHRASES

Elle **a reçu** une lettre de Charlotte. *She received a letter from Charlotte.*

Je ne **reçois** jamais de courrier. *I never get any mail.*

Elle **recevra** une réponse la semaine prochaine. *She'll get an answer next week.*

---

je/j' = I **tu** = you **il** = he/it **elle** = she/it **on** = we/one **nous** = we **vous** = you **ils/elles** = they

rentrer (to go back; to go in)

PRESENT

je	**rentre**
tu	**rentres**
il/elle/on	**rentre**
nous	**rentrons**
vous	**rentrez**
ils/elles	**rentrent**

PRESENT SUBJUNCTIVE

je	**rentre**
tu	**rentres**
il/elle/on	**rentre**
nous	**rentrions**
vous	**rentriez**
ils/elles	**rentrent**

PERFECT

je	**suis rentré(e)**
tu	**es rentré(e)**
il/elle/on	**est rentré(e)**
nous	**sommes rentré(e)s**
vous	**êtes rentré(e)(s)**
ils/elles	**sont rentré(e)s**

IMPERFECT

je	**rentrais**
tu	**rentrais**
il/elle/on	**rentrait**
nous	**rentrions**
vous	**rentriez**
ils/elles	**rentraient**

FUTURE

je	**rentrerai**
tu	**rentreras**
il/elle/on	**rentrera**
nous	**rentrerons**
vous	**rentrerez**
ils/elles	**rentreront**

CONDITIONAL

je	**rentrerais**
tu	**rentrerais**
il/elle/on	**rentrerait**
nous	**rentrerions**
vous	**rentreriez**
ils/elles	**rentreraient**

IMPERATIVE
rentre / rentrons / rentrez

PAST PARTICIPLE
rentré

PRESENT PARTICIPLE
rentrant

EXAMPLE PHRASES

Ne **rentre** pas trop tard. *Don't come home too late.*

Ils **sont rentrés** dans le magasin. *They went into the shop.*

À quelle heure est-ce qu'elle **est rentrée**? *What time did she get in?*

Je **rentre** déjeuner à midi. *I go home for lunch.*

Il **a** déjà **rentré** la voiture dans le garage. *He's already put the car in the garage.*

i Note that **rentrer** takes **avoir** in the perfect tense when it is used with a direct object; see page 114.

répondre (to answer)

PRESENT

je	**réponds**
tu	**réponds**
il/elle/on	**répond**
nous	**répondons**
vous	**répondez**
ils/elles	**répondent**

PRESENT SUBJUNCTIVE

je	**réponde**
tu	**répondes**
il/elle/on	**réponde**
nous	**répondions**
vous	**répondiez**
ils/elles	**répondent**

PERFECT

j'	**ai répondu**
tu	**as répondu**
il/elle/on	**a répondu**
nous	**avons répondu**
vous	**avez répondu**
ils/elles	**ont répondu**

IMPERFECT

je	**répondais**
tu	**répondais**
il/elle/on	**répondait**
nous	**répondions**
vous	**répondiez**
ils/elles	**répondaient**

FUTURE

je	**répondrai**
tu	**répondras**
il/elle/on	**répondra**
nous	**répondrons**
vous	**répondrez**
ils/elles	**répondront**

CONDITIONAL

je	**répondrais**
tu	**répondrais**
il/elle/on	**répondrait**
nous	**répondrions**
vous	**répondriez**
ils/elles	**répondraient**

IMPERATIVE
réponds / répondons / répondez

PAST PARTICIPLE
répondu

PRESENT PARTICIPLE
répondant

EXAMPLE PHRASES

Lisez le texte et **répondez** aux questions. *Read the passage and answer the questions.*

C'est elle qui **a répondu** au téléphone. *She answered the phone.*

Ça ne **répond** pas. *There's no reply.*

je/j' = I **tu** = you **il** = he/it **elle** = she/it **on** = we/one **nous** = we **vous** = you **ils/elles** = they

résoudre (to solve)

PRESENT

je	**résous**
tu	**résous**
il/elle/on	**résout**
nous	**résolvons**
vous	**résolvez**
ils/elles	**résolvent**

PRESENT SUBJUNCTIVE

je	**résolve**
tu	**résolves**
il/elle/on	**résolve**
nous	**résolvions**
vous	**résolviez**
ils/elles	**résolvent**

PERFECT

j'	**ai résolu**
tu	**as résolu**
il/elle/on	**a résolu**
nous	**avons résolu**
vous	**avez résolu**
ils/elles	**ont résolu**

IMPERFECT

je	**résolvais**
tu	**résolvais**
il/elle/on	**résolvait**
nous	**résolvions**
vous	**résolviez**
ils/elles	**résolvaient**

FUTURE

je	**résoudrai**
tu	**résoudras**
il/elle/on	**résoudra**
nous	**résoudrons**
vous	**résoudrez**
ils/elles	**résoudront**

CONDITIONAL

je	**résoudrais**
tu	**résoudrais**
il/elle/on	**résoudrait**
nous	**résoudrions**
vous	**résoudriez**
ils/elles	**résoudraient**

IMPERATIVE
résous / résolvons / résolvez

PAST PARTICIPLE
résolu

PRESENT PARTICIPLE
résolvant

EXAMPLE PHRASES

J'**ai résolu** le problème. *I've solved the problem.*

La violence ne **résout** rien. *Violence doesn't solve anything.*

je/j' = I **tu** = you **il** = he/it **elle** = she/it **on** = we/one **nous** = we **vous** = you **ils/elles** = they

rester (to remain)

PRESENT

je	**reste**
tu	**restes**
il/elle/on	**reste**
nous	**restons**
vous	**restez**
ils/elles	**restent**

PRESENT SUBJUNCTIVE

je	**reste**
tu	**restes**
il/elle/on	**reste**
nous	**restions**
vous	**restiez**
ils/elles	**restent**

PERFECT

je	**suis resté(e)**
tu	**es resté(e)**
il/elle/on	**est resté(e)**
nous	**sommes resté(e)s**
vous	**êtes resté(e)(s)**
ils/elles	**sont resté(e)s**

IMPERFECT

je	**restais**
tu	**restais**
il/elle/on	**restait**
nous	**restions**
vous	**restiez**
ils/elles	**restaient**

FUTURE

je	**resterai**
tu	**resteras**
il/elle/on	**restera**
nous	**resterons**
vous	**resterez**
ils/elles	**resteront**

CONDITIONAL

je	**resterais**
tu	**resterais**
il/elle/on	**resterait**
nous	**resterions**
vous	**resteriez**
ils/elles	**resteraient**

IMPERATIVE
reste / restons / restez

PAST PARTICIPLE
resté

PRESENT PARTICIPLE
restant

EXAMPLE PHRASES

Cet été, je **reste** en Écosse. *I'm staying in Scotland this summer.*

Ils ne **sont** pas **restés** très longtemps. *They didn't stay very long.*

Il leur **restait** encore un peu d'argent. *They still had some money left.*

---

je/j' = I **tu** = you **il** = he/it **elle** = she/it **on** = we/one **nous** = we **vous** = you **ils/elles** = they

retourner (to go back; to turn)

PRESENT

je	retourne
tu	retournes
il/elle/on	retourne
nous	retournons
vous	retournez
ils/elles	retournent

PRESENT SUBJUNCTIVE

je	retourne
tu	retournes
il/elle/on	retourne
nous	retournions
vous	retourniez
ils/elles	retournent

PERFECT

je	suis retourné(e)
tu	es retourné(e)
il/elle/on	est retourné(e)
nous	sommes retourné(e)s
vous	êtes retourné(e)(s)
ils/elles	sont retourné(e)s

IMPERFECT

je	retournais
tu	retournais
il/elle/on	retournait
nous	retournions
vous	retourniez
ils/elles	retournaient

FUTURE

je	retournerai
tu	retourneras
il/elle/on	retournera
nous	retournerons
vous	retournerez
ils/elles	retourneront

CONDITIONAL

je	retournerais
tu	retournerais
il/elle/on	retournerait
nous	retournerions
vous	retourneriez
ils/elles	retourneraient

IMPERATIVE
retourne / retournons / retournez

PAST PARTICIPLE
retourné

PRESENT PARTICIPLE
retournant

EXAMPLE PHRASES

Est-ce que tu **es retournée** à Londres? *Have you been back to London?*
J'aimerais bien **retourner** en Italie un jour. *I'd like to go back to Italy one day.*
Elle **a retourné** la carte pour vérifier. *She turned the card over to check.*
Zoë, **retourne-toi**! *Turn around Zoë!*

i Note that **retourner** takes **avoir** in the perfect tense when it is used with a direct object; see page 114.

➪ See pages 88–91 for information on how to form the reflexive verb **se retourner**.

revenir (to come back)

PRESENT

je	**reviens**
tu	**reviens**
il/elle/on	**revient**
nous	**revenons**
vous	**revenez**
ils/elles	**reviennent**

PRESENT SUBJUNCTIVE

je	**revienne**
tu	**reviennes**
il/elle/on	**revienne**
nous	**revenions**
vous	**reveniez**
ils/elles	**reviennent**

PERFECT

je	**suis revenu(e)**
tu	**es revenu(e)**
il/elle/on	**est revenu(e)**
nous	**sommes revenu(e)s**
vous	**êtes revenu(e)(s)**
ils/elles	**sont revenu(e)s**

IMPERFECT

je	**revenais**
tu	**revenais**
il/elle/on	**revenait**
nous	**revenions**
vous	**reveniez**
ils/elles	**revenaient**

FUTURE

je	**reviendrai**
tu	**reviendras**
il/elle/on	**reviendra**
nous	**reviendrons**
vous	**reviendrez**
ils/elles	**reviendront**

CONDITIONAL

je	**reviendrais**
tu	**reviendrais**
il/elle/on	**reviendrait**
nous	**reviendrions**
vous	**reviendriez**
ils/elles	**reviendraient**

IMPERATIVE
reviens / revenons / revenez

PAST PARTICIPLE
revenu

PRESENT PARTICIPLE
revenant

EXAMPLE PHRASES

Mon chat n'**est** toujours pas **revenu**. *My cat still hasn't come back.*

Je **reviens** dans cinq minutes! *I'll be back in five minutes!*

Ça me **revient**! *It's coming back to me now!*

---

je/j' = I **tu** = you **il** = he/it **elle** = she/it **on** = we/one **nous** = we **vous** = you **ils/elles** = they

rire (to laugh)

PRESENT

je	**ris**
tu	**ris**
il/elle/on	**rit**
nous	**rions**
vous	**riez**
ils/elles	**rient**

PRESENT SUBJUNCTIVE

je	**rie**
tu	**ries**
il/elle/on	**rie**
nous	**riions**
vous	**riiez**
ils/elles	**rient**

PERFECT

j'	**ai ri**
tu	**as ri**
il/elle/on	**a ri**
nous	**avons ri**
vous	**avez ri**
ils/elles	**ont ri**

IMPERFECT

je	**riais**
tu	**riais**
il/elle/on	**riait**
nous	**riions**
vous	**riiez**
ils/elles	**riaient**

FUTURE

je	**rirai**
tu	**riras**
il/elle/on	**rira**
nous	**rirons**
vous	**rirez**
ils/elles	**riront**

CONDITIONAL

je	**rirais**
tu	**rirais**
il/elle/on	**rirait**
nous	**ririons**
vous	**ririez**
ils/elles	**riraient**

IMPERATIVE
ris / rions / riez

PAST PARTICIPLE
ri

PRESENT PARTICIPLE
riant

EXAMPLE PHRASES

On **a** bien **ri**. *We had a good laugh.*

Ne **ris** pas, ce n'est pas drôle! *Don't laugh, it's not funny!*

C'était juste pour **rire**. *It was only for a laugh.*

rompre (to break)

PRESENT

je	romps
tu	romps
il/elle/on	rompt
nous	rompons
vous	rompez
ils/elles	rompent

PRESENT SUBJUNCTIVE

je	rompe
tu	rompes
il/elle/on	rompe
nous	rompions
vous	rompiez
ils/elles	rompent

PERFECT

j'	ai rompu
tu	as rompu
il/elle/on	a rompu
nous	avons rompu
vous	avez rompu
ils/elles	ont rompu

IMPERFECT

je	rompais
tu	rompais
il/elle/on	rompait
nous	rompions
vous	rompiez
ils/elles	rompaient

FUTURE

je	romprai
tu	rompras
il/elle/on	rompra
nous	romprons
vous	romprez
ils/elles	rompront

CONDITIONAL

je	romprais
tu	romprais
il/elle/on	romprait
nous	romprions
vous	rompriez
ils/elles	rompraient

IMPERATIVE
romps / rompons / rompez

PAST PARTICIPLE
rompu

PRESENT PARTICIPLE
rompant

EXAMPLE PHRASES

Elle **a rompu** le silence. *She broke the silence.*
Paul et Jo **ont rompu**. *Paul and Jo have split up.*

savoir (to know)

PRESENT

je	**sais**
tu	**sais**
il/elle/on	**sait**
nous	**savons**
vous	**savez**
ils/elles	**savent**

PRESENT SUBJUNCTIVE

je	**sache**
tu	**saches**
il/elle/on	**sache**
nous	**sachions**
vous	**sachiez**
ils/elles	**sachent**

PERFECT

j'	**ai su**
tu	**as su**
il/elle/on	**a su**
nous	**avons su**
vous	**avez su**
ils/elles	**ont su**

IMPERFECT

je	**savais**
tu	**savais**
il/elle/on	**savait**
nous	**savions**
vous	**saviez**
ils/elles	**savaient**

FUTURE

je	**saurai**
tu	**sauras**
il/elle/on	**saura**
nous	**saurons**
vous	**saurez**
ils/elles	**sauront**

CONDITIONAL

je	**saurais**
tu	**saurais**
il/elle/on	**saurait**
nous	**saurions**
vous	**sauriez**
ils/elles	**sauraient**

IMPERATIVE
sache / sachons / sachez

PAST PARTICIPLE
su

PRESENT PARTICIPLE
sachant

EXAMPLE PHRASES

Tu **sais** ce que tu vas faire l'année prochaine? *Do you know what you're doing next year?*

Je ne **sais** pas. *I don't know.*

Elle ne **sait** pas nager. *She can't swim.*

Tu **savais** que son père était pakistanais? *Did you know her father was Pakistani?*

je/j' = I **tu** = you **il** = he/it **elle** = she/it **on** = we/one **nous** = we **vous** = you **ils/elles** = they

sentir (to smell; to feel)

PRESENT
je	**sens**
tu	**sens**
il/elle/on	**sent**
nous	**sentons**
vous	**sentez**
ils/elles	**sentent**

PRESENT SUBJUNCTIVE
je	**sente**
tu	**sentes**
il/elle/on	**sente**
nous	**sentions**
vous	**sentiez**
ils/elles	**sentent**

PERFECT
j'	**ai senti**
tu	**as senti**
il/elle/on	**a senti**
nous	**avons senti**
vous	**avez senti**
ils/elles	**ont senti**

IMPERFECT
je	**sentais**
tu	**sentais**
il/elle/on	**sentait**
nous	**sentions**
vous	**sentiez**
ils/elles	**sentaient**

FUTURE
je	**sentirai**
tu	**sentiras**
il/elle/on	**sentira**
nous	**sentirons**
vous	**sentirez**
ils/elles	**sentiront**

CONDITIONAL
je	**sentirais**
tu	**sentirais**
il/elle/on	**sentirait**
nous	**sentirions**
vous	**sentiriez**
ils/elles	**sentiraient**

IMPERATIVE
sens / sentons / sentez

PAST PARTICIPLE
senti

PRESENT PARTICIPLE
sentant

EXAMPLE PHRASES
Ça **sentait** mauvais. *It smelt bad.*
Je n'**ai** rien **senti**. *I didn't feel a thing.*
Elle ne **se sent** pas bien. *She's not feeling well.*

⇨ See pages 88–91 for information on how to form the reflexive verb **se sentir**.

je/j' = I **tu** = you **il** = he/it **elle** = she/it **on** = we/one **nous** = we **vous** = you **ils/elles** = they

servir (to serve)

PRESENT

je	sers
tu	sers
il/elle/on	sert
nous	servons
vous	servez
ils/elles	servent

PRESENT SUBJUNCTIVE

je	serve
tu	serves
il/elle/on	serve
nous	servions
vous	serviez
ils/elles	servent

PERFECT

j'	ai servi
tu	as servi
il/elle/on	a servi
nous	avons servi
vous	avez servi
ils/elles	ont servi

IMPERFECT

je	servais
tu	servais
il/elle/on	servait
nous	servions
vous	serviez
ils/elles	servaient

FUTURE

je	servirai
tu	serviras
il/elle/on	servira
nous	servirons
vous	servirez
ils/elles	serviront

CONDITIONAL

je	servirais
tu	servirais
il/elle/on	servirait
nous	servirions
vous	serviriez
ils/elles	serviraient

IMPERATIVE
sers / servons / servez

PAST PARTICIPLE
servi

PRESENT PARTICIPLE
servant

EXAMPLE PHRASES

On vous **sert**? *Are you being served?*

Ça **sert** à quoi ce bouton? *What is this button for?*

Servez-vous en viande. *Help yourself to meat.*

⇨ See pages 88–91 for information on how to form the reflexive verb **se servir**.

je/j' = I **tu** = you **il** = he/it **elle** = she/it **on** = we/one **nous** = we **vous** = you **ils/elles** = they

sortir (to go out)

PRESENT		**PRESENT SUBJUNCTIVE**	
je	**sors**	je	**sorte**
tu	**sors**	tu	**sortes**
il/elle/on	**sort**	il/elle/on	**sorte**
nous	**sortons**	nous	**sortions**
vous	**sortez**	vous	**sortiez**
ils/elles	**sortent**	ils/elles	**sortent**

PERFECT		**IMPERFECT**	
je	**suis sorti(e)**	je	**sortais**
tu	**es sorti(e)**	tu	**sortais**
il/elle/on	**est sorti(e)**	il/elle/on	**sortait**
nous	**sommes sorti(e)s**	nous	**sortions**
vous	**êtes sorti(e)(s)**	vous	**sortiez**
ils/elles	**sont sorti(e)s**	ils/elles	**sortaient**

FUTURE		**CONDITIONAL**	
je	**sortirai**	je	**sortirais**
tu	**sortiras**	tu	**sortirais**
il/elle/on	**sortira**	il/elle/on	**sortirait**
nous	**sortirons**	nous	**sortirions**
vous	**sortirez**	vous	**sortiriez**
ils/elles	**sortiront**	ils/elles	**sortiraient**

IMPERATIVE
sors / sortons / sortez

PAST PARTICIPLE
sorti

PRESENT PARTICIPLE
sortant

EXAMPLE PHRASES

Je ne **suis** pas **sortie** ce week-end. *I didn't go out this weekend.*

Aurélie **sort** avec Bruno. *Aurélie is going out with Bruno.*

Elle **est sortie** de l'hôpital hier. *She came out of hospital yesterday.*

Je n'**ai** pas **sorti** le chien parce qu'il pleuvait. *I didn't take the dog out for a walk because it was raining.*

ⓘ Note that **sortir** takes **avoir** in the perfect tense when it is used with a direct object; see page 114.

suffire (to be enough)

PRESENT

je	**suffis**
tu	**suffis**
il/elle/on	**suffit**
nous	**suffisons**
vous	**suffisez**
ils/elles	**suffisent**

PRESENT SUBJUNCTIVE

je	**suffise**
tu	**suffises**
il/elle/on	**suffise**
nous	**suffisions**
vous	**suffisiez**
ils/elles	**suffisent**

PERFECT

j'	**ai suffi**
tu	**as suffi**
il/elle/on	**a suffi**
nous	**avons suffi**
vous	**avez suffi**
ils/elles	**ont suffi**

IMPERFECT

je	**suffisais**
tu	**suffisais**
il/elle/on	**suffisait**
nous	**suffisions**
vous	**suffisiez**
ils/elles	**suffisaient**

FUTURE

je	**suffirai**
tu	**suffiras**
il/elle/on	**suffira**
nous	**suffirons**
vous	**suffirez**
ils/elles	**suffiront**

CONDITIONAL

je	**suffirais**
tu	**suffirais**
il/elle/on	**suffirait**
nous	**suffirions**
vous	**suffiriez**
ils/elles	**suffiraient**

IMPERATIVE
suffis / suffisons / suffisez

PAST PARTICIPLE
suffi

PRESENT PARTICIPLE
suffisant

EXAMPLE PHRASES

Ça te **suffira**, 10 euros? *Will 10 euros be enough?*
Ça **suffit**! *That's enough!*
Il **suffisait** de me le demander. *You only had to ask.*

je/j' = I tu = you il = he/it elle = she/it on = we/one nous = we vous = you ils/elles = they

suivre (to follow)

PRESENT

je	**suis**
tu	**suis**
il/elle/on	**suit**
nous	**suivons**
vous	**suivez**
ils/elles	**suivent**

PRESENT SUBJUNCTIVE

je	**suive**
tu	**suives**
il/elle/on	**suive**
nous	**suivions**
vous	**suiviez**
ils/elles	**suivent**

PERFECT

j'	**ai suivi**
tu	**as suivi**
il/elle/on	**a suivi**
nous	**avons suivi**
vous	**avez suivi**
ils/elles	**ont suivi**

IMPERFECT

je	**suivais**
tu	**suivais**
il/elle/on	**suivait**
nous	**suivions**
vous	**suiviez**
ils/elles	**suivaient**

FUTURE

je	**suivrai**
tu	**suivras**
il/elle/on	**suivra**
nous	**suivrons**
vous	**suivrez**
ils/elles	**suivront**

CONDITIONAL

je	**suivrais**
tu	**suivrais**
il/elle/on	**suivrait**
nous	**suivrions**
vous	**suivriez**
ils/elles	**suivraient**

IMPERATIVE
suis / suivons / suivez

PAST PARTICIPLE
suivi

PRESENT PARTICIPLE
suivant

EXAMPLE PHRASES

Mon chat me **suit** partout dans la maison. *My cat follows me everywhere around the house.*
Il **a suivi** un cours d'allemand pendant six mois. *He did a German course for 6 months.*
Elles n'arrivent pas à **suivre** en maths. *They can't keep up in maths.*

se taire (to stop talking)

	PRESENT		PRESENT SUBJUNCTIVE
je	**me tais**	je	**me taise**
tu	**te tais**	tu	**te taises**
il/elle/on	**se tait**	il/elle/on	**se taise**
nous	**nous taisons**	nous	**nous taisions**
vous	**vous taisez**	vous	**vous taisiez**
ils/elles	**se taisent**	ils/elles	**se taisent**

	PERFECT		IMPERFECT
je	**me suis tu(e)**	je	**me taisais**
tu	**t'es tu(e)**	tu	**te taisais**
il/elle/on	**s'est tu(e)**	il/elle/on	**se taisait**
nous	**nous sommes tu(e)s**	nous	**nous taisions**
vous	**vous êtes tu(e)(s)**	vous	**vous taisiez**
ils/elles	**se sont tu(e)s**	ils/elles	**se taisaient**

	FUTURE		CONDITIONAL
je	**me tairai**	je	**me tairais**
tu	**te tairas**	tu	**te tairais**
il/elle/on	**se taira**	il/elle/on	**se tairait**
nous	**nous tairons**	nous	**nous tairions**
vous	**vous tairez**	vous	**vous tairiez**
ils/elles	**se tairont**	ils/elles	**se tairaient**

IMPERATIVE
tais-toi / taisons-nous / taisez-vous

PAST PARTICIPLE
tu

PRESENT PARTICIPLE
se taisant

EXAMPLE PHRASES

Il **s'est tu**. *He stopped talking.*
Taisez-vous! *Be quiet!*
Sophie, **tais-toi**! *Be quiet Sophie!*

tenir (to hold)

PRESENT

je	**tiens**
tu	**tiens**
il/elle/on	**tient**
nous	**tenons**
vous	**tenez**
ils/elles	**tiennent**

PRESENT SUBJUNCTIVE

je	**tienne**
tu	**tiennes**
il/elle/on	**tienne**
nous	**tenions**
vous	**teniez**
ils/elles	**tiennent**

PERFECT

j'	**ai tenu**
tu	**as tenu**
il/elle/on	**a tenu**
nous	**avons tenu**
vous	**avez tenu**
ils/elles	**ont tenu**

IMPERFECT

je	**tenais**
tu	**tenais**
il/elle/on	**tenait**
nous	**tenions**
vous	**teniez**
ils/elles	**tenaient**

FUTURE

je	**tiendrai**
tu	**tiendras**
il/elle/on	**tiendra**
nous	**tiendrons**
vous	**tiendrez**
ils/elles	**tiendront**

CONDITIONAL

je	**tiendrais**
tu	**tiendrais**
il/elle/on	**tiendrait**
nous	**tiendrions**
vous	**tiendriez**
ils/elles	**tiendraient**

IMPERATIVE
tiens / tenons / tenez

PAST PARTICIPLE
tenu

PRESENT PARTICIPLE
tenant

EXAMPLE PHRASES

Tiens-moi la main. *Hold my hand.*

Elle **tenait** beaucoup à son chat. *She was really attached to her cat.*

Tiens, prends mon portable si tu veux appeler chez toi. *Here, have my mobile if you want to call home.*

Tiens-toi droit! *Sit up straight!*

⇨ See pages 88–91 for information on how to form the reflexive verb **se tenir**.

je/j' = I **tu** = you **il** = he/it **elle** = she/it **on** = we/one **nous** = we **vous** = you **ils/elles** = they

tomber (to fall)

PRESENT

je	**tombe**
tu	**tombes**
il/elle/on	**tombe**
nous	**tombons**
vous	**tombez**
ils/elles	**tombent**

PRESENT SUBJUNCTIVE

je	**tombe**
tu	**tombes**
il/elle/on	**tombe**
nous	**tombions**
vous	**tombiez**
ils/elles	**tombent**

PERFECT

je	**suis tombé(e)**
tu	**es tombé(e)**
il/elle/on	**est tombé(e)**
nous	**sommes tombé(e)s**
vous	**êtes tombé(e)(s)**
ils/elles	**sont tombé(e)s**

IMPERFECT

je	**tombais**
tu	**tombais**
il/elle/on	**tombait**
nous	**tombions**
vous	**tombiez**
ils/elles	**tombaient**

FUTURE

je	**tomberai**
tu	**tomberas**
il/elle/on	**tombera**
nous	**tomberons**
vous	**tomberez**
ils/elles	**tomberont**

CONDITIONAL

je	**tomberais**
tu	**tomberais**
il/elle/on	**tomberait**
nous	**tomberions**
vous	**tomberiez**
ils/elles	**tomberaient**

IMPERATIVE
tombe / tombons / tombez

PAST PARTICIPLE
tombé

PRESENT PARTICIPLE
tombant

EXAMPLE PHRASES

Attention, tu vas **tomber**! *Be careful, you'll fall!*

Nicole **est tombée** de son cheval. *Nicole fell off her horse.*

Elle s'est fait mal en **tombant** dans l'escalier. *She hurt herself falling down the stairs.*

je/j' = I **tu** = you **il** = he/it **elle** = she/it **on** = we/one **nous** = we **vous** = you **ils/elles** = they

traire (to milk)

PRESENT		PRESENT SUBJUNCTIVE	
je	**trais**	je	**traie**
tu	**trais**	tu	**traies**
il/elle/on	**trait**	il/elle/on	**traie**
nous	**trayons**	nous	**trayions**
vous	**trayez**	vous	**trayiez**
ils/elles	**traient**	ils/elles	**traient**

PERFECT		IMPERFECT	
j'	**ai trait**	je	**trayais**
tu	**as trait**	tu	**trayais**
il/elle/on	**a trait**	il/elle/on	**trayait**
nous	**avons trait**	nous	**trayions**
vous	**avez trait**	vous	**trayiez**
ils/elles	**ont trait**	ils/elles	**trayaient**

FUTURE		CONDITIONAL	
je	**trairai**	je	**trairais**
tu	**trairas**	tu	**trairais**
il/elle/on	**traira**	il/elle/on	**trairait**
nous	**trairons**	nous	**trairions**
vous	**trairez**	vous	**trairiez**
ils/elles	**trairont**	ils/elles	**trairaient**

IMPERATIVE
trais / trayons / trayez

PAST PARTICIPLE
trait

PRESENT PARTICIPLE
trayant

EXAMPLE PHRASES

À la ferme, on a appris à **traire** les vaches. *We learnt to milk cows on the farm.*
Elle **trait** les vaches à six heures du matin. *She milks the cows at 6 am.*

vaincre (to defeat)

PRESENT

je	vaincs
tu	vaincs
il/elle/on	vainc
nous	vainquons
vous	vainquez
ils/elles	vainquent

PRESENT SUBJUNCTIVE

je	vainque
tu	vainques
il/elle/on	vainque
nous	vainquions
vous	vainquiez
ils/elles	vainquent

PERFECT

j'	ai vaincu
tu	as vaincu
il/elle/on	a vaincu
nous	avons vaincu
vous	avez vaincu
ils/elles	ont vaincu

IMPERFECT

je	vainquais
tu	vainquais
il/elle/on	vainquait
nous	vainquions
vous	vainquiez
ils/elles	vainquaient

FUTURE

je	vaincrai
tu	vaincras
il/elle/on	vaincra
nous	vaincrons
vous	vaincrez
ils/elles	vaincront

CONDITIONAL

je	vaincrais
tu	vaincrais
il/elle/on	vaincrait
nous	vaincrions
vous	vaincriez
ils/elles	vaincraient

IMPERATIVE
vaincs / vainquons / vainquez

PAST PARTICIPLE
vaincu

PRESENT PARTICIPLE
vainquant

EXAMPLE PHRASES

L'armée **a été vaincue**. *The army was defeated.*
La France **a vaincu** la Corée trois buts à deux. *France beat Korea 3 goals to 2.*

je/j' = I **tu** = you **il** = he/it **elle** = she/it **on** = we/one **nous** = we **vous** = you **ils/elles** = they

valoir (to be worth)

PRESENT

je	**vaux**
tu	**vaux**
il/elle/on	**vaut**
nous	**valons**
vous	**valez**
ils/elles	**valent**

PRESENT SUBJUNCTIVE

je	**vaille**
tu	**vailles**
il/elle/on	**vaille**
nous	**valions**
vous	**valiez**
ils/elles	**vaillent**

PERFECT

j'	**ai valu**
tu	**as valu**
il/elle/on	**a valu**
nous	**avons valu**
vous	**avez valu**
ils/elles	**ont valu**

IMPERFECT

je	**valais**
tu	**valais**
il/elle/on	**valait**
nous	**valions**
vous	**valiez**
ils/elles	**valaient**

FUTURE

je	**vaudrai**
tu	**vaudras**
il/elle/on	**vaudra**
nous	**vaudrons**
vous	**vaudrez**
ils/elles	**vaudront**

CONDITIONAL

je	**vaudrais**
tu	**vaudrais**
il/elle/on	**vaudrait**
nous	**vaudrions**
vous	**vaudriez**
ils/elles	**vaudraient**

IMPERATIVE
vaux / valons / valez

PAST PARTICIPLE
valu

PRESENT PARTICIPLE
valant

EXAMPLE PHRASES

Ça **vaut** combien? *How much is it worth?*

Ça **vaudrait** la peine d'essayer. *It would be worth a try.*

Il **vaut** mieux ne pas y penser. *It's best not to think about it.*

---

je/j' = I **tu** = you **il** = he/it **elle** = she/it **on** = we/one **nous** = we **vous** = you **ils/elles** = they

vendre (to sell)

PRESENT
je	vends
tu	vends
il/elle/on	vend
nous	vendons
vous	vendez
ils/elles	vendent

PRESENT SUBJUNCTIVE
je	vende
tu	vendes
il/elle/on	vende
nous	vendions
vous	vendiez
ils/elles	vendent

PERFECT
j'	ai vendu
tu	as vendu
il/elle/on	a vendu
nous	avons vendu
vous	avez vendu
ils/elles	ont vendu

IMPERFECT
je	vendais
tu	vendais
il/elle/on	vendait
nous	vendions
vous	vendiez
ils/elles	vendaient

FUTURE
je	vendrai
tu	vendras
il/elle/on	vendra
nous	vendrons
vous	vendrez
ils/elles	vendront

CONDITIONAL
je	vendrais
tu	vendrais
il/elle/on	vendrait
nous	vendrions
vous	vendriez
ils/elles	vendraient

IMPERATIVE
vends / vendons / vendez

PAST PARTICIPLE
vendu

PRESENT PARTICIPLE
vendant

EXAMPLE PHRASES

Il m'**a vendu** son vélo pour 50 euros. *He sold me his bike for 50 euros.*
Est-ce que vous **vendez** des cartes SIM? *Do you sell SIM cards?*
Elle voudrait **vendre** sa voiture. *She would like to sell her car.*

venir (to come)

PRESENT

je	**viens**
tu	**viens**
il/elle/on	**vient**
nous	**venons**
vous	**venez**
ils/elles	**viennent**

PRESENT SUBJUNCTIVE

je	**vienne**
tu	**viennes**
il/elle/on	**vienne**
nous	**venions**
vous	**veniez**
ils/elles	**viennent**

PERFECT

je	**suis venu(e)**
tu	**es venu(e)**
il/elle/on	**est venu(e)**
nous	**sommes venu(e)s**
vous	**êtes venu(e)(s)**
ils/elles	**sont venu(e)s**

IMPERFECT

je	**venais**
tu	**venais**
il/elle/on	**venait**
nous	**venions**
vous	**veniez**
ils/elles	**venaient**

FUTURE

je	**viendrai**
tu	**viendras**
il/elle/on	**viendra**
nous	**viendrons**
vous	**viendrez**
ils/elles	**viendront**

CONDITIONAL

je	**viendrais**
tu	**viendrais**
il/elle/on	**viendrait**
nous	**viendrions**
vous	**viendriez**
ils/elles	**viendraient**

IMPERATIVE
viens / venons / venez

PAST PARTICIPLE
venu

PRESENT PARTICIPLE
venant

EXAMPLE PHRASES

Elle ne **viendra** pas cette année. *She won't be coming this year.*

Fatou et Malik **viennent** du Sénégal. *Fatou and Malik come from Senegal.*

Je **viens** de manger. *I've just eaten.*

---

je/j' = I **tu** = you **il** = he/it **elle** = she/it **on** = we/one **nous** = we **vous** = you **ils/elles** = they

vêtir (to dress)

PRESENT

je	vêts
tu	vêts
il/elle/on	vêt
nous	vêtons
vous	vêtez
ils/elles	vêtent

PRESENT SUBJUNCTIVE

je	vête
tu	vêtes
il/elle/on	vête
nous	vêtions
vous	vêtiez
ils/elles	vêtent

PERFECT

j'	ai vêtu
tu	as vêtu
il/elle/on	a vêtu
nous	avons vêtu
vous	avez vêtu
ils/elles	ont vêtu

IMPERFECT

je	vêtais
tu	vêtais
il/elle/on	vêtait
nous	vêtions
vous	vêtiez
ils/elles	vêtaient

FUTURE

je	vêtirai
tu	vêtiras
il/elle/on	vêtira
nous	vêtirons
vous	vêtirez
ils/elles	vêtiront

CONDITIONAL

je	vêtirais
tu	vêtirais
il/elle/on	vêtirait
nous	vêtirions
vous	vêtiriez
ils/elles	vêtiraient

IMPERATIVE
vêts / vêtons / vêtez

PAST PARTICIPLE
vêtu

PRESENT PARTICIPLE
vêtant

EXAMPLE PHRASES

Il **était vêtu** d'un pantalon et d'un pull. *He was wearing trousers and a jumper.*

Il faut se lever, se laver et **se vêtir** en 10 minutes. *You have to get up, get washed and get dressed in 10 minutes.*

⇨ See pages 88–91 for information on how to form the reflexive verb **se vêtir**.

je/j' = I **tu** = you **il** = he/it **elle** = she/it **on** = we/one **nous** = we **vous** = you **ils/elles** = they

vivre (to live)

PRESENT

je	**vis**
tu	**vis**
il/elle/on	**vit**
nous	**vivons**
vous	**vivez**
ils/elles	**vivent**

PRESENT SUBJUNCTIVE

je	**vive**
tu	**vives**
il/elle/on	**vive**
nous	**vivions**
vous	**viviez**
ils/elles	**vivent**

PERFECT

j'	**ai vécu**
tu	**as vécu**
il/elle/on	**a vécu**
nous	**avons vécu**
vous	**avez vécu**
ils/elles	**ont vécu**

IMPERFECT

je	**vivais**
tu	**vivais**
il/elle/on	**vivait**
nous	**vivions**
vous	**viviez**
ils/elles	**vivaient**

FUTURE

je	**vivrai**
tu	**vivras**
il/elle/on	**vivra**
nous	**vivrons**
vous	**vivrez**
ils/elles	**vivront**

CONDITIONAL

je	**vivrais**
tu	**vivrais**
il/elle/on	**vivrait**
nous	**vivrions**
vous	**vivriez**
ils/elles	**vivraient**

IMPERATIVE
vis / vivons / vivez

PAST PARTICIPLE
vécu

PRESENT PARTICIPLE
vivant

EXAMPLE PHRASES

Ma sœur **vit** en Espagne. *My sister lives in Spain.*

Il **a vécu** dix ans à Lyon. *He lived in Lyons for 10 years.*

Les gorilles **vivent** surtout dans la forêt. *Gorillas mostly live in the forest.*

je/j' = I **tu** = you **il** = he/it **elle** = she/it **on** = we/one **nous** = we **vous** = you **ils/elles** = they

voir (to see)

PRESENT
je	**vois**
tu	**vois**
il/elle/on	**voit**
nous	**voyons**
vous	**voyez**
ils/elles	**voient**

PRESENT SUBJUNCTIVE
je	**voie**
tu	**voies**
il/elle/on	**voie**
nous	**voyions**
vous	**voyiez**
ils/elles	**voient**

PERFECT
j'	**ai vu**
tu	**as vu**
il/elle/on	**a vu**
nous	**avons vu**
vous	**avez vu**
ils/elles	**ont vu**

IMPERFECT
je	**voyais**
tu	**voyais**
il/elle/on	**voyait**
nous	**voyions**
vous	**voyiez**
ils/elles	**voyaient**

FUTURE
je	**verrai**
tu	**verras**
il/elle/on	**verra**
nous	**verrons**
vous	**verrez**
ils/elles	**verront**

CONDITIONAL
je	**verrais**
tu	**verrais**
il/elle/on	**verrait**
nous	**verrions**
vous	**verriez**
ils/elles	**verraient**

IMPERATIVE
vois / voyons / voyez

PAST PARTICIPLE
vu

PRESENT PARTICIPLE
voyant

EXAMPLE PHRASES

Venez me **voir** quand vous serez à Paris. *Come and see me when you're in Paris.*

Je ne **vois** rien sans mes lunettes. *I can't see anything without my glasses.*

Est-ce que tu l'**as vu**? *Did you see him?* or *Have you seen him?*

Est-ce que cette tache **se voit**? *Does that stain show?*

⇨ See pages 88–91 for information on how to form the reflexive verb **se voir**.

je/j' = I **tu** = you **il** = he/it **elle** = she/it **on** = we/one **nous** = we **vous** = you **ils/elles** = they

vouloir (to want)

PRESENT

je	**veux**
tu	**veux**
il/elle/on	**veut**
nous	**voulons**
vous	**voulez**
ils/elles	**veulent**

PRESENT SUBJUNCTIVE

je	**veuille**
tu	**veuilles**
il/elle/on	**veuille**
nous	**voulions**
vous	**vouliez**
ils/elles	**veuillent**

PERFECT

j'	**ai voulu**
tu	**as voulu**
il/elle/on	**a voulu**
nous	**avons voulu**
vous	**avez voulu**
ils/elles	**ont voulu**

IMPERFECT

je	**voulais**
tu	**voulais**
il/elle/on	**voulait**
nous	**voulions**
vous	**vouliez**
ils/elles	**voulaient**

FUTURE

je	**voudrai**
tu	**voudras**
il/elle/on	**voudra**
nous	**voudrons**
vous	**voudrez**
ils/elles	**voudront**

CONDITIONAL

je	**voudrais**
tu	**voudrais**
il/elle/on	**voudrait**
nous	**voudrions**
vous	**voudriez**
ils/elles	**voudraient**

IMPERATIVE
veuille / veuillons / veuillez

PAST PARTICIPLE
voulu

PRESENT PARTICIPLE
voulant

EXAMPLE PHRASES

Elle **veut** un vélo pour Noël. *She wants a bike for Christmas.*

Ils **voulaient** aller au cinéma. *They wanted to go to the cinema.*

Tu **voudrais** une tasse de thé? *Would you like a cup of tea?*

---

je/j' = I **tu** = you **il** = he/it **elle** = she/it **on** = we/one **nous** = we **vous** = you **ils/elles** = they

How to use the Verb Index

The verbs in bold are the model verbs which you will find in the Verb Tables. All the other verbs follow one of these patterns, so the number next to each verb indicates which pattern fits this particular verb. For example, **aider** (to help) follows the same pattern as **donner** (number 29 in the Verb Tables).

All the verbs are in alphabetical order. For reflexive verbs like **s'asseoir** (to sit down) or **se taire** (to stop talking), look under **asseoir** or **taire**, not under **s'** or **se**.

Superior numbers (¹, ² etc) refer you to notes on page 105. These notes explain any differences between the verbs and their model.

With the exception of reflexive verbs which always take **être**, all verbs have the same auxiliary (**être** or **avoir**) as their model verb. There are a few exceptions which are indicated by a superior number ¹ or ².

An asterisk (*) means that the verb takes **avoir** when it is used with a direct object, and **être** when it isn't.

For more information on verbs that take either **avoir** or **être**, see page 114.

abaisser	29	accomplir	39	adorer	29	aiguiser	29
abandonner	29	accorder	29	adosser	29	aimanter	29
abattre	10	accoter	29	adoucir	39	aimer	29
abêtir	39	accoucher	29	adresser	29	ajouter	29
abîmer	29	accouder (s')	29	advenir³	90	ajuster	29
abolir	39	accourir⁵	17	aérer	35	alarmer	29
abonder	29	accoutumer	29	affaiblir	39	alerter	29
abonner	29	accrocher	29	affairer (s')	29	alimenter	29
aborder	29	accroître⁶	22	affaisser (s')	29	allécher	35
aboutir	39	accroupir (s')	39	affamer	29	alléger	67
aboyer	54	accueillir	23	affermir	39	alléguer	35
abréger	67	accumuler	29	afficher	29	**aller**	**4**
abreuver	29	accuser	29	affirmer	29	allier	20
abriter	29	acharner (s')	29	affliger	46	allumer	29
abrutir	39	acheminer	29	affoler	29	altérer	35
absenter (s')	29	**acheter**	**2**	affranchir	39	alterner	29
absorber	29	achever	44	affréter	35	alunir	39
absoudre⁴	71	**acquérir**	**3**	affronter	29	amaigrir	39
abstenir (s')	84	actionner	29	agacer	13	ambitionner	29
abstraire	86	activer	29	agenouiller (s')	29	améliorer	29
abuser	29	adapter	29	agir	39	aménager	46
accabler	29	additionner	29	agiter	29	amener	44
accaparer	29	adhérer	35	agrandir	39	ameuter	29
accéder	35	adjoindre	43	agréer	19	amincir	39
accélérer	35	admettre	48	ahurir	39	amoindrir	39
accepter	29	admirer	29	aider	29	amollir	39
accompagner	29	adopter	29	aigrir	39	amonceler	5

	/	suer	29	tournoyer	54	**vendre**	**89**
	24	**suffire**	**81**	tousser	29	venger	46
	29	suggérer	35	tracasser	29	**venir**	**90**
	44	**suivre**	**82**	tracer	13	verdir	39
s...ir	78	supplier	20	traduire	24	verdoyer	54
séparer	29	supposer	29	trahir	39	vérifier	20
serrer	29	surcharger	46	traîner	29	vernir	39
sertir	39	surenchérir	39	**traire**	**86**	verrouiller	29
servir	**79**	surfaire	37	traiter	29	verser	29
sévir	39	surgeler	2	transcrire	31	**vêtir**	**91**
sevrer	44	surgir	39	transférer	35	vexer	29
siéger	67	surmonter¹	49	transformer	29	vibrer	29
siffler	29	surpasser	59	transmettre	48	vider	29
signaler	29	surprendre	66	transparaître	57	vieillir	39
signer	29	surveiller	29	transpirer	29	violer	29
signifier	20	survenir	90	transplanter	29	virer	29
simplifier	20	survivre	92	transporter	29	viser	29
simuler	29	susciter	29	traquer	29	visiter	29
soigner	29	suspendre	89	travailler	29	visser	29
sombrer	29	tacher	29	traverser	29	vitrifier	20
sommeiller	29	tâcher	29	trébucher	29	vitupérer	35
songer	46	tailler	29	trembler	29	vivifier	20
sonner	29	**taire (se)**	**83**	tremper	29	**vivre**	**92**
sortir°	**80**	taper	29	tricher	29	vociférer	35
souffrir	55	tâter	29	tricoter	29	voiler	29
souhaiter	29	taxer	29	trier	20	**voir**	**93**
souiller	29	teindre	61	triompher	29	voler	29
soulager	46	teinter	29	tripoter	29	vomir	39
soulever	44	téléphoner	29	tromper	29	voter	29
souligner	29	téléviser	29	troquer	29	vouer	29
soumettre	48	témoigner	29	trotter	29	**vouloir**	**94**
soupçonner	29	tendre	89	troubler	29	vouvoyer	54
soupeser	44	**tenir**	**84**	trouer	29	voyager	46
sourire	75	tenter	29	trouver	29	vrombir	39
souscrire	31	terminer	29	truffer	29	vulgariser	29
sous-entendre	89	ternir	39	truquer	29	zébrer	35
soustraire	86	terrasser	29	tuer	29	zézayer	60
soutenir	84	terrifier	20	tutoyer	54	zigzaguer	29
souvenir (se)	90	téter	35	ulcérer	35		
spécialiser	29	tiédir	39	unifier	20		
spécifier	20	timbrer	29	unir	39		
standardiser	29	tirer	29	urbaniser	29		
stationner	29	tolérer	35	user	29		
stériliser	29	**tomber**	**85**	usiner	29		
stimuler	29	tondre	70	utiliser	29		
stupéfier	20	tonner	29	vacciner	29		
subir	39	tordre	50	**vaincre**	**87**		
submerger	46	torpiller	29	**valoir**	**88**		
subsister	29	tortiller	29	vanter	29		
substituer	29	torturer	29	varier	20		
subvenir¹	90	toucher	29	végéter	35		
succéder	35	tourmenter	29	veiller	29		
sucer	13	tourner	29	vendanger	46		